The Sweethearts *in the War*

Lynn Russell & Neil Hanson

The Sweethearts *in the War*

The bittersweet true story of
the fearless women who brought
hope to hardship

HARPER
element

HarperElement
An imprint of HarperCollins*Publishers*
1 London Bridge Street
London SE1 9GF

www.harpercollins.co.uk

First published as *The Sweethearts* by HarperCollins*Publishers* 2013
This edition published 2020

1

A catalogue record for this book is
available from the British Library

ISBN: 978-0-00-839273-4

Printed in Great Britain by CPI Group (UK), Croydon

For Madge, Florence, Eileen,
Dorothy and Maureen

Prologue

Some places announce themselves by a distinctive smell in the air, long before the town or city itself is reached: the hoppy aroma of brewing from Burton, the lingering smell of the old fish docks in Grimsby, the sulphurous fire and brimstone of the forges that used to announce Sheffield, or the acrid stink of the Billingham chemical works. York greets its visitors with an altogether sweeter and more enticing smell: the rich, mouth-watering aroma of chocolate drifting on the breeze from the Rowntree's factory just to the north of the city centre. The company, by some distance the city's largest employer, was taken over by Nestlé in 1988, but to the citizens of York it will always be known as 'Rowntree's'.

This is the story of some of the Rowntree's Sweethearts – the women workers from the company's Golden Age, which spanned the half-century from the 1930s to the 1980s. That era began at a time when a woman's right to vote had at last been established, but her right to choose her career path, manage her own money, live her own life and follow her own destiny was far from certain. In the 1930s and the decades that followed, many of the women employed at Rowntree's found a degree of financial independence, self-confidence and self-reliance through the money they earned at the factory, the skills they acquired and, of no lesser importance, the bonds they formed with other women workers. For some unhappy women, whose lives were blighted by poverty, illness, bad housing and even bad husbands, their working days at the factory also offered a much-needed refuge and respite from their domestic turmoil – a place where they could be happy, respected and valued by their workmates.

The women to whom we spoke in the course of our research were all unstintingly generous with their time and their memories, but it's a sobering thought that, had this book not been published, their extraordinary, moving and inspirational stories might well have gone untold and unrecorded. They loved their time at Rowntree's and still regard the factory and the company with great affection. It was, they said, 'a great place to work and a real community'. They had the Yorkshire virtues: warmth, compassion, honesty, truthfulness, thrift and the capacity for hard graft. They did a fair day's work in return for a fair day's pay, shared laughter and tears, hardship and good times, and in the process they helped to make Rowntree's – and York – what it is today.

Lynn Russell and Neil Hanson, April 2013

1

Madge

On a warm Monday morning in July 1932, Madge Fisher stood fidgeting in the hallway of her terraced house while her mother, Margaret, pinned up her hair and then inspected her from top to toe. 'Hands,' her mother said, and Madge presented them meekly for inspection, glad that she'd remembered to wash them at the kitchen sink. She was a petite blonde girl with a quick wit and a ready smile, but her mum was a force of nature, a big, powerful woman, warm and loving, but leaving no one in any doubt that she was the boss of her own household. At seventeen stone, she dwarfed her diminutive daughter, and one look from her was enough to let Madge know when she'd done something wrong.

The front door, opening straight onto Rose Street, stood ajar, and the sun streaming through it cast a long rectangle of light onto the threadbare strip of carpet in the hall and the scuffed toes of the hand-me-down shoes Madge had inherited from one of her sisters. She fidgeted even more as her mum straightened the collar of her dress and repinned her hair for the third time. 'I'm going to be late if I don't go now, Mam,' Madge said, so with a last critical glance at her daughter, Margaret hugged her and then stood on the doorstep to wave her off.

There was the sound of horse's hooves and a brief, warm smell of stables as a horse and cart plodded slowly past, the rag and bone man's cry of 'Rag and Bo-o-o-o-ne' echoing from the walls. He sat with the reins held loosely in his lap, the open cart behind him already littered with a few bundles of rags and a heap of thick beef bones left over from Sunday joints. Nothing was wasted in those days. Madge's mum collected used brown-paper bags, carefully smoothing and folding them and putting them in the kitchen drawer for later use. They shared the drawer with bits of string, coiled and tied like small bowties, and rubber bands and paperclips that were stored in neatly labelled old tobacco tins. Food was never thrown away but used and reused, so that Sunday's roast meat would be served cold on Monday (washday), reheated in a stew on Tuesday, then minced and cooked as a shepherd's pie on Wednesday, and the last of it served up as rissoles on Thursday. Friday, of course, was always a fish day.

The rags collected by the rag and bone man would go to the 'shoddy merchants' in the Heavy Woollen district around Batley and Dewsbury, to be spun back into blankets or cheap yarn, while the bones went to the glue factories, the eye-watering stink revealing their presence long before the factories came into sight. The rag and bone man exchanged this near worthless waste, not for money, but for little muslin bags of 'dolly blue', used to whiten the sheets and shirts on washday, or donkey stones like the ones Madge's mum and her neighbours used to scour a neat white strip onto the edge of their front steps. Some even did the edges of the kerb stones at the side of the street. It was not just a sign that the owners were houseproud; on winter evenings and early mornings the white edges shone faintly and helped them to avoid stumbling over the kerbs or the steps in the darkness.

As Madge reached the corner of the street she glanced back. Her mum was still standing on the step, and although she was already deep in conversation with their next-door neighbour as usual, she gave an answering wave to her daughter before she disappeared from sight. Fourteen years old and just two days after she had left the Haxby Road School that stood at the end of the street, Madge was about to enter the world of work for the first time. The flood of workers who had been walking and cycling up the Haxby Road only minutes before had now dwindled to a trickle. The last few, half a dozen women in turbans and white overalls, hurried past Madge, two of them smoking a last cigarette before they reached the factory gates.

The walk to Rowntree's should have held few terrors for Madge, for Rose Street was so close to the factory that the smell of chocolate was always in the air, a constant thread in her childhood memories. Her family and Rowntree's were as closely linked as the lettering in a stick of rock, and in fact confectionery was arguably as much a family business for the Fishers as it was for the Rowntrees. Madge's father worked as a fireman in the Rowntree's Fire Brigade, and every single one of Madge's nine brothers and sisters was already at Rowntree's as well. There had never been any question that Madge would also be going to the factory or, like most girls in York, that she would leave school at the legal minimum age. Very few parents could afford the luxury of continuing to subsidize children who wanted to further their education. It was a straightforward economic necessity: as soon as you were old enough to earn your keep, that is what you had to do. When each of her brothers and sisters had left school, at the end of the spring or summer term, depending on when their fourteenth birthday fell during the year, straight to the factory they all went. Now she was treading the same path.

Yet despite her brothers and sisters already being at Rowntree's, as Madge walked up the Haxby Road, she found her footsteps slowing at the daunting thought of what lay ahead. Even more than York Minster, Rowntree's dominated the city. The factory's countless buildings sprawled over a site that spanned the whole area between Haxby Road and Wigginton Road, extending well over a mile from north to south. It was so vast that there was even room for allotments on the Wigginton Road side, while to the north of the factory buildings there were acres of sports grounds and open fields. Rowntree's even had its own network of railway sidings inside the factory grounds, a small station, Rowntree's Halt, on the main line, and its own wharf on the Foss Lock – the navigable part of the River Foss. Barges with gleaming brass, varnished woodwork and buckets and watering cans painted in the traditional 'canal' style shuttled between York and the deep-water port of Hull on the Humber, bringing cocoa beans from Ghana and Nigeria, gum arabic – the sap of the acacia tree – from Sudan, hazelnuts from Turkey, Ethiopian coffee, vanilla from Tahiti, Jamaican honey and a score of other exotic ingredients. They were discharged into the factory's huge bonded warehouses on the waterfront in Hungate, and the barges would then depart laden with chocolates and confectionery for export.

The Rowntree's factory was a town within the town: 'You could almost have lived your life there and never left,' one former worker said. 'There was everything you could ever need right there,' including a shop, a post office, a library, a cinema, a gymnasium, tennis courts, sports fields, a swimming pool and a dining hall. Built in 1913, and used as a military hospital during the First World War, the Dining Block spread over three floors and could seat well over 2,000 people at a time, yet that was just a fraction of the thousands employed at the factory. There were around 8,000 at the time that Madge began work, and by the end of the decade that had grown to over 12,000 – 30 per cent of York's entire working population. Rowntree's employed so many people that at 5.30 every evening the Haxby Road was swamped by an avalanche of men and white-clad women pouring out of the factory on foot and on bicycles, while the queue of buses waiting to take home those who lived further afield extended for half a mile along the road. So narrow was the bridge over the railway that two buses could pass each other with only inches to spare, increasing the congestion still more and endangering the crowds of pedestrians spilling out from the pavement into the roadway.

As Madge crossed the bridge over the railway line, passing the little shop where another latecomer had paused to buy a newspaper and a packet of five cigarettes, a billowing cloud of steam and smoke from an engine waiting at the signals below swirled around her and a few black smuts drifted down to the pavement around her feet. The train that brought hundreds of workers from Selby every morning was discharging the last of its passengers at Rowntree's Halt, and in the sidings she could see lines of goods wagons waiting for a shunting engine to haul them into the factory.

Her walk led her alongside the dark-blue-painted iron railings that surrounded the factory, and as she passed the first set of gates she quickened her pace when she saw the time on the large clock set into a tall, white-painted concrete pillar just inside the gates. There were similar clocks at all the entrances to the factory, perhaps as a warning to late-arriving employees of how much pay they were about to lose, for if you were even two minutes late for work at Rowntree's, you would find the doors shut and locked until lunchtime and your wages would be docked a full morning's pay. It was now five minutes before her interview and she did not want to be late; she had heard of girls who had been turned away and refused a job without even being given an interview if they failed to arrive on time.

Just beyond the first gates, facing the road but still within the confines of the factory site, she passed the Joseph Rowntree Memorial Library, a quaint-looking, red-brick Arts and Crafts building dedicated to the man who had ruled the company for over half a century until his death in 1925. With its arched leaded windows and stone pillars framing the entrance, it looked rather like a small church, perhaps an apt reflection of the reverence that its founder had felt for education and self-improvement through learning.

Smoothing an imaginary crease from her dress, she turned in through the main gates on the north side of the library and passed along an avenue of trees next to the Rose Lawn, an area of grass and flowerbeds that contained another memorial to Joseph Rowntree. Three small oak lampposts and a row of oak benches stood around the lawns, all carved by Robert Thompson, 'The Mouseman of Kilburn', with his signature, a small carved mouse, on each of them, as on every piece of oak furniture he ever made. Every summer, men from the Rowntree's Joiners department would carefully sand down the benches and then revarnish them to preserve them in perfect condition through the coming winter.

Madge had no time to admire them, let alone sit on them, and she hurried on towards the doors of the building. As she entered the lobby she was greeted by the smell of polish and the scent of the cut flowers that stood in two large vases at either side of the entrance. Just inside the doors there was also a life-size statuette of 'Plain Mr York', a smiling, bespectacled figure, wearing a top hat and tails and holding a tray of souvenir postcards that visitors to the factory were encouraged to take.

The timekeeping office stood just beyond the lobby on the left-hand side of the entrance corridor, flanked by some of the time clocks on which every employee had to clock in and out at the start and finish of the working day. The timekeeper, a florid-faced man with a thick, grey moustache, kept a watchful eye on the comings and goings of the staff from a hatchway set into the wall. Madge hung on her heel for a moment as he dealt with someone else, but then he looked up and winked at her. 'You're new,' he said. 'Here for the interview?' He turned his head to glance at the clock. 'Cutting it fine, aren't you? And I'm afraid you're in the wrong place, love. The interviews are in the Dining Block across the road.' He pointed back the way she had just come. 'You can take the tun–' But terrified that she would now be late, Madge had already turned and run back out of the doors.

She sprinted across the road, dodging a bus and a bicycle on the way, and burst in through the doors of the Dining Block just as the minute hand of the clock on the end wall clicked round to 7.30. A woman with a self-important air and a sheaf of papers in her hand glanced from the clock to Madge, pink-faced from exertion and still breathing hard from the run across the road, and pursed her lips in disapproval. But she only asked 'Interview?' and then pointed to the bench on the other side of the corridor, next to a small staircase, where another young girl was already seated. 'Wait there a moment and someone will come down for you.'

Madge did as she was told, exchanging a nervous smile with the other girl. They sat in silence for a couple of minutes, with Madge glad of the chance to get her breath back, and then there was the clatter of heels on the stone stairs and a girl appeared. She looked scarcely older than them, but already had the bored and slightly condescending air of a hard-bitten veteran. 'You waiting for Mrs Sullivan?' she said.

They looked at each other, uncertain of who they were waiting for.

'You are here for an interview, aren't you?' the bored-looking girl said, not even bothering to conceal her irritation. 'Well come on then.' She jerked her head to signal them to follow her and then went back upstairs without waiting to see if they were behind her.

They hurried after her and at the top of the stairs found themselves in an open area lined with glass cases displaying some of the beautiful commemorative chocolate boxes the workers in the Card Box department had made for special occasions such as Valentine's Day, Easter and Christmas, or for members of the Royal Family; Queen Mary had a standing order for a dozen elaborate boxes of Rowntree's chocolates as Christmas gifts.

The girl handed Madge and the other interviewee over to Mrs Sullivan, a middle-aged woman with wire-rimmed glasses and grey hair tied back in an immaculate bun. She gave them a brief welcoming smile and then led them into a small office furnished with hard wooden chairs and plain wood desks, just like the ones at Madge's school, right down to the steel-nibbed pens, the inkwells and the sheets of well-used, dark-green blotting paper. Mrs Sullivan told them to sit down and then handed them each a form on which they entered their name, address, age, the school they'd attended, their hobbies and their other personal details. The tip of her tongue protruding from the corner of her mouth, Madge completed her form with painstaking care, desperate not to smudge it or drop ink blots on it.

Mrs Sullivan looked up as the sound of scratching pen nibs ceased. 'Now,' she said, as she collected the completed forms from them, 'we have a series of tests for you to complete, but don't worry.' Again there was the flicker of a smile. 'They're not like exams that you pass or fail, these are simply to give us a good idea of what you can and can't do, and what you're best at, so that we can decide – everything else being satisfactory, of course – which department to allocate you to. You'll also have a medical and our dentist will check your teeth.' She gave another thin smile at the look of panic that crossed Madge's face.

'I've never been to a dentist before,' Madge said.

'Then it's high time you went,' the woman said. 'But don't be alarmed. It's perfectly routine and quite pain-free.'

The two girls were separated and Madge was led into another, larger room, where three people, two men and one woman, were waiting. All wore white lab coats, giving them the air of doctors or scientists, and each carried a stopwatch and a clipboard. They were industrial psychologists, whose role was to study working methods and identify the most suitable new recruits for any given task. Industrial psychology was a still-novel quasi-science much admired by Seebohm Rowntree, who had succeeded his father as chairman of the company, and its stated aims were not just to use scientific methods to increase efficiency, but to produce a 'correspondingly higher standard of comfort and welfare for the workers' and eliminate 'all the unhappiness caused by what is popularly called putting the round peg in the square hole'. Laudable though those aims may have been in theory, their practical application via 'time and motion' studies almost invariably led to employees being required to do more work, more quickly, for little or no more reward, and the individuals with their stopwatches and clipboards soon became hated figures.

To help them assess potential employees, the industrial psychologists devised home-spun tests and pieces of 'home-made' apparatus, including colour-recognition tests and a formboard like the child's toy in which different shapes have to be matched to the right holes on a wooden board, enabling them to 'weed out those girls who are unlikely to become efficient packers'. It was to remain the yardstick by which Rowntree's graded potential production line employees for thirty years.

Madge was to be the latest new recruit to be graded by these methods. The leader of the group, a man with dark hair flecked with grey and a small goatee beard, explained each test to Madge and then one of his assistants placed the equipment in front of her. 'These tests are to assess your aptitude for the different kinds of work you might be doing here,' he said. 'Please complete them accurately and as quickly as you can. The first test is to place these wooden shapes into the correct spaces in the formboard. Some of the shapes are incorrect, either because they are the wrong size or because they are damaged, and those you should place on one side. Now if you are ready? But please do not begin until I tell you to.'

His assistants then placed a wooden board with different-shaped indentations in front of her and a tray containing the wooden shapes to her right, and a moment later the man with the goatee said 'Go' and clicked his stopwatch. As Madge began sorting the shapes and fitting them into the recesses on the board, she could see from the corner of her eye that they were watching her intently and making occasional notes on their clipboards, but she did her best to ignore that and carried on sorting the shapes. She tried one in a couple of different places before consigning it to the reject pile, but eventually she filled the last recess and heard the faint metallic click as they stopped their watches in unison. She glanced at their faces, but their expressions remained impassive as they compared their notes and figures, making it impossible for her to read how well or badly she had done.

The next test involved sorting items by colour, which she did by posting different coloured cards into the correct matching boxes, and then she had to fit shaped pieces of wood into a square frame. There were a series of other tests, including a paper with puzzles to solve and a set of mathematical problems that again made Madge feel as if she had been transported back to the school classroom. They also took her temperature and measured how warm her hands were, something she might have found alarming had one of her sisters not told her that they did this because you could not go into chocolate piping – hand-piping designs onto the top of individual chocolates using an icing bag – if your hands were too warm, because it made the chocolate go white as it cooled.

Finally she was asked to pack some dummy chocolates into a box while once more they timed her with stopwatches. 'The chocolates are actually made of plaster of Paris, so I advise you not to taste them,' the leader of the group said, permitting himself a small smile, though the expressions on his companions' faces showed it was a joke that had grown whiskers from constant repetition. 'Pack them in exactly the same order as the box on your left, and once more, please do not begin until I tell you to.' His assistants then placed a full chocolate box on her left, an empty one in front of her and set down a wooden tray containing the plaster 'chocolates' on her right. Madge sat studying the layout of the full box, her hands poised over the dummy chocolates until she heard the word 'Go' and the faint click from their stopwatches, then scrambled to pack the chocolates into the individual frilled paper cups inside the box as quickly as she could.

When she had completed all the tests, the three of them conferred briefly, their impassive faces still giving Madge no hint of how well or badly she had done. The woman added something to the notes she had been making on Madge's form and then ushered her back into the corridor. Mrs Sullivan was waiting for her, and having studied the form – Madge herself was not permitted to see it – she gave a brief smile and said, 'Congratulations. Subject to a satisfactory medical, you have been passed as suitable for employment at Rowntree's.'

Madge felt no elation or excitement at that, only relief that she would not have to go home and tell her parents that, uniquely among the members of her very large family, she would not be working at the factory. Whether because Madge's hands were too warm, or because she hadn't shown enough dexterity and speed when posting shapes on the form-board, or simply because it was the only place where they were currently short-staffed, Mrs Sullivan told her that, providing her medical examination did not reveal any unexpected problems, she would be assigned to work in the Card Box Mill, where they made the boxes for the Rowntree's chocolate assortments and made and printed the packaging for all the company's brands.

She then led Madge along the corridor to a suite of rooms with a sign reading 'Occupational Health Department', and left her in the care of a nurse. The rooms were light and airy, with a strong background smell of carbolic disinfectant. Madge was first seen by an optician, a man in his thirties wearing horn-rimmed spectacles and a spotted bowtie, who shone a light into her eyes and then had her read a series of letters of diminishing size from a chart on the wall. She rattled them off right down to the end of the bottom line, and would have told him the manufacturer's name in tiny print at the bottom had he not held up a hand and said, 'Thank you, Miss Fisher, your eyesight is marvellous.'

She returned to the nurse, who scrutinized Madge with the air of a horse dealer assessing a filly, and then rattled off a series of questions. 'Ever had any serious medical complaints? Ever been in hospital? Ever suffered fits, blackouts or seizures? Any of your family suffer from TB? Any family history of mental illness? Do you suffer from ringworm or any other skin complaint?' As Madge replied 'No' to each question, the nurse made a note on the pad in front of her. 'Now,' she said, 'take off your dress so I can examine you. If you've got any skin complaints, then we'll have to treat them before you can begin work.'

Madge hesitated, embarrassed, but then took off her outer clothes and stood there in her underwear, acutely aware of how old, patched and mended it was. 'Hold out your hands,' the nurse said. 'And now turn them over so I can see the other side.' She also checked Madge's back, neck and legs for signs of any skin conditions, felt the glands in her neck and parted the hair on her scalp. 'Just checking for nits,' she said. 'All right, no problems there. Now I just need to measure your height and weigh you.'

Madge stood in front of the wooden measure fixed to the wall while the nurse checked her height. When Madge stood on the scales, she saw the nurse frown as she adjusted the weights until the scale was in balance, and then read the figure. 'Seven stone four,' she said. 'A bit light for your height. You need to put a bit of weight on.'

'Why's that?' Madge asked.

'Because if you're too thin, you're more likely to be ill. That means you're more likely to be off work and that costs Rowntree's money.'

'Not me,' Madge said. 'I'm never ill.'

'Just the same,' the nurse said. 'Tell your mam that I said you need a bit more weight on your bones. Now, get dressed, and then you just need to see the dentist and you're done. It's the next room down the corridor from this one. Just knock and walk in.'

The dentist had a fully equipped surgery and Madge looked around with interest, tinged with more than a little fear. She might never have been to the dentist herself, but she'd heard enough scare stories from people who had to be very nervous about it. The dentist bustled in, all brisk efficiency. 'Now, let's have a look at those teeth of yours, shall we, Miss Fisher?' he said, steering her into the leather chair and then pressing a foot pedal to recline it. 'All right, open wide.'

She felt herself go rigid as he leaned over her with a dental mirror in one hand and a thin steel probe in the other. 'Just relax,' he said. 'I promise you, I've done this before and I'm not going to hurt you.' She was grateful for his attempt to put her at ease, though it did little to soothe her nerves. He fell silent as he began to probe her teeth. Madge had just begun to relax a little when she felt a stab of pain as he tested one of her back teeth. A few moments later, she yelped at another twinge from the opposite side of her mouth.

The dentist checked the last few teeth, then brought the chair upright again. 'I'm afraid those two teeth are going to have to come out,' he said.

Madge felt the blood drain from her face at the thought. 'But it's the first time I've ever had teeth out,' she said, with a tremor in her voice. 'In fact it's the first time I've ever been to a dentist.'

'From the state of your teeth, I rather thought it was,' he said. 'But don't worry. We'll give you an anaesthetic – some gas – and you won't feel a thing.' He gave her a brief professional smile that did little to reassure her. He then asked her when she'd last eaten, and luckily – if that was really the word, Madge thought, as she peered over his shoulder at the frightening-looking steel implements in the sterile cabinets behind him – she'd been too nervous to eat breakfast before she left the house that morning. The dentist studied her pale, frightened face for a moment. 'Do any of your family work here?'

She nodded. 'My father, three brothers and six sisters.'

He smiled. 'Then I'm sure we can spare one of them from their work for half an hour. I'll send word for one of your sisters to come and sit with you.'

The dental nurse took her back out to the waiting room and sent for Madge's sister Rose, the next in age to her, to come from the Card Box Mill. Rose arrived ten minutes later, glad of any interruption to the monotonous routine of the working day, and sat with Madge, making nervous small talk until it was time for her to go back into the surgery.

The nurse helped Madge into a white gown and settled her back in the chair. She felt like a very small child as two men loomed over her, the dentist behind her and a red-faced anaesthetist with the ruptured veins of a heavy drinker in front of her. He wheeled a metal stand with two tall gas bottles over to the chair and checked the gauges and settings. 'Is that laughing gas?' Madge asked, half frightened and half intrigued.

'No,' he said. 'This one puts you completely to sleep.' He unhooked the mask with a flexible hose attached to it and placed it over her nose and mouth, then told her, 'Now, just close your eyes and breathe deeply.' The mask was cold and hard and smelled of rubber, and it also had a slightly acrid tang, like the cupboard under the kitchen sink at home where Madge's mum kept the bleach and lye soap. She heard a faint hissing sound and took a tentative breath and then another, her palms prickling with a nervous sweat. The gas felt cold in her nose and mouth and a feeling of dizziness and nausea crept over her. She couldn't remember anything after that.

Rose had stayed in the waiting room, but she could see the blurred movements of the dentist through the frosted glass, and heard the murmured conversation of the two men and then the gruesome, grinding sounds as the steel forceps gripped and twisted Madge's teeth and pulled them out one by one. Madge herself saw and heard none of that, and remembered nothing else until she came round a few minutes later. As she regained consciousness, still half drugged by the gas, she began shouting for her sister and saying, 'I remember, Rose. I remember.'

At the sound of her sister's voice, Rose jumped up, knocked on the door and without waiting for an answer, pushed it open and ran in. 'What do you remember, Madge?' she said, squeezing her sister's hand.

In her gas-fuelled dreams, Madge had been seeing herself as a piece of confectionery on the Rowntree's production line.

'I was coming down this chute,' she said. 'And I saw you at the end of the chute waiting for me.' She tried to sit up but was still very groggy. Her mouth tasted foul and as she probed with her tongue, she felt the soft fleshy cavities in her gums where the two teeth had been removed. The dental nurse had meanwhile steered Rose back to the waiting room while the dentist made a final check of Madge's mouth.

'Everything's fine,' he said. 'They'll heal up perfectly well, but don't eat or drink anything until teatime and, tempting though it is, don't keep testing the cavities with your tongue, because if you do, they'll start bleeding again. And Miss Fisher? If you don't want to be coming back to see me again, you need to take better care of those teeth. Brush them twice a day, morning and night, and don't eat so many toffees.'

'I don't eat toffees,' Madge protested.

'Well, chocolates then, or gums, or whatever sweets you do eat.' He paused, studying her face. 'All right now? Then let's see if we can get you back on your feet and into the waiting room. You may be a little unsteady at first, but the nurse will help you.'

Later, Madge would look back on her first taste of dentistry with relief that the experience had not been worse, because the stories circulating around the factory about the company dentist cast serious doubts over his competence. One of her fellow workers, Muriel, recalls that 'After a visit to have a tooth removed, it put me off going to any dentist for life, as he broke it so many times and even then left a bit of tooth stuck in my gum,' necessitating several visits to a different dentist to repair the damage. Others suffered even more at his hands. One girl, Marjorie Chapman, had to have five teeth out before she could start work at Rowntree's. As she went under the anaesthetic, the last thing she remembers seeing was 'a tram going by with all the faces looking at me'. The extraction was a prolonged, messy and very bloody affair, and Marjorie ended up having to be taken to hospital to have her gums stitched. 'It was rough,' she says. 'My mouth was dreadful and I was only fourteen. It was about eight weeks before I could start work and the dentist got in terrible trouble over it.'

With Rose walking alongside them, the nurse steered Madge back to the waiting room and then, after she'd had a few more minutes to recover, took her out to the main office area, where Mrs Sullivan was still sitting at her desk. She peered at Madge over her glasses, then turned to Rose. 'Your sister seems fine now,' she said. 'So you'd better be getting back to work, hadn't you?'

Rose gave a reluctant nod, squeezed Madge's hand and walked off down the corridor as Mrs Sullivan turned her attention to Madge's form. She made another note on it, then nodded to herself and added her signature at the bottom.

'Right,' she said. 'You'll start in the Card Box Mill tomorrow morning at 7.30 a.m. prompt. Your pay will be eleven shillings a week for a forty-four hour week.' She took a printed booklet from her desk drawer and handed it to Madge. 'This is a copy of the *Works Rules and Regulations*. We expect you to read it, know the rules and abide by them at all times. Any breach of them will be treated as a matter for disciplinary action.'

She paused and gave Madge a questioning look, making sure the message had been received. 'Now, you'll need two white turbans and two overalls with no pockets in them. We don't supply them, you have to provide your own, but if you've no money and can't afford them, we have an arrangement with the stores in town. You can get them there and we'll deduct the money from your wages, a shilling a week, until you've paid for them. You'll need to wear stockings and flat shoes, no high heels, no sandals and no jewellery other than wedding rings.' She paused again. 'Though you'll not have one of those just yet, will you? No make-up and no perfume allowed, no pins or small objects of any kind, and no food to be brought into the working areas. You'll need money for a drink at break time, and a little "sailor bag" to hang around your neck to keep your money in. There's a ten-minute morning break and you get an hour at dinnertime. If you're not going home for your dinner, you can buy a meal in the Dining Block – the food is good and it's cheap, too. Any questions? No? Then we'll see you tomorrow at 7.30 a.m. sharp. Don't be late or you'll be locked out and lose your morning's pay. Report to the timekeeper's office just inside the main doors and someone will meet you there and take you over to the Card Box Mill.'

As Madge turned into Rose Street on her way home, with the metallic taste of blood in her mouth, she saw her mother on the step, still chatting to her neighbour. 'Well?' she said, as Madge walked up to her.

'I've had two teeth out,' Madge said, opening her mouth to show her mother her sore and bleeding gums.

'Never mind that,' her mum said. 'Did they take you on?'

'Yes, in the Card Box Mill.'

Her mum nodded to herself as if she'd known it all along. 'Good. Well, you'll not lack for company, will you? You've got two sisters already working there.'

Madge felt a little crestfallen that her mother was treating her success at gaining a job so matter of factly – paid work of any kind wasn't exactly thick on the ground in 1932 – and her disappointment must have shown in her face, because a moment later her mum's expression softened and she gave Madge a hug. 'I'm proud of you,' she said. 'Now get yourself changed and go and enjoy your afternoon off. It's the last one you'll be having on a weekday for quite a while.' She winked at their neighbour. 'About fifty years, if all goes to plan.' Madge could hear them still laughing at the joke as she hurried upstairs to get changed.

Madge was even excused helping with the tea that night, though she and Rose were quite adept at dodging those duties anyway. The next sister, Laura, always did more than her share, and as she was making the tea she would often say plaintively to her sisters, 'Come on, you two, I've been at work the same as you, give me a hand,' but Rose and Madge would usually find ways to sneak off and not reappear until tea was actually on the table, and most of the time they would get away with nothing worse than a reproachful look from Laura.

Madge was born in the house in Rose Street on 29 May 1918 – Royal Oak Day. The First World War was still raging and her father was away fighting on the Western Front. He didn't set eyes on his new daughter until eight months later, when he was demobbed after the end of the war. Madge was the youngest of ten children – seven girls and three boys. Her dad had ginger hair and her mum was fair, he was right-handed and she was left-handed, and their ten children were split along similar lines: five of them had ginger hair and five of them – including Madge – had fair hair; five of them, again including Madge, were left-handed and five of them were right-handed.

Rose Street was about 200 yards long, running the full distance between Haxby Road and Wigginton Road. There were fifty identical terraced houses on either side of the street, with a narrow back lane behind them. There was virtually no traffic in the street at all – only one of all the occupants of the houses in the street had a car, and even that was used only at weekends – so the local kids could play in the street all day long. Madge and her friends had a skipping rope, fixed to a hook in the wall and stretching from one side of the street to the other, and she can still remember the skipping rhyme she and her friends used to sing on her birthday.

Twenty-ninth of May,
Royal Oak Day,
If you don't give us a holiday,
We'll all run away.

Where shall we run to?
Down the lane,
To see the teacher with the cane.

The girls would play rounders in the street as well, while the boys played cricket in summer with an old tennis ball and a wooden crate for stumps, and in winter they kicked an old, scuffed leather football around, and when that was lost they used a bundle of rags, tightly bound together with string, as a substitute.

There was a corner shop at the end of Rose Street. When Madge was small it was a sweet shop, and her parents or one of her older sisters would sometimes give her and Rose a penny to go and buy some sweets. 'I used to think I could buy the whole shop for a penny,' Madge says. 'Rose and I would stand there for ages trying to decide what to buy.'

The rooms in the two-up, two-down houses were very small, so much so that a tall man could stand with his arms outstretched in any of the rooms and almost touch the opposite walls simultaneously. Downstairs there was a kitchen at the back with a floor of bricks, and a coal fire with an oven alongside it where Madge's mum used to do her baking. As a child, one of Madge's jobs was to polish the oven once a week with black lead. There were twelve mouths to feed, and every other day her mum would make up big bowls of bread dough, leave it to rise and then bake it in the fire oven, filling the house with the delicious aroma of fresh-baked bread. The big wooden table where she made the bread was also used to scrub the clothes on washday – Monday – the day of the week the girls used to dread. All of them were roped in to help with the task of washing and airing the sheets and clothes from the week, and with their mum too busy washing to cook, the Monday evening meal was usually an unappetizing cold spread of the leftovers from Sunday.

Madge's mum and dad didn't go out often – aside from anything else they couldn't afford it – but once in a while they would get dressed up in their Sunday best clothes and go to the Grand picture house to see a film. Madge and Rose would sit on the edge of their mum's bed, watching her putting on her make-up, and they'd say to each other, 'We'll do that when we're older.' Once their parents had gone out, despite all their promises of good behaviour, the children would go wild around the house, with Madge's brother Jimmy and sister Laura getting up on the wooden table in the kitchen and dancing like mad.

The front room was kept for best and only used on Sundays. One Sunday, Madge's sister Ginny was coming through from the kitchen with a shovelful of coals to light the little fire when Madge came running out of the room, straight onto the edge of the red-hot shovel. It could have blinded her, but it missed her eyeball by millimetres and she escaped with a bad burn on her eyelid. There was a piano in the front room and Madge was sent to a music teacher for piano lessons, but she was so desperate to get out and play with her friends in the street that she barely ever practised at home. She used to sit in the front room and bang away on the piano, while her mum, who had a tin ear for music, would call out from the kitchen, 'That's good, our Madge.' The truth was, the family had wasted their money, because Madge could only just about play 'Chopsticks' and nothing else.

Upstairs there were two and a half bedrooms: two bedrooms and a tiny boxroom where her brother Dick slept. He made a hole in the door and used to spy on his sisters and tease them, usually leading to a noisy chase down the stairs. Madge's mum and dad had one room, though they shared it with their youngest children when they were small, and the rest of the kids slept three and four to a bed, topped and tailed, with two at the top of the bed and two at the bottom. Madge slept that way every night for five years. Only when the eldest boy, John, and their eldest sister, Edna, had both left home and got married did the congestion ease a little. Somehow there was also room in the tiny house for a large collie dog as well.

There was no bathroom in the house, just a tin bath hanging on a hook on the outside wall next to the back door; the toilet was also outside, next to the coal shed at the end of the long, narrow yard. It was what was called a 'duckett' toilet, like a bucket with a wooden seat over it. When they were younger, Madge and her sister Rose used to go out there with a candle after dark and drop candle wax on the backs of their hands, then go in and say, 'Look at all the spots we've got!' in the hope of persuading their mother that they had gone down with measles or some other infectious disease that would have got them a few days off school. Madge's mum was not born yesterday, however, and was not so easily fooled. 'I'll give you spots,' she'd say, and chase them out of the room.

Madge was a little scared of the dark out in the yard, with the wind blowing, rustling the dead leaves and making the door creak, and if she wanted to go to the toilet at night, she always waited for Rose and went with her. When Rose had finished with the toilet and it was Madge's turn, Rose used to say, 'Right, I'm going now,' and pretend she was going to go back into the house, while Madge was crying and saying, 'I'm going to tell my mam if you don't stop it.'

There was a little raised flowerbed in one corner of the yard where her mum grew flowers such as geraniums and pansies, and a home-made pigeon loft where one of Madge's brothers used to keep a few fan-tailed doves. Madge's mum would block up the grate in the middle of the yard and fill it with water so that the pigeons could have a drink and a bathe. They also kept an old drake that lived in a pen at the end of the yard. It had a vicious streak, and if it got out it used to chase Madge and the other small children out of the yard and down the back lane. They wouldn't come back until one of the grown-ups had rounded it up and shooed it back into its pen.

A cobbled lane ran along the rear of the house, flanked by Parson's Wall, a high stone wall surrounding the garden of the vicarage, which contained an orchard full of apple trees. In late summer, Madge and her sisters and brothers would climb over the wall and help themselves to the apples, even though the parson seemed an intimidating, almost sinister figure when they were young. He was very tall and dressed all in black, with a long black frock coat and broad-brimmed black hat; he looked more like an undertaker than a priest to them. However, their fear did not stop Madge and her friends from playing tricks on him sometimes. They would sneak through his garden, tiptoe up to his front door and knock loudly on it. Then they would wait, peering through the letterbox, until they saw him appear from his study at the far end of the hall, and then they would turn and run like mad, sprinting away through the orchard and over the wall, arriving back home more out of breath from laughter than from running.

They also had a rusting black bicycle – one of the old-fashioned, heavy iron 'sit up and beg' types – that they named 'Black Bess' after Dick Turpin's steed, and they used to take turns to go round and round the block on it, pedalling down the street and round the back lane, while the others counted loudly the minutes and seconds it took. That simple pastime could occupy them for hours until the gang gradually lost interest and drifted away in search of the next game or amusement.

Being the youngest of the ten children, Madge was, she says, 'really spoilt', and her sisters Marian and Ginny even used some of their wages from the factory to pay by weekly instalments for a top-of-the-range Silver Cross dolls' pram for her, together with two beautiful dolls. One of her other sisters, Mabel, used to do a lot of knitting and she chipped in by knitting all the dolls' clothes. Madge hardly ever used to play with that pram or those dolls, but she was not being a spoilt brat, for she had a friend across the road whose family were even poorer than Madge's and couldn't buy her any sort of dolls' pram to play with. Consciously or subconsciously, Madge decided that she did not want to be playing with her expensive toys in front of a friend who did not have any, and instead the two friends played with a little rag doll. They got a cardboard shoebox and made cushions and blankets out of scraps of fabric to put inside it, then poked a hole through the end of the box and tied a piece of string through it. While the Silver Cross pram and the expensive dolls remained almost untouched, Madge and her friend would play for hours pulling the shoebox along the street behind them as if it were a pram and they were taking their baby out for some fresh air. If it was a wet day and the box started to disintegrate, they just went and found another one.

Madge's dad – his name was John, but everyone called him Jack – was a jolly-looking, apparently extrovert character with a bushy moustache and stocky build, but appearances could be deceptive, because he was quiet, shy and softly spoken and, like the rest of the family, he was never in any doubt as to who was the boss of the household. Madge's mum was a real hard worker. She more than had her hands full with a family of twelve to look after, but she used to take in washing as well, trying to earn a bit of extra money to help make ends meet. She did not have a washing machine or anything like that; it was all hand-washing, done with a boiler, a dolly tub and a washboard, and her big, powerful hands were always reddened from the work, the constant immersion in water and the cheap, rough soap she had to use.

Madge's mum could be formidable, but she was warm and loving to her children and she had a kind heart, as well as a soft streak for those down on their luck. There were plenty of 'gentlemen of the road' – tramps – on the streets in those days, many of them veterans of the Great War, too rootless, too injured or too traumatized to settle easily back into normal civilian life – and they all knew Madge's mum. Madge remembers them coming down the street, heralding their approach by singing at the tops of their voices. They would walk round into the back lane at the side of the house and wait there, and after a couple of minutes Madge's mum would always come out and give them a mug of tea and a big lump of home-made custard tart or apple pie; they all knew where to go for a hot drink and a bite to eat.

It had probably never occurred to Madge or her mum to wonder why York had become such a 'chocolate city', but throughout the twentieth century, the city's three big confectionery firms – Rowntree's, Terry's and Craven's – employed about three times as many people as York's other great industry, the railway. The reason was partly an accident of history and partly of geography. Sited on a principal junction of the east coast mainline and straddling one of the main tributaries of the River Humber, the railways and the barges plying the waterways between York and the port of Hull gave the confectionery manufacturers cheap transport for raw materials like cocoa beans and sugar, and easy access for their finished products to the great industrial populations of Yorkshire, the Northeast and the Northwest. York also happened to be the site of a long-established Quaker community, and Quaker and non-conformist industrialists in York and elsewhere dominated the confectionery trade.

One of the most famous names in that trade began life in very humble circumstances, when Joseph Rowntree Senior established a small grocer's shop at 28 Pavement, York, in 1822. A devout Quaker, he was given an immediate reminder of the evils of the demon drink when he attended the auction of the shop premises at a nearby pub and found the auctioneer so drunk that Joseph had to sober him up by repeatedly plunging his head into a bucket of cold water before the sale could even begin. Despite – or perhaps because of – that treatment, the auctioneer then sold the property to him.

In time, his two eldest boys joined him in the business, but it was not large enough to support the third son, Henry, as well. Instead, he began working for Tuke and Company in Castlegate, another Quaker-owned business, importing and manufacturing tea, coffee and cocoa, until, in 1862, he bought and renamed the Tukes' business. A lively, gregarious personality, Henry had great ambition and charm, but rather less business sense. Despite total sales of no more than £3,000, he promptly splashed out on 'a wonderful new machine for grinding cocoa' and a collection of ramshackle buildings on the bank of the River Ouse to house a new factory. It was always a dark, dingy and damp place, and often worse than damp; whenever the river was high, it flooded the cellars. Within seven years, Henry's elder brother, also called Joseph – who was cautious and prudent where Henry was impulsive and spendthrift – had to take over the running of the company to save his brother from the shame of bankruptcy, and succeeded in turning the business around.

During the latter half of the nineteenth century, the falling price of cocoa as Britain and the other imperial powers forced down the price of raw materials from their colonies, coupled with the rising wages paid to industrial workers, paved the way for a boom in the consumption of cocoa and chocolate. Once barely affordable luxuries for the working classes, both were now within the reach of almost everyone.

Employing just a handful of workers in 1869, Rowntree's labour force swelled so rapidly that by 1890 it had far outgrown the original factory at Tanners Moat, and construction began on a new factory, a steadily expanding sprawl of fortress-like red-brick buildings on a site that eventually covered a square mile between Haxby Road and Wigginton Road in the north of the city. By 1909, 4,000 people were employed there.

Even while the firm was still struggling, Joseph Junior's brand of Quaker philanthropy had led him to seek a means of improving the social condition of his workforce and, in 1901, his son Seebohm, who shared his father's concerns, produced a report revealing the scale of the deprivation in the slums that had developed in York and other cities during the previous century. It had a powerful impact on the young Winston Churchill: 'I have been reading a book which has fairly made my hair stand on end,' he said, 'written by a Mr Rowntree who deals with poverty in the town of York ... I see little glory in an Empire which can rule the waves and is unable to flush its sewers.'

Spurred on by his son's report, Joseph acquired 150 acres of land in open country between the Rowntree's factory and what is now the York outer ring road for a new 'garden village' – New Earswick – echoing existing developments at Bournville, Port Sunlight and Saltaire for Cadbury's, Lever Brothers and Salts Mill workers respectively. Joseph insisted that the houses were to be spacious, 'sanitary and thoroughly well built', with large gardens. Rents were low and New Earswick was a genuine mixed community, with housing for both workers and managers. There were allotments, a local community centre – the Folk Hall – sports facilities, a library, a doctor's surgery, shops and a post office. The village was open to anyone, not just Rowntree's employees, but the majority of residents earned their living at the factory, and it proved enormously popular.

In line with Joseph's progressive ideas, all employees at Rowntree's also had access to sports, social clubs and other facilities, free education, a company doctor – the first one was appointed to the staff in 1904 – and a team of nurses. There was a dentist, an optician and a chiropodist, and Rowntree's even had its own social workers, ambulance and a fire brigade with its own fire engines; with 14,000 employees at its peak and some highly inflammable products stored at the factory, Rowntree's was a greater fire risk than the city itself.

Joseph also introduced a Works Council in an effort to replace the 'us and them' industrial relations that blighted so many other industries. In 1906 he established one of the first ever occupational pension schemes in the world, holidays with pay were introduced in 1918, and the following year the working week was reduced to forty-four hours, with no Saturday working, long before the vast majority of other British factories followed suit. Soon afterwards, Rowntree's brought in a profit-sharing scheme for employees, again one of the first in the country.

Like the other great Quaker industrialists of his era, Joseph Rowntree is now often accused of paternalism and excessive meddling in the lives of his employees, but he undoubtedly felt an acute sense of responsibility for their welfare and, whatever his motives, the results were not in doubt: his employees were better paid, better housed, better fed and clothed, and had better medical and social care than almost any others in the country. He remained chairman of Rowntree's until 1923 and died two years later at the age of eighty-eight. He was buried in the Quaker burial ground at The Retreat in York, and despite his fame and fortune, in accordance with Quaker traditions, his gravestone is identical to all the others in that cemetery; if not always so in life, all were equal in death.

Joseph's son and successor, Seebohm, also combined a strong social conscience with a hard head for business, but the effects of the Great Depression in the late 1920s and early 1930s pushed Rowntree's to the brink of bankruptcy. In 1931 large numbers of workers in the Card Box Mill were laid off and the company cut the wages of its remaining workforce, replaced many of the male workers with lower-paid women and for a while worked a three-day week.

Rowntree's remained in serious financial trouble throughout 1932, but within twelve months, from bleak-looking prospects and shedding its workers in droves, Rowntree's was transformed into a fast-expanding and hugely profitable business. This was the company that Madge had now joined.

2

Florence

Madge was already nineteen and beginning to feel like a seasoned veteran at Rowntree's when, in 1937, another nervous fourteen-year-old followed in her footsteps through the main gates of the factory. Florence Clark was born in 1923 and grew up in Layerthorpe, just to the east of the city centre, in a two-up, two-down terraced house with a front door that opened straight onto Bilton Street. There were ten of them all together: Florence's mum, Barbara, and dad, Harry, and her four brothers and three sisters, with Florence the youngest of them all by five years. The house was tiny and, like Madge's family, the children slept three and even four to a bed, with two at the top and two at the bottom. 'You were lucky to get a blanket,' she says, 'and we had to use overcoats for blankets on cold winter nights, though if it was really cold, my mum would give us the shelf out of the fireside oven, wrapped in a piece of cloth, as a hot-water bottle. She'd put it right in the middle of the bed where all four of us could get our feet on it.'

There was no bathroom and no hot water in the house, just a tap for cold water that was shared with the neighbouring houses. There was an outside toilet – a wooden seat perched on top of a bucket – but it was more than a little precarious and Florence was always a bit frightened to sit on it when she was young in case it overbalanced. She was lucky she didn't have to use the outside toilet at night, because there was a 'gazunder' – a chamber pot, so-called because it goes under the bed – in the bedroom she shared. They did not have luxuries like toilet paper, just bits of newspaper, and as the youngest, one of Florence's jobs when her dad and mum had finished reading the paper was to tear it into squares, make a hole in the corner of them, slot a string through, and then hang them up in the outside toilet.

They had a wash house in the yard as well, a lean-to built onto the back wall of the house containing a concrete and steel boiler with a fireplace underneath and a galvanized pipe poking out through the roof to serve as a chimney. Once a week, on Fridays after school, they used to light the fire under the boiler to heat up the water for their weekly bath – the tin tub they used as a bath hung on the back wall in the yard because there wasn't room for it in the house. They would all share the same water, so by the time the last of them got in – and as the youngest and smallest, Florence was in no position to argue about the pecking order – the water was tepid at best, and so grey and with so much soap scum on the surface that it was questionable whether they were any cleaner when they got out than when they got in.

Inside the house were hard floors of bricks laid on edge directly onto the earth beneath them, with oilcloth like a thin linoleum placed on top of them, and a scrubbed pine table and a few mismatched hard chairs in the kitchen. They used sheets of newspaper instead of tablecloths – it did at least give them something to read while they ate – and there were not enough seats for all the family to sit down together; since they all ate at the same time, the younger children had to eat standing up.

With so many mouths to feed, there was never any food to spare. 'I always remember,' Florence says with a rueful smile, 'that my dad had two boiled eggs for his breakfast and all I ever used to get were the tops of the eggs when he'd cut them off.'

Florence and the other local children all played in the street; they had to do so because there was nowhere else to play except for a bit of rough ground called Ropery Walk a few streets away. The girls played skipping with a long rope tied at one end to a lamppost or a house wall, hopscotch or a curious game called 'peggy stick' that was a bit like the old Yorkshire game of 'knurl and spell'. It was played with a big stick and a wooden peg, shaped at both ends. You had to hit one end of the peg with the stick to flick it up into the air, and then before it dropped to the ground you had to swing back the stick and hit the peg again, knocking it as far as you could. In a narrow street lined on both sides with houses opening directly onto the pavement, misdirected hits of the peg sometimes led to the ominous sound of breaking glass. The girls also had 'whipping tops' that spun with the flick of a bit of string or cord, and Florence and her friends would spend ages decorating them with paints or drawing pins pushed into the top and polishing them until they shone, so that they would catch the light and sparkle like gold. In summer the boys would run down to the river at the end of the next street and go splashing and swimming in it, but Florence and the other girls never went down there.

Although there weren't any cars in the street – no one could afford to run one, let alone buy one, in that impoverished district – over the course of the day there was a steady trickle of horses and carts with people buying and selling goods. Some only came once or twice a year, like the swarthy knife grinder with a thick moustache and eyes so dark they looked black even in bright daylight, who always wore a red-spotted handkerchief like a scarf around his neck, fastened with a gold clasp. He had an enclosed cart like a small showman's wagon and a Heath Robinson contraption on the back: a rickety-looking metal frame, like a bicycle, with a grindstone precariously balanced where the handlebars should have been. Having drawn up his cart, the knife grinder would shout his rallying cry to alert the women of the street, and then sit on the bicycle seat. The women would bring out kitchen knives, carving knives, scissors, scythes or garden shears – no one had a garden, but some had allotments – anything with an edge in need of sharpening. He'd pocket a few coppers from his first customer and then begin to pedal his 'bike'. The grindstone spun faster and faster, and as he drew the edge of each knife or tool across it, a shower of sparks flew upwards, drawing squeaks of excitement from Florence and the crowd of other children who had gathered to watch.

The chimney sweep would also make his rounds by horse and cart, with his brushes and sacks of soot stacked on the back. His skin was permanently ingrained with soot, and wisps of his incongruously fair hair peeped out from under a flat cap that was as black as the chimneys he swept. Sweeps were thought – by the superstitious at least – to bring good luck, and brides-to-be would position themselves so that he had to cross their path. Some even invited him to their wedding for luck, and having pocketed his fee, he would kiss the bride and make a black smudge on her cheek that she would leave untouched as a token of her future good fortune.

When the coalman came down the street with his big, powerful horse dragging the high cart piled with sacks of coal and coke, the boys used to rush out and use the back of the cart as a swing as it bumped along over the cobbles. When the rag and bone man was on his rounds, like the other kids, Florence would run inside and see if she could find any old rags or pester her mum for the bones from the Sunday roast. In those hard times and mean streets, very little was thrown away, but apart from his two staples, the rag and bone man would also take scrap metal, such as aluminium pans with holes burned through the bottom, empty tins, broken toys, cracked china, scrap wood, worn-out shoes, and almost anything else that might have a scrap value, no matter how slight. In theory, if the children brought him enough, the rag and bone man would give them a goldfish, but in fact the goldfish in its little glass bowl appeared to be only for show, or perhaps the rags they brought were of too poor a quality, as the most that Florence or any of the other kids in the street ever seemed to receive was a balloon.

An ice-cream van also used to come round once a week, and the driver, Mac, did a brisk trade in halfpenny cornets. On winter evenings there was the 'hot pea man', and when she heard his call, Florence's mother would sometimes send her out with a halfpenny and an empty cup. The pea man would ladle the hot, mushy marrowfat peas into the cup and put a spoonful of mint sauce on top. Florence would carry it back inside, the cup so hot it almost burned her hands, and then she and her sisters would sit in front of the fire with it and take turns to eat small spoonfuls of the peas, trying to make them last as long as possible.

On Friday nights a man came round with a little roundabout on the back of a horse and cart. He would tether the horse to a lamppost, swing out the roundabout on its steel support, and then hand-crank a handle to turn it. It was very basic, there was no music and it only had four hard metal seats, but the little kids loved to ride on it. Even though he charged just a halfpenny a ride, it was often more than Florence's parents could afford to spend, so the halfpenny cornets and the roundabout rides were very occasional treats. Money was so tight in their house that every time the gas man came to read the meter and empty the coin box – all the houses in the street had coin meters for the gas – Florence would wait until he had gone, and then rush to search the space under the stairs where the meter was in case he had dropped a penny or a halfpenny. He never had, but she never gave up looking, just in case.

When Florence was seven, the entire street was demolished under the slum clearance programme and the family was moved to a brand-new council house in Pottery Lane. Florence was delighted when they went to see it and she discovered that it had the luxury of a handbasin with taps. Even then they still had to use an outside toilet – it wasn't until they eventually moved to a four-bedroom house in Foss Way years later that they had a bathroom as well: 'We thought we'd died and gone to heaven when we got there!' Florence says.

Florence had started school at St George's, but then went to St Wilfrid's when they moved house, and stayed there until she left school at fourteen. There was little doubt about where she would work when she grew up. Her dad was one of only two members of the family not employed by Rowntree's – he worked at the electricity station on Foss Islands Road – but all her brothers and two of her sisters worked there; even her mum had worked there as well before she got married. She was one of the first 'pipers', using an icing bag full of liquid chocolate to pipe swirls onto the chocolate assortments, in the original Rowntree's factory at Tanners Moat by the river.

Florence finished school on a Friday in July 1937 and started work at Rowntree's the following Monday. 'There was only Rowntree's, Terry's and the railways in York really,' she says. 'If you didn't go to one of them, you'd have struggled to find work at all. Mind, you couldn't walk straight into Rowntree's like you could at Terry's; you had to pass the tests that they gave you, but you knew if you passed the medical and the tests, that's where you'd be going. It was seen as the best place to work; they were good to you, Rowntree's, with medical care and everything.'

Even those girls who did not at first follow the well-trodden route straight from school through the factory gates at Rowntree's often turned up there within a couple of years. One of Florence's workmates, Dot Edwards, started at Terry's instead when she was fourteen, and spent two and a half years there. 'I Cellophaned a lovely big fancy box for the Queen while I was there,' she says. 'It was on display in Terry's window for a while, but then they went on short-time working, where you did two weeks on, but then you were off for two weeks. There was no unemployment money then so I only had half the money I'd had before – and at age fourteen it was only nine shillings and eightpence a week, even when I was working full time – so I decided to leave and went to Rowntree's instead. I had a brother and a sister already working there and that was how you got on to work at Rowntree's in those days; if you had relatives working there, you had preference over everyone else.'

Girls without family connections often found themselves drawn to Rowntree's by peer pressure or the gravitational pull of the city's biggest employer. The mother of another of Florence's contemporaries, Madge Tillett, had planned a career for her daughter in hairdressing and had even secured her an apprenticeship. 'My mum used to go to a hairdressers in Clarence Street,' she says, 'and she got me a place there, and in those days you had to pay a premium to learn. But when they asked us at school, "Where do you want to go?" all my friends said "Rowntree's", and when they got to me I said "Rowntree's" as well, because if all my schoolfriends were going to be there, I wanted to be there, too. I thought, "Whatever am I going to say to my mum?" and she was really furious with me, but luckily my dad stuck up for me and said, "Let her go where she wants to." So, like almost all of my friends, I went to work at Rowntree's.'

Another girl, Marjorie Cockerill, was planning to join the Co-op and work in the kitchens, but when she told her father, he said, 'You're not going into the kitchens – you're that clumsy, you'll cut your hands off. Get yourself to Rowntree's and get a job there.' Muriel Jones, who had lost both of her parents within ten months of each other when she was young, and had been taken in by her aunt and uncle, saw a similar lack of sympathy from her guardian. 'When I left school,' she says, 'and had "had a rest", as my uncle called it, over the weekend, he said, "Right, now get yourself over to Rowntree's and see if you can get a job."'

Rowntree's also gave employment to people from other areas of the country. One of them, eighteen-year-old Gwen Barrass, left her home in Cramlington, Northumberland, to work at Rowntree's in 1938 without knowing a single soul in York. At the railway station she had to find the girls who were to be lodging at the same address as her – one girl from Washington, County Durham, and two from Newcastle – none of whom she had ever met before. They shared a room in a boarding house and were each charged one pound a week for full board at their lodgings, but it was very poor quality and the food they were given was almost inedible. Her wage as an adult was one pound eighteen shillings a week and she tried to send a few shillings home to her mother every week, so she did not have much left to spend on herself.

For other girls, a move to York was rooted in a family tragedy. Sheila Hawksby's great-grandparents came from Derbyshire, where they had worked as domestic servants in a country house, but both caught cholera and died, leaving Sheila's grandmother and four other children as orphans. The three oldest, including her grandmother, were old enough to work and so moved to Yorkshire in search of jobs, but the two youngest, aged just five and seven, were taken in by Barnardo's and then sent to Canada. Once there, the two children were separated and sent to homes thousands of miles from each other. Sheila's grandmother never saw either of them again.

Before she moved to York and found work at Rowntree's, Sheila's early life had been spent among the coalfields of South Yorkshire. After years in the grimy colliery districts, with the smoke-belching chimneys, the clanking winding-wheels at every pit head, the black dust that coated every surface no matter how many times the house was swept and cleaned, and the pall of smoke that seemed to hang permanently over the pit villages, York was a revelation to her. 'I thought it was a beautiful place,' she says. 'Going down Coney Street with all the lovely shops, I'd never experienced anything like that before. I thought York was a wonderful city, and I still do.'

Even though Florence had lived in York all her life and nearly all of her family already worked at Rowntree's, she still found it 'quite a scary experience' when she went into the factory for the first time for her interview. Blonde-haired and so petite that she looked even younger than her fourteen years, she drew a little comfort from the fact that a large number of other young girls were also being interviewed at the same time. Boys tended to be taken on sporadically at the factory, on an ad hoc basis, but Rowntree's need for female workers had steadily increased to cope with the rising demand for their new Black Magic assortments and Aero and Kit Kat bars, and they tended to recruit them at mass interviews and hirings, usually coinciding with the end of the Easter and summer terms, when the fourteen-year-olds were leaving school.

Most of them would have been as intimidated as Florence by the sheer scale of the Rowntree's factory and the vast numbers of people already employed there. 'There were so many people pouring in through the gates,' Florence recalls, 'and the whole place was so huge – even the rooms were enormous – that I couldn't imagine how I was ever going to find my way around the place.'

Like the other girls applying for jobs, Florence went through an interview, a 'very stiff' medical examination and also underwent a psychological evaluation. Her medical history and general state of health were assessed, and the nurse examining her searched her scalp for nits, checked her teeth and eyes, and examined her skin, taking a very close look at her hands and arms. 'They wanted to make sure that you were good and healthy before they took you on!' Florence says. She was also weighed to make sure she was not too thin for her height. Another girl, Lillian, remembers them 'playing steam' with her for being underweight – she was only six stone ten at the time.

The industrial psychologists then took over, with a series of tests designed to evaluate Florence's memory and her basic mathematical abilities – packers had to be able to count the number of chocolates going into certain products and also weigh items to ensure they were not below the minimum weight printed on the outside of the box. They also assessed her hand-eye coordination, her attention span – how long she could carry out a monotonous, repetitive task before she grew bored and began to make errors – and her ability to spot and reject misshaped or otherwise defective chocolates. Florence was given 'quite a few other tests as well. There were practical tests to see how nimble you were with your fingers and that sort of thing. There was a box filled with all different shapes that you had to quickly put into the right compartments in another box, and there was a test for piping, too, making shapes and patterns by squeezing chocolate out of an icing bag, but my hand was shaking that much through nerves that I made a right mess of it.'

The tests, first introduced by the Institute of Industrial Psychology in 1923, were continually being refined and developed by Rowntree's industrial psychologists, and since Madge's interview they had added new sections to test interviewees' reactions and agility. In the reaction test, they recorded how quickly Florence responded to a red light as it flickered on and off. She did that well enough, but the agility test was a larger version of the child's game where you have to move a metal hoop along a wire. If you allowed the hoop to touch the wire, it completed an electrical circuit and sounded a buzzer. Just as in the piping test, Florence's hand was shaking so much from nerves that her attempts to move the hoop along the wire were accompanied by a relentless succession of buzzing noises, each of which only served to make her nerves worse and her hand shake even more.

'There were quite a few other things I had to do,' she says, 'and after they had tried you out with all these different things, they then decided what sort of job to offer you. When I finished, they must have decided that I was all thumbs and much too clumsy for the production line, because I saw them write on my paper in block capitals "NO MACHINE WORK" – no piping or setting chocolates, or any of the other jobs in the Machine Room.'

3

Madge

Madge was almost too excited to sleep the night before her first full day at the Rowntree's factory, and although she knew that she had dropped off for a while during the fleeting hours of summer darkness, she was wide awake as the morning sunshine grew brighter on the edge of the curtains, listening to her two sisters breathing steadily on either side of her. Being the youngest and smallest girl, Madge had to sleep in the middle of the bed between her sisters and there were many times that she cursed her misfortune at having to do so, but not that morning. She felt cosy and safe and warm, lying next to her sisters as she thought ahead to what the day might hold. She smiled to herself when she heard the knocker-up rattling their bedroom window with her long pole, as she pictured the familiar figure of Mrs Ettenfield standing in the street below. Ample-bosomed and no more than four feet ten inches tall, she was almost as tall as she was wide, and Madge's dad always joked, 'She needs a pole to reach the parlour window, never mind the bedrooms upstairs.'

Mrs Ettenfield was the last of a dying breed, one of only a handful of knocker-ups left in the whole of the North of England by the early 1930s, and very few of them were women. Before that time, not many families in the street owned an alarm clock, because even the cheapest ones were quite expensive and unreliable, and with stiff financial penalties for being late for work, a lot of families relied instead on the traditional knocker-up to rouse them. Knocker-ups were often the older residents of a neighbourhood, doing one of the few jobs still open to them, earning a few extra coppers by banging on doors and windows to wake people up in time for work; or the lamplighters who came round the streets lighting the gas lamps in the evenings and extinguishing them again at dawn; or even the local policemen, supplementing their wages on their early-morning beats. Now clocks were becoming cheaper, and within a few years the knocker-ups, like parlourmaids and rag and bone men, would fade into history.

Madge got out of bed, provoking a sleepy mumble of complaint from Rose as she clambered over her. By the time she went downstairs, her mum was already busy, riddling out the ashes and coaxing the fire back to life to boil the smoke-blackened kettle she had filled. Madge washed her face and hands at the sink, shivering at the chill of the water. She dressed in her new overall and spent ages tying and retying her turban in front of the mirror in the hall, but each time it looked a mess. 'I just can't seem to get it right,' she said, as her sister came clattering down the stairs.

'Here, I'll do it for you,' Rose said, 'but you'll soon get the hang of it.' She retied it, gave a nod of satisfaction and then hurried through to the kitchen. Madge submitted patiently to her mum's inspection, then walked up to the factory with Rose, both of them eating a slice of bread as their breakfast on the way. Madge's gums were still sore and she tore the crusts off her bread and gave them to her sister.

Haxby Road was packed with people, all moving in the same direction. Most of the men were on bicycles, with the women on foot, a tide of white-overalled and turbaned workers flooding through the gates. They slowed to a jostling queue as they passed through the double doors into the main building. Rowntree's rules on timekeeping were strict. Everyone had to record their exact starting and finishing times by putting their time card into one of the four clocking-in machines by the timekeeper's office inside the main entrance, or in the time clocks in the individual departments. The process of clocking-in was known to the girls as 'blicking-in', because the Rowntree's time clocks were made by a company called Blick Time Recorders Ltd, and the word 'BLICK' was prominently displayed in block capitals on the face of the clocks. To encourage good timekeeping, Rowntree's gave a 'Blue Riband' award to those with 100 per cent attendance over the course of a year.

There was a 'ping' sound as each employee's card was time-stamped by the machines, and the whole entrance lobby echoed with the tinny noise. Madge gave her name to the timekeeper, who riffled through a handful of new blicking-in cards and handed her one with her name and department typed neatly at the top. Rose could have showed Madge the way to the Card Box Mill, but the company rules about introducing new employees to their workplace were as precise and unbreakable as every other aspect of Rowntree's operations, so Rose went on ahead while Madge was greeted by her designated guide and led through the factory towards the Card Box Mill.

It was a long walk, because the Card Box Mill was at the northeastern corner of the factory site. The corridor that led to Madge's workplace was windowless, flanked by offices all the way down the right-hand side, and by a vast, concrete-floored storage area on the other side. At the far end they took a staircase up to the first floor, the main card box production area, where the beautiful fancy boxes for the chocolate assortments were made. As Madge reached the top of the stairs and looked around the vast room, she was met by a wall of sound. The noise of the clattering machines on every side was deafening, and the women working there were shouting above the din just to make themselves heard.

Built ten years before, the Card Box Mill housed about 500 workers, the vast majority of them women. They worked in a huge, wood-floored open space, interrupted only by the steel pillars supporting the roof, with electric lights hanging from the steel girders that spanned the full width of the enormous room. The overhead lighting was harsh and it was always bright in there, and often extremely hot. Along with the eye-watering smell of the glue they used to stick the boxes together, there was also a rather fusty odour, suggesting a lack of care in cleaning and dusting that would never have been tolerated in the food production areas. The same applied to the pigeons that often found their way into the Card Box Mill and became trapped there. As fast as one lot were caught or killed and removed, others found their way in through broken windows or gaps around the roof edges, or by flying in through the main doors that were always left open in hot weather to provide much-needed ventilation, for it was one of the least comfortable places in the entire factory to work.

The roof – a series of steep-pitched ridges and troughs – was entirely glazed, and as a result the mill was freezing in winter, while in summer the heat was almost unbearable. Every door and window was left open to try to create a draught, and the women workers wore nothing but underwear or even swimsuits beneath their overalls, but it had little effect and sweat dripped steadily from their foreheads as they worked. Even when the glass roof was eventually whitewashed to reflect the sun's rays a little, the Card Box Mill remained ferociously hot.

Madge's guide stood over her while she pushed her card into the time clock and then showed her where to place it in the wooden racks. She then handed Madge over to the teacher – there was one in every department – whose duties included showing new girls how to do the jobs to which they had been allocated, and inspecting the work that all the women were producing, checking it for quality, making sure that materials were not being wasted and that the girls were working fast and neatly enough; 'And they soon let you know if you weren't!' one such worker, Muriel, recalls with a rueful smile. As well as the teacher, there were examiners, overlookers – Grade A and Grade B – and charge-hands, and all of them were women. The various grades were distinguished by the different coloured bands on the caps they wore: teachers had a red band, Grade A overlookers a blue one, and Grade B overlookers a green one.

In the employment of women, as in much else, Rowntree's had always been more progressive than almost any other manufacturer. The Quaker belief that God was in everyone, men and women alike, gave women as much right as men to testify or take part in the ministry at gatherings of the Society of Friends, as the Quakers were properly known, and also to seek employment if they chose. As a result, women had always worked alongside men in the Rowntree's factory – albeit on lower wages and with fewer privileges than their male counterparts. Rowntree's was also one of the first factories in Britain where women were allowed to progress beyond menial tasks to supervisory and managerial roles; the first, a 'Lady

Welfare Supervisor', had been appointed by Joseph Rowntree as far back as 1891. He also allowed production line workers a say in the appointment of their immediate supervisors – charge-hands and overlookers – an example of industrial democracy that few modern industrialists have been willing to contemplate even to this day.

The teacher took Madge to an empty space on a workbench, talked her through the work she was to do and showed her how to do it once, then left her to learn it properly by watching the woman next to her and following her instructions. The cardboard pieces were cut for them, and Madge and the other box-makers' job was to fix them together, cover them with glue – there was a pot of glue and a brush on each bench – and stick the lining paper to them, pulling it taut and shaping it to fit the curves and angles of the box they were making. She had to fashion the lid in the same way, glue the printed illustration to it, and add any ribbons or decorations that were needed.

As she watched the quick, sure movements of the woman alongside her as she created a beautiful box, lining it, shaping the lid and fixing ribbons and tassels to it, Madge had a sinking feeling. If she did the job for a hundred years, she could not imagine how she was ever going to be able to make something as perfect as that. She was so disheartened that the thought of leaving and finding other work somewhere else crossed her mind for a moment, but the thought of the volcanic reaction that would provoke from her mother was enough to dispel that idea, and she buckled down to the task of learning the job.

For the first few days, as the newest junior in the department, she was kept busy on subsidiary tasks, keeping the box-makers supplied with card, paper and the other materials they needed, and topping up their glue pots with the foul-smelling liquid glue they used. The glue pots sat bubbling away on small Bunsen burners and the fumes would not only get on the girls' chests, but also left a foul taste in their mouths. The smell and the fumes made Madge feel nauseous at first, so much so that she nearly had to run to the toilet to throw up at one point, but slowly she got used to them as she began to learn the craft of box-making.

Her first few efforts were something of an embarrassment, with the paper lining full of lumps, bumps and creases, the folds in the card not sharp enough or in the wrong place, and with dribbles of glue on the outside, but she rapidly improved and before long her work was drawing admiring glances from her fellow workers and even compliments from the overlookers. Although there were no formal apprenticeships for women in the factory, as there were for the men learning skilled trades like carpentry, bricklaying, painting, decorating and electrical engineering at Rowntree's, work such as box-making was highly skilled and a genuine trade, and despite her earlier misgivings Madge ultimately proved to be one of the most skilful of all. The skills that she and the other Rowntree's girls acquired at work increased their self-confidence, and that confidence often extended into their home lives as well. Many felt more able to stand up for themselves and argue their corner with a father or husband, though a woman who was thought by men to be too 'pushy' or 'gobby' was often deemed a 'factory girl' – shorthand for a loud, crude and foul-mouthed woman.

Rowntree's paid workers a week in hand – the girls were paid on Thursday afternoons for the work they had done the previous week – so Madge had to wait eleven days before she received her first wages. Early on the Thursday afternoon, a woman from the pay office appeared in the Card Box Mill, pushing a trolley along the aisle between the clanking machines and pausing at each workbench to hand out a pay packet. A man walked alongside her, his eyes darting everywhere, as if he was riding shotgun on a wagon train and expecting an attack by outlaws at any moment.

The system of paying wages had been rather less formal in Rowntree's early days. In the old factory at Tanners Moat, everyone kept their own note of the hours they had worked and at the end of each week the foreman went round with a hat full of coins, asked each of them, 'How much time has thou got?' and then paid them accordingly.

Madge had been trying to imagine what it would feel like to hold her first ever pay packet, and the feeling did not disappoint. She signed her name in the ledger to show that she'd received her wages, and then held the small brown paper packet unopened in her hands, savouring the moment. She turned it over and was about to rip it open when Rose called across to her, 'Tear off the corner and check it first. Once you've opened it, you can't go to the pay office and complain, even if your wages are short. They might just say you've pocketed it and are trying it on.'

Madge tore off a corner of the pay packet and fingered the edge of one crisp, new ten-shilling note. She shook the packet, heard the rattle of a coin and tipped the packet to let the coin slide to the top so that she could make sure it was a shilling. She turned the packet over again, ripped it open and took out her wages. The ten-bob note, the first she'd ever had in her hands, was pristine, straight from the bank and without a crease in it, and it almost felt like sacrilege to fold it up and put it in the little blue sailor bag hanging around her neck, where she kept her money for her tea because they were not allowed to have pockets in their overalls.

Madge had been taken on as a junior at the minimum Rowntree's wage of eleven shillings a week, and she didn't even see much of that because, like all her sisters and brothers, she had to march straight home on pay day and hand her wage packet to her mum. She would keep ten shillings (fifty pence) for Madge's keep and then give her back the odd shilling as spending money. From then on, every week Madge spent sixpence (two and a half pence) on the price of admission to a dance at the New Earswick Folk Hall or the Assembly Rooms in the centre of York, and used the other sixpence to buy make-up: 'I always loved my make-up,' she says, 'and I would far rather spend my money on that than the sweets, drinks or stockings that my sisters often bought with their money.' However, Madge didn't even have a shilling to spend during her first few weeks at Rowntree's, because she had to pay for her own uniforms for work – the white overall and turban to cover her hair – and she had to have two of them, so that she had one to wear while the other was in the wash.

As in most other industries of that era, the rules about uniforms for work were more strict for women employees than for men, and the male authors of the Rowntree's rule book also made patronizing attempts to link the requirements of food hygiene to attractiveness and style, including the comment that: 'A Clean Cap and Overall Properly Worn Make an Attractive Uniform. A Workmanlike Appearance is the Best of Styles for the Workroom.' Although admittedly far less men worked on the production lines, rules about covering hair with a cap were not applied to them until 1953, and it is probably no coincidence that from that date onwards, the company itself provided and paid for staff uniforms, whereas previously, women employees had been expected to provide their own, at their own expense.

The women didn't wear hairnets – the rules requiring them to be worn at work were not introduced until the 1960s – but without exception, all the women production workers, even in areas like the Card Box Mill where no edible items were produced, had to wear turbans, and as Madge had discovered, there was an art to tying these. There was also often a conflict between the factory regulations and the dictates of fashion: the rules stated that all the woman's hair had to be tucked under the turban, but most women left at least a fringe of hair exposed, and often much more than that.

During Madge's early days in the Card Box Mill, an overlooker came marching along the production line one day, brandishing a couple of hairs that had found their way into a completed chocolate box. Madge's sister Rose had beautiful, lustrous long hair, and when not at work had it arranged in ringlets down her back – 'She used to win prizes for it at the Rialto,' Madge says. Rose was now singled out and told to report to the manager's office.

She returned to the house that lunchtime in floods of tears. Their mum looked up from her cooking and said, 'Now then, our Rose, what's wrong with you?'

'I've been told off about my hair,' Rose said. 'They found a hair in one of the boxes and they think it's one of mine.'

Madge's mum gave her a look that was somewhat lacking in sympathy and then said, 'Come here a moment, then.' Rose gave her a puzzled look, but did as she was told, and Madge's mum immediately took out her kitchen scissors and cropped off all of Rose's long ringlets, saying, 'There you are. Problem solved!' However, when she'd finished snipping away with the scissors, and saw all those beautiful ringlets lying on the floor, Madge's mum joined in with Rose's tears and sobbed even louder than her daughter.

Juniors like Madge were paid lower rates when they were young, and they didn't go on to the full adult wage until they were twenty-one. Like many other manufacturers, at times when there was no shortage of labour Rowntree's used to save money by getting rid of workers when they were old enough to qualify for a full adult wage and taking on another fourteen-year-old instead. Men received higher pay than women, even when performing exactly the same task, but they were just as vulnerable to being sacked as soon as they qualified for the full adult wage. Madge's three brothers were all fired by Rowntree's when they reached their twenty-first birthdays. One of them, Ted, the second eldest, couldn't find other work around York and in the end emigrated to Australia. That was in the days of the 'Ten Pound Poms', when it cost you ten pounds to emigrate there on voyages that were heavily subsidized by the Australian government. Neither Ted nor his parents had that kind of money, but their neighbours heard about it, held a collection in the street and raised seven pounds for him. Madge's dad then told Ted, 'I'll give you the other three pounds.' So Ted and another boy from the street went out to Australia together on a steamer packed with Ten Pound Poms. It was a ten- to twelve-week journey, and once out there the emigrants had to remain there for at least two years or repay the full cost of their passage – the huge sum of £120. As a result, most emigrants did not return to Britain for many years, even for a brief visit, and some never came back at all.

Madge was nine years old when Ted left. It was to be forty-seven years before she or any other member of the family saw him again, and it was several years before they had news of him at all. Madge's mum wrote regular letters to the last address she had for him, but they all came back unopened, because neither his family nor the Australian authorities had any idea where he was. Like thousands of others in those bitter years of the 1930s, he was unemployed for a long time, wandering the outback trying to eke out a living and find some work somewhere, even if it was just an hour or two's labour in return for food or a roof over his head for the night. Without work, Ted was reduced to eating out of bins, or anything he could find. He did not write to his family, partly because he didn't even have money for a stamp, but also because he didn't want to write with a tale of failure, preferring to leave them in ignorance of the dire straits he was in.

However, Ted came to an outback farm one day and asked the farmer's wife for work or something to eat. She pointed to a pile of logs and told him that if he split those for her, she'd give him some food. He chopped the logs for her and did a few more odd jobs around the farm over the next few days, and eventually he was taken on as a permanent worker. The farmer's wife had a daughter, Maud, and she and Ted started courting and in time they got married.

Madge was a married woman with children of her own long before Ted returned to Britain, but finally, forty-seven years after emigrating as a Ten Pound Pom, he came home on a visit, bringing Maud to meet his mum, who by then was in her late eighties. Madge's mum had always said, 'Whatever else, I'll live to see our Ted come back,' and she was as good as her word, and in fact lived for many years after that, dying at the ripe old age of ninety-five. However, her husband had died of a stroke some years before Ted came home, and was never to see his son again. A few years after that visit, Madge and her sister Ginny went out to Australia together and stayed with Ted and Maud on the farm, which by then they'd inherited.

When Madge started at Rowntree's in 1932, Ginny was working as a tour guide, showing visitors around the factory. There were seventy women working in the Guides department, a reflection of the huge popularity of the Rowntree's factory tours. School parties, clubs and all sorts of other organizations – 70,000 people a year in total – took the free tours, coming from all over the North of England and far beyond, by train, charabanc and later, as affluence increased, by car. People coming by train arrived at Rowntree's Halt and the guides, dressed in cream overalls edged with brown piping and wearing navy-blue court shoes, would walk through the factory to meet them there. Other arrivals were dropped off by bus outside the guides' office in part of the Dining Block.

Ginny was a lively character and very popular with the visitors. Their dad used to say, 'There's always one devilish one in a family,' and in the Fishers it was Ginny, though Madge herself was not far behind. Ginny was, Madge says, 'a real devil, always cracking jokes, playing tricks and bending the rules whenever she could'. Rowntree's tour guides were strictly forbidden to accept tips, but many visitors, especially the Americans, were accustomed to tipping everywhere they went and Ginny was certainly not going to look such a gift horse in the mouth. As she was showing the visitors around the factory, she would glance behind her to make sure there were no supervisors or managers within earshot and then say, 'We're not supposed to accept tips, you know, but in case you're interested, that's my pocket right there!'

As a tour guide, Ginny often had to work very long hours. The tours didn't start until 8.30 a.m. but the guides still had to turn up for work at 7.30, and spent the first hour of their day working on the production lines. They then assembled in a long line and were given one of the five routes: A, B, C, D or E. Each guide would take a small group, usually about eight people, and lead them on a three-mile walk around the factory that took two hours to complete. One tour started at the Card Box Mill, another in the Gum department, another at the Cream Block, another at the offices, and the last one at the Melangeur Block. The name Melangeur (the workers pronounced it 'mullanja') had been adopted from a term used by the French and Swiss confectioners who had perfected the art of chocolate-making. *Mélangeur* meant 'mixer' in French and the Melangeur Block was where all the chocolate for the factory was made.

As well as the general public, Rowntree's also used factory tours to strengthen the company's links with wholesalers and retailers. Once a year a train would set off from London and 'stop at just about every station' to pick up local shopkeepers and bring them to York for a factory tour. The guides would go down to Rowntree's Halt to meet them and show them around the factory, and then serve them tea. There were evening tours too, and dinners, and Ginny would sometimes work till midnight, having been there since 7.30 a.m., though if they worked that late, Rowntree's did at least pay for taxis to make sure that all the guides got home safely.

While Ginny led factory tours, Madge and her sister Rose were hand-making fancy boxes, but their other sister in the

Card Box Mill, Laura, was at the machine end of the room, doing much less interesting work, making plain boxes and the 'outers' – the large cartons in which the completed boxes were shipped. She would have loved to have been working in the same section as Madge and her other sisters, making boxes of all shapes and sizes, as it was interesting work and very skilled. There were heart-shaped boxes for Valentine's Day, and special ones for Christmas and Easter, as well as for one-off presentations. When Madge was eighteen she was chosen to make four beautiful boxes to be presented to Queen Mary and her three ladies in waiting during a visit to the factory, all in ruched satin with drawers with silk tassels, and each box a different colour: gold for the Queen, and red, green and blue for her ladies in waiting. The Queen spent some time standing at the end of the bench, right next to Madge, watching her work, and it was all Madge could do to stop her hands trembling with nerves.

Even though Madge and the other girls had stools at their workbenches, they usually used them to hold their work because, with boxes stacked while they waited for the glue to dry, there wasn't enough space on their benches for everything. They preferred to stand anyway – it wasn't possible to do the work while sitting down – but they were more than ready for a rest and a sit down by the end of the day. They had a ten-minute break in the morning – there was no afternoon break – but they did not have time to go to the dining hall during break time, so they would all buy a mug of tea or cocoa, or a glass of milk or squash from the trolley brought round to each department by one of the servers from the Dining Block. Rather than sit on their high stools in full view of the overlookers, Madge and the other girls used to lay their stools on their sides, flat on the floor next to the machines, and then perch on the legs and chat until they finished their drinks. Sometimes they would even crawl underneath the benches where they worked, out of sight of the overlookers, but they had to crawl back out as soon as the bell went to signal the end of the break, and get cracking again straight away.

As they were doing hand-work, Madge and her workmates could go for a short toilet break whenever they needed one, whereas Madge's sister Laura at the other end of the room had to wait for break time. Like those at many other factories, she and her workmates could only leave their work stations during official rest periods, because if anyone left at other times they had to stop the machines. 'You all had to go to the toilet together,' one of them recalls. 'We worked from half past seven to half past five, and you kept working until the conveyor stopped.'

Another woman, Kath, who worked in Cream Packing, putting the chocolate assortments into the boxes that Madge and her workmates made, recalls that:

> *We used to get a ten-minute toilet break when they'd stop the machines and we all had to go to the toilet together, because when the conveyor was running you had to be working. One charge-hand was a real stickler. She would look at the clock and say, 'Right, ten minutes, no longer,' and then turn the machine off. Precisely ten minutes later, whether or not everyone was back from the toilet, she'd turn the machine back on again. Down would come all the chocolates, and the last few girls would be scrambling to get back to their places in time. With the time it took to get there and back, you'd only have six minutes' break time, but it was amazing what you*

could get up to in those six minutes, especially my friend Joyce. She used to draw black lines on bits of white paper, stick them on her eyelids, like giant false eyelashes, and walk down the aisle between the machines, fluttering her eyelids at the men she passed going down the room.

The girls were not allowed food on their workbenches, so if they wanted something to eat at break time, they either had to eat it sitting on the floor or go downstairs to the room where they kept their coats. Again, as soon as they had finished eating, they had to rush to the toilets and then be back at the machines ready to start work as soon as they started running. 'If you weren't there,' says one of them, 'that was your lookout and you'd be struggling to catch up.'

Some of Madge's workmates in the hand-work section took advantage of their relative freedom compared to the machine box-makers stuck at their workplaces on the conveyor belt, and they often used a toilet break as an excuse to go for a crafty smoke outside, since smoking was forbidden anywhere within the factory buildings. Madge did not smoke, but her friend Alice would often pretend to have period pains in order to take a break; if the overlookers had been more alert, they might have noticed that she appeared to be having two or three periods a month.

There was a rest room as well, where women could go if they weren't feeling well. They could have an hour's sleep and then, if they still didn't feel any better, they could go home. This was also open to a certain amount of abuse, and sometimes Madge or one of the other girls would either elude the overlookers and sneak off to the rest room or pretend an illness they didn't really feel, and then go and have a quick forty winks.

Until the age of eighteen, like all the other juniors at Rowntree's, Madge spent a few hours a week at what were known as 'Day Continuation' classes, another of Joseph Rowntree's liberal innovations, aimed at extending the education of his workforce for a few years beyond their schooldays. Employees had to attend classes one day a week for boys and one afternoon a week for girls. For the most part, the classes were not aimed at improving their working skills, but rather as an end in themselves, giving them a taste of music and drama, for example, that they might otherwise never have experienced.

Miss Birkenshaw took the drama group, and while most of the girls and women at Rowntree's wore plain-coloured, utilitarian clothes in more or less drab shades of green, brown, grey or black, she was an altogether more exotic specimen. Her hair was immaculately coiffed and she wore thick make-up with heavily rouged cheeks that made her look a little like a Japanese geisha, and she always dressed in heavily frilled blouses and suits in vivid shades of pink, red and orange. Her reading style was equally dramatic and her choice of mainstream, middlebrow books such as *Jamaica Inn* proved very popular with Madge and the other girls.

Miss Johnson, the music teacher, was a much less flamboyant character but no less well liked by her pupils. She was a Scot, with a soft Highlands accent, and taught the girls everything from traditional Scottish ballads to light opera and classical music. She wore her long, dark hair in a bun, but as she waved her hands about conducting an imaginary orchestra while the music played, her hairpins would often fall out and her hair would tumble around her shoulders while the class collapsed in fits of giggles.

The girls were also expected to improve their physical condition through PT (physical training) sessions, and Miss Birkenshaw often took those classes as well. In winter or in poor weather, the sessions were held in the factory gymnasiums – one for each sex – in the long glass veranda along one side of the Dining Block, but in summer the classes were held out of doors, often on the Rose Lawn near the main gates of the factory. Madge and the other girls, shivering and self-conscious, had to go outside and over the road, wearing their shorts that looked like navy-blue knickers, and they had to do their exercises on the lawn with everyone peering out of the windows at them, as one of them later recalled: 'I always hated PT because of that.' Those who were keener on exercise could also do fitness and athletics classes after working hours, some of them run by Audrey Kilner-Brown, who worked in the Personnel department but was well qualified to coach athletics, having won a silver medal in the 100 metres at the 1936 Berlin Olympics.

The Day Continuation classes took place in the Dining Block, where the junior employees were also taught skills for life. In the case of girls, such skills were often, though not always, linked to their supposed future roles as wives and mothers. In autumn 1938, the company's house journal *Cocoa Works Magazine* noted 'a strong demand for courses of instruction in the domestic field, helpful to brides to be', and ten years later the magazine was still proudly claiming that they helped 'the natural ambition of the normal girl for marriage and motherhood'.

However, the girls' classes were not confined to the domestic duties that wives and mothers were expected to carry out; they were also taught a variety of subjects that appeared to vary from year to year according to the skills, interests and sometimes the hobbies of those appointed to teach them. Many girls seem to have been taught English and natural sciences but, perhaps surprisingly in the context of the times, many also learned woodwork, making wooden trays, stools or other small items for their homes.

Madge and her classmates were also taken to see the glazed hot house near the Dining Block, where the gardeners grew tropical fruits like bananas, as well as vanilla pods and cocoa beans, though the latter were for demonstration purposes, not for production. During the war years, when imports of fruit from the Caribbean virtually ceased, that hot house was one of the few places in Britain where you could actually find a banana. There were also grass tennis courts between the hot house and the Haxby Road, one of several leisure facilities that women employees on short-time working were encouraged to use, and behind the tennis courts there were flowerbeds where the gardeners grew the cut flowers for the vases spread throughout the factory.

4

Florence

Like Madge, Florence was sent to work in the Card Box Mill, where they made the fancy cardboard boxes for the chocolate assortments, and the plainer ones for Black Magic and Dairy Box. Her heart sank when she saw her workplace for the first time that summer day in 1937, because there were so many machines and the noise they made was deafening. As if that wasn't daunting enough for a shy girl like Florence, the overlookers were also very strict. 'They used to sit in the middle of the room at right high desks,' she says, 'so that they could see everybody and everything that was going on, and when you were just starting and very young like me, I daren't do anything wrong, because I was really frightened of them.'

Two of the overlookers, Miss Price and Miss Sanderson, were 'both tartars really', according to Joan Martin, one of Florence's workmates, who also worked under their hawk-like gaze:

> *Everything had to be done just right or you were in trouble. Miss Sanderson was very tall and very straight-laced. She was in charge of inspecting your work and if you got one thin mint too many in a box, or whatever it was, you were in trouble. And if Miss Sanderson came round the corner and caught you*

putting a chocolate in your mouth, you'd really be in for it. Miss Price was shorter and tubbier, but pretty strict too, though the foreman, Mr Walker, was even worse. He was a holy terror and a lot of the girls were frightened of him. Miss Price and Miss Sanderson could be a bit too demanding, but they were nice enough away from the factory. They shared a house in Fountain Street, just off Haxby Road near the factory. They were living together, but in those days nobody thought anything much about that; if they thought about it at all, they probably just assumed they were friends.

When Florence and the other new girls started work, Rowntree's invited their mothers to come in during their first week, to look round the factory and see what their daughters were doing. In fact, although Florence had been interviewed on her own, throughout most of the 1930s the girls' mothers or sometimes a friend of the family would sit alongside them during their interviews. The system was changed in 1938, so that girls were interviewed without their mothers being present, though they were still invited into the factory on the afternoon of their daughters' first day at work, to have tea with them in the café annexe and talk through their first experience of paid work. History does not relate whether this was to reassure the mothers that their daughters were being well trained and looked after, or to stiffen the backbones of daughters who had found their first taste of the workplace unpleasant and were looking for a way out.

The parents of boys starting apprenticeships were also invited to the factory. A huge range of skilled tradesmen were employed by Rowntree's, and every craftsman, joiner, engineer, bricklayer, plasterer, electrician, plumber, painter and decorator had an apprentice. Their mothers and fathers would look round the factory and then go over to the dining hall and have tea with their boy's overlooker, just to get to know the man who was to be in charge of their son for the five- to seven-year term of his apprenticeship.

Florence's mum came in one afternoon soon after she had started work, but Florence was so scared of the overlookers and so fearful of doing something wrong that she did not even look up when her mum walked past her workbench, but kept her eyes down, fixed on her work. When she started, she was too frightened to do anything but get on with her work, but 'it was a learning experience there,' Florence says, 'and I soon got a bit braver and a bit bolder, and I came out of there knowing a lot more than when I went in – and not just about work!'

It was all piecework – the quicker you worked, the more you could earn – and there was very little training. New girls like Florence were not set to work with an experienced woman who could have shown them the ropes and helped them get up to speed; they were shown once what they were supposed to be doing and that was it, they were thrown in at the deep end and left to sink or swim. Rather than making her less error prone, Florence's nervousness and her desperation not to make mistakes made her even more fallible, and there was precious little sympathy for her from some of her more experienced workmates. She recalls:

> *It took a while to learn everything, but if they thought you were going too slow and costing them money, some of the women you were working with could be pretty impatient with you … and some a bit more than impatient. My job was to keep a woman supplied with cardboard to make the boxes and*

at first I couldn't keep her going fast enough with them. She thought I was being too slow, so she threw a box at me and one of the corners hit me in the eye. I had a real shiner of a black eye and a scratch on the eyeball itself and she panicked a bit then, and said, 'I'll never do that again.' I think she was worried stiff that I'd report it, but I was far too frightened of her to do that. Anyway, my eye was all right, and I soon got up to speed with the work; it was amazing how quickly you learned. It was funny, when we started, the experienced women didn't want us juniors anywhere near them, because they thought we'd be costing them money, but by the time we got moved to other departments, we'd got that good at it that they didn't want us to go.

Nearly all the production line workers in the factory were paid at piecework rates, and there were sometimes astonishing differences in the speed at which some of the more dexterous women could perform their tasks. One woman was legendary for the speed with which she could chop cherries for the Cherry Cup chocolates (known as Liquid Cherry in the 1930s) for the Black Magic assortments. Normal workers picked up a cherry from the pile on their left, placed it on the chopping board in front of them, cut it in half with their knife and then picked up the two halves and dropped them into the container on their right. However, this particular woman had evolved a system where she flicked cherries across from her left, trapping them against the blade of her knife, cut them in half with a blow of the knife and then flicked the halves into the container on her right with the knife blade. She worked so fast that she reached her targets and achieved the maximum piece-rate income well before the end of the working week, and after that she would surreptitiously shift some of her surplus cherries to the containers of her workmates so that they too could earn more.

As elsewhere in the factory, in addition to their lunch break, Florence and the other girls had a ten-minute break in the morning, though none at all in the afternoon. The break was taken at or near their workbenches and conveyors, since there was insufficient time to go anywhere else. A woman from the kitchens came round with the trolley of hot and cold drinks – tea, coffee, cocoa, milk, lemonade or lime juice – though they weren't provided free; the girls had to pay for them. Although there was a choice of drinks, the trolley did not contain any food. In some of the food production areas, employees were not allowed to bring in anything to eat in case crumbs or other debris contaminated the confectionery or attracted vermin; in others they were merely forbidden to eat at their work tables, but could eat sitting on the floor or in the changing room downstairs, or there was a 'corridor kitchen' where they could buy sandwiches or scones that had been made in the Dining Block. Less strict rules applied in areas of the factory where no food was produced, like the Card Box Mill and the Saw Mill, which may help to explain the Card Box Mill's near-permanent population of pigeons.

At first Florence and her fellow juniors used to sit under the bench during their break and try to turn out some more boxes while they were there, to keep up to the rate that had been set, but even during their breaks the overlookers used to watch them, and would shout at them, 'This is a break. You're supposed to sit and rest and not do any work,' and the girls had to stop. Like many others, Florence used to go home for her lunch because she lived so close to the factory, so she did not use the Dining Block regularly until much later on when she was put on night shifts, but occasionally, if her mother was away for the day visiting a relative, Florence would have her lunch at work.

The Dining Block was on the other side of Haxby Road from the factory, and at dinnertime – lunchtime to those born outside of the North – although some made the dash across the road, most of the thousands of workers opted to reach the block by means of the tunnel that ran right under the Haxby Road. On the night shift, when the factory was largely deserted and the gates locked, there was no option but to use the tunnel. The entrance was near the Rose Lawns, and the first time she used it Florence thought that from the outside it looked like an overgrown bike shed, but inside, to her amazement, she found that there was a grand double staircase leading down into a broad tunnel. At the far end Florence followed the crowd of chattering workers up another double staircase into the three-storeyed dining hall.

The Dining Block was on the same giant scale as the rest of the factory. The offices and the Health department that had occupied part of the building when Madge was interviewed had now been moved to the newly built Cream Block on the other side of the road, and almost all of the Dining Block was now given over to feeding the army of Rowntree's workers. There was a café and servery, and a 500-capacity men's dining hall on the ground floor, a women's dining hall seating 2,000 on the first floor, and an executive dining room with waitress service on the top floor, where the firm's managers and directors could eat. Florence and her workmates would join the queue, and as they approached the servery, wooden railings at hip height funnelled them into single file. Having ordered their food, they then sat at long, thin wooden benches to eat their lunch, usually soup, meat and two veg and a steamed pudding, though on Fridays the main course was always fish. Whether served at midday or in the middle of the night, it cost less than a shilling, with meat and two veg for sevenpence halfpenny and fish and chips fourpence or sixpence.

The Dining Block was packed from noon to 2 p.m. every day, with the peak at 12.30 p.m. when the women's dining hall was usually full to bursting. Men and women were always segregated, eating in separate canteens, a practice that continued until the 1950s. Contact between the male and female workers at any time during the working day was very limited. Apart from an occasional sighting of a manager hurrying past, as a rule the only men that the women on the conveyor belts would see were those who brought in the tubs of chocolate or heavier materials and took out the empty ones, or wheeled away the trolleys of completed boxes or outers.

Although some of the older workers recall Seebohm Rowntree, 'a little man with white hair and a gold chain across his waistcoat', walking round the factory and greeting all the women employees he passed with a courteous 'Good morning ladies,' many of the later generations of managers, who were all 'quite posh' according to Florence, used to walk around the factory without speaking. The manager of the Card Box Mill, Ned Sparkes, rarely showed his face at all, much to the regret of Florence and some of the other girls, because he was very good-looking. 'He had the looks of a 1940s matinée idol,' Florence says, trying not to sigh at the recollection, 'and quite a few of the girls had crushes on him.'

The overlookers were a different matter. There was a strict hierarchy in each department. The production line workers were at the bottom of the pyramid, and above them were the teachers who taught the new employees how to do their jobs, supervised them to make sure they were doing it right and also made sure that the work of the existing workers was up to standard. Next in the hierarchy were the examiners and check-weighers, who checked the completed products coming off the end of the line, and then there were the charge-hands and finally the overlookers, who ruled the roost on the production lines and reported directly to the departmental manager.

Rowntree's policy of promoting women to supervisory roles was still unusual in that era, but although welcomed by most women, it could also prove a source of friction. Some preferred male bosses and did not like being supervised by another woman, though in some cases that might have been because of resentment that the woman had been preferred to them for promotion. Even the overlookers' high stools – necessary so that they could see everything that was going on in the room – were strongly resented by some workers, one woman complaining that a particular overlooker was 'like the Queen of Sheba' as she kept watch over them.

The overlookers had all worked on the line themselves, but a feeling of 'us and them' usually began to develop with their former workmates almost as soon as they were promoted. Room examiners, check-weighers, charge-hands and overlookers had more status but little more pay than their fellow workers, and after being promoted out of the 'ranks', they were separated from the community of girls on the machines and conveyors and so missed out on much of the gossip and the tales. 'We didn't really socialize with the charge-hands and overlookers anyway,' Florence says, 'but most of them were all right, though there was one with delusions of grandeur who started elocution lessons as soon as she became an overlooker! She didn't want to know us then, but when she retired she was suddenly keen to spend time in our company again.'

One of Florence's contemporaries, Joan Martin, who ended up as a teacher, still harbours regrets that she accepted promotion instead of remaining an ordinary worker on the production line. 'I'd rather have stayed in packing really. You had to be a bit keen on how they did things if you were a teacher and there was sometimes a little bit of friction. I didn't really enjoy that. I'd rather have stayed as just one of the workers.' Another called it 'like a prefect type of thing. Some of them got carried away with it. We used to say, "Look at her. She's got a few more brownie points today, she's told off someone."'

Another of Florence's workmates, Dot Edwards, also became a teacher, even though she also says that she did not really want to:

I was happy just looking after myself, rather than looking after others, but it was a choice between becoming a teacher or going into the Machine Room and I couldn't bear the smell of chocolate flopping [the curtain of liquid chocolate constantly falling inside the enrober]. It sounds strange for someone working in a chocolate factory, but I wasn't the only one; that sweet, sickly smell could be overpowering. I worked in piping for a bit but I'd only been there for a short while when I offered to leave. I'd only gone in as a volunteer and I said, 'I'll never volunteer for anything again in my life.' I went in the office and said, 'I can't bear the smell of that chocolate flopping,' so they sent me back to packing and I became a teacher there instead. When you started, you didn't get long to learn how to do it, you got shown by the teacher and then you just had to get on with it and some teachers were better than others. A friend of mine was being taught by a man and I said to him, 'She'd learn a lot quicker if I showed her how to do it instead.'

Even though one newly promoted overlooker, Brenda Gray, was told, 'Although you're a supervisor, you're still a worker,' – which she took to mean 'Don't be getting too big for your boots and start thinking you're better than the others' – some of the overlookers lorded it over the girls working on the line. All of them were strict and one of them, called Mabel, was particularly fierce, with a very fiery temper. When she first started at Rowntree's, Florence kept her head down and wouldn't have dreamed of answering back to any of the overlookers, least of all to Mabel, but as she grew more mature and experienced, she felt more able to stand up for herself. There was a vivid demonstration of how much Florence had grown in self-confidence from the shy, timid fourteen-year-old she had been, after an argument developed between her and another fiery overlooker one day. The overlooker had been promoted only recently and was perhaps keen to make her mark, so she shouted at Florence and then threatened her, saying, 'I'll knock your block off.'

Florence matched her look for look. 'I don't think you will,' she said. 'I'm stronger than you, so if anyone is going to get their block knocked off, I don't think it's going to be me.' There was a long silence and then the overlooker backed down and stalked off, muttering to herself, while Florence's workmates crowded around to congratulate her. The overlooker steered a wide berth around Florence from then on.

At the end of the working day Florence would join the jostling crowds of men and women walking or sprinting out of the gates. 'There'd be buses galore parked up and down the Haxby Road,' she remembers, 'and bikes galore and people galore, and as soon as that buzzer went at the end of the day, they all used to run and there was a mad rush to get out of the gates. The Haxby Road bridge was only a little one then and it would be absolutely choked with bicycles.' Some girls cycled from the far side of York. Dot Edwards used to bike to Rowntree's from Dringhouses on the south side of the city, beyond the Knavesmire racecourse, leaving home at 6.45 a.m. and getting to the factory just in time to start work at 7.30. The bikes she and the other girls rode were heavy, steel-framed machines with fixed gears and, she says, 'It used to be hard work in bad weather, and that Mount [virtually York's only hill] seemed to get higher every day.'

The parts of the factory where continuous production was needed operated on a three-shift system – 6 a.m. to 2 p.m.; 2 p.m. to 10 p.m.; 10 p.m. to 6 a.m. – but, like most of the workforce, Florence's normal hours of work were 7.30 a.m. to 5 p.m. on Monday and Friday, and 7.30 a.m. to 5.30 p.m. on Tuesday, Wednesday and Thursday. With an hour for lunch each day, that made the normal working week one of forty-four hours, with Saturdays off. When the five-day week was introduced at Rowntree's in April 1919, it was highly unusual (most factories treated Saturday as another working day) and at first Rowntree's introduced it only on a six-month trial basis. As a young woman, Florence's mum had always worked Saturday mornings in the factory and she told Florence that she wouldn't have wanted it any other way. 'Why would I have wanted to be at home doing chores and housework for nothing,' she said, 'when I could be at work and earning?' One of the reasons for Rowntree's caution was the thought that many employees might feel the same as Florence's mum about substituting unpaid domestic drudgery for paid work at the factory, but the five-day week proved popular with almost everyone and was permanently adopted at the end of the six-month trial. It was not introduced for the vast majority of other British workers until after the Second World War, over a quarter of a century after Rowntree's had pioneered it.

As a junior, Florence was paid eleven shillings for her forty-four-hour week. Like Madge, she used to give it all to her mother, who would keep ten shillings and give Florence the odd shilling back as pocket money. She used to go to the pictures once a week on a Saturday afternoon. It was threepence to get in and Florence and her friends used to call it 'The Threepenny Rush' because there was such a mad scramble to get the best seats when the doors opened. She spent another penny on a Mountain Maid – a bar of toffee with chocolate on – to eat during the film, and she kept the rest of the money to see her through the remainder of the week, although if she and her friends were feeling rich on a Saturday night, they used to live the high life by going to the fish and chip shop for a tuppenny (fish) and a pennorth (of chips).

As well as their work, juniors had to do Day Continuation classes, but the hours had been reduced from when Madge started work. Boys now did one afternoon a week, while Florence and her fellow juniors just did two hours: one hour of English and one hour of Greek dancing. Like Madge, Florence was taught by Miss Birkenshaw, who took her for English, 'and a few lessons were certainly needed in my case,' she says, 'though I must have been a hopeless case because I'm no better at it now.' Her other lesson, Greek dancing, was a rather more surprising one. 'I can't remember who took us for that,' she says, 'some Greek goddess, I suppose! God knows why they taught us that, but there was no choice about it, that's what we had to do.' Florence and her friends had to wear green slip-on tabards with slits up the sides, and the infamous shorts like navy-blue knickers, and then go across the road from the girls' gym room to the Rose Lawn in front of the factory and do their dancing there. 'All the workmen used to be whistling at us,' she says, 'and we used to feel such fools. When we'd finished we had to go back to the changing rooms and we were all supposed to have a bath in the slipper baths before going back to work, but they didn't give you time to bath, dry yourself and put your clothes on. The teacher would always be shouting, "Aren't you ready yet girls?" when you hadn't been in there two minutes. So we often just used to dip our feet in the water, stamp around on the duckboards to make them wet and pretend we'd had a bath, but she used to peer through the gap under the door from time to time and say, "I can see you're not having a bath, you know."'

Greek dancing was the only dancing Florence ever did, because, unlike most of the other girls, she never used to go dancing in her free time. Even when they were on night shift and had their 'lunch' break at one o'clock in the morning, Florence would go over to the Dining Block for her meal with the other girls, but after they had eaten, when the rest of the girls put records on and started dancing, Florence would just sit and watch. However, she insists it was not because of her shyness. 'I used to love to watch so much that I never really learned how to dance properly – though I can dance by myself all right!' At weekends most of the other girls would go to dances at the De Grey Rooms or the Assembly Rooms in the centre of York, or walk or pedal their bikes to New Earswick for the dances at the Folk Hall there, but Florence never joined them. She and her best friend rarely had any money to spend anyway, and so they used to walk round the streets in the evenings instead. There was always the thought, never voiced, that they might meet a couple of boys while they were out walking, but although they might risk a glance from under their eyelashes, both Florence and her friend were so shy that they never actually dared to talk to any of the boys they did pass on the streets.

5

Madge

Working in the Card Box Mill, Madge and her sisters never saw a chocolate or a sweet while they were at work, except when their sister Ginny was showing visitors around the factory. Ginny would sometimes fill her pocket with chocolates in the Cream Packing department, and when the tour reached the Card Box Mill, she would put her hand in her pocket as she got to Madge's workbench and discreetly drop a handful on the end of the bench as she walked past. Madge didn't mind which chocolates they were, because she liked all of them!

Apart from that rare treat, all Madge and Rose usually encountered at work was cardboard and foul-smelling glue balls, but once in a while, when the orders for fancy boxes dried up, Madge and Rose were transferred to other departments for a few weeks. Near Christmas every year extra girls were drafted into the Fresh Fruit department to pack the crystallized orange and lemon slices that came in a round box with a little wooden fork. Madge and Rose were also sometimes sent to the Machine Room, where the chocolate assortments were packed into the boxes they had made, and the two girls even spent a few weeks working on the production line for a brand-new chocolate assortment called Black Magic, introduced after one of the most extensive – and expensive – market research campaigns that had ever been mounted at that time.

Seebohm Rowntree had not lost his faith in industrial psychologists and in 1931, even as Rowntree's struggled to survive at all, he had been so impressed by the 'psychological approach to market research' of a precocious young Cambridge graduate and self-proclaimed genius, Nigel Balchin, that he promptly hired him as a consultant to the company. Seebohm's judgement was rapidly vindicated, because Balchin proved to be one of the saviours of Rowntree's.

Balchin's talents were not confined to industrial psychology. He was already writing humorous articles for *Punch* magazine and would later become a highly successful novelist and Hollywood screenwriter, but while at Rowntree's he also turned his prodigious imagination to developing new products. He at once pointed out that, while new products were introduced after extensive consultations with the company's different departmental heads and its experts in design and production, the opinions of the public who were expected to buy them were rarely, if ever, canvassed.

In July 1932, the same month that Madge began work at the factory, Balchin persuaded Seebohm and the cash-strapped Rowntree's board to invest the then considerable sum of £3,000 – up to a quarter of a million pounds today – in a survey of 7,500 people, asking about their tastes and preferences in chocolate assortments, from the chocolates themselves to the design and colour of the box. The survey identified the types of centres the sample customers preferred and the ones they hated, and revealed the previously undiscovered or disregarded facts that chocolate assortments were primarily bought for women by men, and that younger men and women preferred a modern Art Deco-inspired design, hinting at luxury, albeit at a mass-market price, rather than the traditional floral and pictorial boxes that Rowntree's had been producing. The survey also showed that consumers of both sexes wanted a diagram inside the box to identify the different chocolate centres, something which, surprisingly, had not been provided before.

Balchin found a temporary ally in another highly egotistical character, George Harris, who had married Henry Rowntree's granddaughter and, as a member of the extended family, had been given a job by the company in 1923. He was sent to America to study the confectionery business there and had formed a friendship with Forrest Mars, whose great innovation was to develop a brand – the Mars bar – with a strong identity and 'personality' distinct from that of the parent company. When Harris returned to York, he was appointed as Rowntree's Marketing Director in 1933, and began to put his new-found ideas into practice, applying American-style market research, product testing, marketing and promotion to the development of distinctive new brands that, promoted by relentless marketing and advertising, would sell through their associations with glamour and a relaxed, modern, carefree lifestyle.

Commonplace today, those ideas were something of a revelation to 1930s industrialists, and a radical departure for Rowntree's, but the directors were eventually persuaded to test the waters with a new brand of chocolate assortment – Black Magic – and a new form of 'aspirational' marketing, featuring affluent-looking, elegant couples in upmarket settings. Boxes of chocolates had previously been hand-made and priced well beyond the reach of ordinary families; they were so expensive that a box of chocolates was a significant gift – giving a box of chocolates to your girlfriend was tantamount to a marriage proposal! However, boxes of Black Magic were reasonably priced and the marketing emphasized that they were to be regarded as an everyday gift, not just a rare treat for a special occasion. After an uncertain start, Black Magic became a huge success and, along with a series of other aggressively marketed, new 'niche' brands, transformed the company's fortunes.

Harris and Balchin both had great talents but even greater egos, and both loudly proclaimed their own primacy in the success of Black Magic. They were even louder in their claims as to their roles in the development of the chocolate bar that became Rowntree's most successful brand ever – but in fact it owed its origins completely to chance. There were suggestion boxes at various places around the factory and any worker who came up with an idea that was subsequently utilized was paid a cash reward of a few pounds. One of the suggestions put into the box in the early 1930s was: 'Why can't you make a bar of chocolate that a man can put in his "pack-up" (lunch box)?'

The result of that question was the Kit Kat bar. Retailing at twopence, it was marketed as 'The biggest little meal' and 'The best companion to a cup of tea'. It was a cheap product to make because the wafer it contained was much less expensive to produce than the chocolate that surrounded it, but the wafer also had an unexpected and very valuable side effect. Wafer is a palate cleanser, and eating it partly neutralized the cloying, slightly sickly effect on the palate that eating a solid bar of chocolate could produce. As a result, people could eat more of them, more often, without feeling full.

Launched in 1935 and originally called Chocolate Crisp, the first Kit Kats (the name came from an eighteenth-century club whose members met in a tavern owned by Christopher Catling and which adopted his abbreviated name 'Kit Cat') were wrapped in very austere, plain packaging, like a modern supermarket own-brand. The Kit Kat name had been trademarked as far back as 1911, and was probably used as a result of the debacle that surrounded the name Rowntree's had given to their new Aero bar when it was launched. It turned out that the name had already been registered as a trademark by Cadbury's, and the Rowntree's board had to make a humiliating, cap-in-hand pilgrimage to Paul Cadbury's office and beg for permission to use the name. The two firms' shared Quaker heritage and Paul Cadbury's personal acquaintance with the Rowntree family did not prevent him from keeping them dangling for quite some time before he finally agreed to allow them the continued use of the name, in exchange for two of Rowntree's own registered brand names. Had he realized at the time how successful Aero would prove to be, he would probably either have refused altogether or demanded an eye-watering sum of money in compensation.

As a result of that near disaster, when Harris cast about for a new name for the Chocolate Crisp bar – so as to give it a proper brand name, rather than its temporary descriptive one – Rowntree's thought it safest to use a name that they had already registered, and Kit Kat, which had previously been tried on an unsuccessful chocolate assortment, was brought out of retirement, dusted off and put back into use. The rest, as they say, is history. Customers liked Kit Kats, ate more and more of them, and a phenomenon was born; it is still one of the UK's most popular confectionery brands today.

Other brands were developed and manufactured in conditions of such secrecy that it bordered on paranoia. Ivy Marshall, whose father Herbert worked all his life as the timekeeper for Rowntree's, went to work at the factory herself in 1933, aged fourteen, and was put to work in the Walnut Whip section. On her first day, Ivy was surprised to discover that the door to the room where they were made was locked. She was even more startled when, having unlocked the door to let in Ivy and her workmates, the overlooker immediately locked the door again behind them. If they wanted to leave the room for any reason, they had to wait for the overlooker to come and unlock the door. Such was the fear of a rival manufacturer stealing a march on Rowntree's by copying the product or the production process that Ivy was also told that, on pain of dismissal, she and her workmates were not allowed to discuss any aspect of their work with other Rowntree's workers, let alone with any outsiders, and 'certainly not to tell them what they did or how they got that walnut in the bottom'. According to her daughter, Ivy took the lesson to heart so much that 'she never even told me – that's how well she kept the secret!'

Nigel Balchin was probably too mercurial to be comfortable for long within the staid confines of the corporate world, and also too much of a loose cannon to be tolerated indefinitely by Rowntree's directors, and he eventually parted company with them in 1935, on his way to Hollywood fame and fortune. The company he left behind also went from strength to strength. Black Magic, introduced in 1933, ushered in a Golden Age for Rowntree's as a raft of other new brands was launched. Not all took off – Cokernut, Three Aces and Barcelona Caramel sank without trace – but Aero, launched in 1935, closely followed by Kit Kat in the same year, Dairy Box in 1936, and Smarties in 1937, were spectacular successes, and the near bankrupt and moribund company of 1932 was a hugely profitable enterprise before the end of the decade.

The new Black Magic assortments were only just beginning production when Madge and Rose were sent to pack chocolates in the Machine Room, where they worked on orange creams. The centres came down the belt in rows ten to twelve deep across the conveyor and the two girls, standing either side of the belt, had to arrange them so that they all faced the same way before they went under the enrobing machine that covered them with chocolate. But the conveyor belt moved very fast and, not being used to the work, Madge was a bit slower than the others and kept dropping behind. The charge-hands would come round, stand behind Madge and nudge her in the back, saying, 'Go on! Quicker! Get two hands going!' but even with practice, Madge found the speed of the conveyor belt so fast that she had 'all on' to keep pace with it, and she didn't even have time to get her money out for the union woman when she came round collecting the subs for the week. Instead, Madge just kept working while the union rep put her hand in the sailor bag round Madge's neck and helped herself to the money.

A lot of Madge's fellow workers refused to join the union, and disputes at the factory were very rare. Madge could only remember one strike in all her years at Rowntree's, and it was, she says, 'a bit of a giggle anyway. It was the first strike ever at Rowntree's, as far as I know, and it only lasted four hours. I couldn't even tell you what it was about now, but the machines were all stopped and the charge-hands and overlookers came round and told us we all had to go out of the building, but then we all just milled around in the yard for a while, with no one really telling us what was going on. We were all giggling about it and eventually, a couple of hours later, they said it was all settled and we all shuffled back inside, the machines started up again and we all got back to work.'

The generally friendly relations between management and workers did not prevent women from being laid off if demand for Rowntree's products fell. There was a company rule that if work was short and there was more than one member of the family working there, the youngest had to leave, and in times of recession many young girls who had only just been taken on at Rowntree's found themselves thrown out of work again. Nor were older workers immune from being sacked. One woman remembers being one of 300, all aged over fifty and with many years' service to the company, who were abruptly sacked without compensation when sales of chocolates failed to match the company's expectations. There was also a general and perhaps correct belief among the women that the unions in that era were more interested in defending male workers' rights than those of women. 'It was still very much a man's world then,' one says. 'It wasn't a woman's world at all. And I'm not sure how much it's changed even now.'

On another occasion, when orders for fancy boxes had slowed, Madge and Rose were sent to the Gum department to pack Fruit Pastilles. They had to put the pastilles into the tubes, always in exactly the same sequence of colours, and every now and then the overlooker would come down the line, pick out one tube out and check it, and if Madge had one colour in the wrong place, the overlooker would reject the entire box and make her repack all of them. They were on piece rate and had to complete a certain number of boxes in an hour to make their money, so to achieve the rate they had to work fast – 'be sharp', as they used to say in Yorkshire. Having a box rejected was a potential disaster.

The sugar crystals on the pastilles were another unexpected hazard. By the end of the day both girls' finger ends were red raw from rubbing against the sharp crystals. There were no rubber gloves then, so Madge and Rose just had to put up with the soreness until the skin on their fingers toughened up. On that first day, by the time they got home, they had covered every one of their finger ends with bits of tape to protect them from any further damage when they were doing their chores at home.

Like the other girls, they had to clean their machines at the end of their shifts and, after they had done so, a Hygiene Adviser went round to check them. If she was not satisfied, Madge and Rose, who by then had already gone to the changing rooms or the snack room, found themselves rounded up and taken back to their machines to finish the job properly.

Just as in Cream Packing, women working on the Fruit Gum and Fruit Pastille production lines were not supposed to eat any of the sweets, and the charge-hands and overlookers were always 'very keen' to keep a close watch on them. Though she could take or leave chocolates, Madge used to love gums and pastilles, and she was dying to eat one, so she palmed one from the conveyor belt, got herself down under the bench, out of sight of the overlooker, and popped it into her mouth. Rose saw her do it and was hissing at her, 'Stop it, our Madge. Stop it. You'll get into trouble. They'll finish you if they catch you.' Fortunately they didn't.

It was a rare flash of defiance from Madge, because she was usually so shy that she would keep a very low profile. The boss of the Card Box Mill, Peter Luger, was a suave and good-looking man with a 'right posh' accent, as they called it on the production line. He was also a gifted pianist in his spare time, and Madge had a serious crush on him. The overlooker for Madge's section was a woman called Fanny Hall, who sat at a high desk so she could watch everything that was going on.

Her desk was directly opposite Madge, and although she was fond of her, Fanny also had a strong mischievous streak; knowing how shy Madge was, and how keen she was on Peter Luger, she would lose no opportunity to send Madge to his office on some errand or another.

'Madge,' she would say, with the hint of a smile, 'just a minute. Would you mind just going and telling Peter I want to see him?' And poor Madge would already be blushing crimson as she put down her work and set off along the room, between the machines, with the ribald comments of her workmates ringing in her ears. She would try to compose herself, knock on Peter Luger's office door, go in and pass on the message, the words tumbling out of her as she tried to end the ordeal as quickly as possible. 'MrLugerMissHallwantstoseeyouaboutsomething,' she would say, scrambling her words together as she rushed to get the sentence out before her face got any more crimson with embarrassment, and then she would scuttle back to her work-bench, still blushing like mad. Peter Luger would come out of his office, walk to the overlooker's desk and start talking to Fanny Hall, but they would keep looking across at Madge and chuckling to themselves while they were doing so. She could tell they were talking about her, which only made her blush even more. 'Peter Luger actually thought a lot of me,' she says now, 'and I think that he would have liked to have taken me out, but I used to be so shy then – and perhaps he was, too – that it never happened.' Though she was painfully shy then, she insists that she's over it now: 'I'm not shy now! I'm a little devil and I speak my mind!'

At home time each day, Madge and her sisters would hurry down from the Card Box Mill and, like the hordes from the other departments, they would line up by the time clocks, waiting for the siren that signalled the end of the working day, and then it was mayhem. They were not allowed to leave their departments until the charge-hands told them they could go, and then there was a rush for the stairs to get to the cloakroom and put on their hats and coats, but then, with the exception of invalids, they had to stand in the corridor outside the time-keeper's office until the timekeeper said they could go, at which point there was a stampede for the gates.

The time clocks would rattle out a symphony of 'pings' as the women jostled to blick-out, and then Haxby Road, deserted one minute apart from the queues of works buses lined up and waiting, would be deluged the next moment with a flood of people pouring out of the factory, thousands on foot and thousands more on bicycles. The footpaths and the two bridges would be jammed with people, and the roads were wall to wall with bikes, half of which – including Madge's – didn't seem to have any brakes. 'If you had any sense,' she says, 'you wouldn't have been trying to go against the tide of people at home time or you might have been killed in the rush.'

Madge had little spare time during the week. It was a long working day and by the time she had eaten her evening meal and done her share of the household chores under the eagle eye of her mum, there was little time to do anything else before curling up in bed. At weekends, however, after the bliss of a lie-in on Saturday morning – albeit a very brief one, because Madge's mum thought that laziness was a habit that was easily acquired and very hard to lose, and chased them out of bed if they lingered there – Madge and Laura would often buy a yard or two of cloth from the market and make clothes for themselves and their sisters. Laura was a very good seamstress and she and Madge used to make exotic hats for everybody, a bit like the 'fascinators' women wear to weddings and glamorous occasions today.

'We inherited that creative streak from our mother,' Madge says, 'because she was very good at making things. She showed us how to make little dolls. The arms, legs and body were made separately from scrap cloth and stuffed with rags before being sewn together. We would buy little shaped faces ready-made from a shop called Booth and Barr and stitch them onto the heads, and spend hours making outfits for them. There were shortages of everything after the war, and there was a real demand for the dolls because people just could not get hold of things like that unless they made them themselves.'

Madge's mum also used to make beautiful paper flowers. She would cut out squares of paper and then carefully concertina them into strips, using a bit of wire to pinch each strip in the middle. She then pulled out the concertina at either end and finished up with something looking like a carnation. She could make roses, too, by fixing paper flower petals round and round a central stem. Using thread, the flowers were fastened together into a long string with real greenery woven in as well; trying to dodge the thorns, Madge and Rose would pick the leaves from a sprawling rambling rose in the orchard beyond Parson's Wall. On special occasions, like street parties or coronations, Madge's mum would hook the strings of paper roses up with a couple of nails banged into the wall outside and, Madge says, 'We had to keep hold of her as she hung out of the bedroom windows to fix the flowers and crinkled paper twists into place.'

Madge still has a photograph of herself and her sisters, with their mum and dad, all grouped together on the doorstep outside their house on the day of King George VI's coronation, 12 May 1937. All are dressed in their Sunday best clothes with the hats that Madge and Laura made perched on the girls' heads. There is a flower basket hanging above the door under a framed picture of the King and Queen, beautifully decorated flower boxes on all the windowsills, paper garlands and streamers, and her mum's paper flowers arranged up the walls like the stems of climbing roses.

When Madge had finished work for the week, she loved to go dancing more than anything else. She would sometimes go to the Rowntree's dances – the girls called them the 'Penny Hops' – in the gym on Friday nights (though Friday was usually hair-washing night), but on Saturday nights Madge and her friends always went dancing at the New Earswick Folk Hall or the Assembly Rooms in York. It cost sixpence to get into the dance and the girls would share a bottle of port between them that cost two shillings and elevenpence. 'I'd smuggle in the port inside my handbag,' Madge says, 'and we'd hide it in the toilet, because you weren't supposed to be drinking there at all – we were too young to drink legally and anyway the New Earswick Folk Hall was strictly teetotal – so we'd have a dance for a while and then we'd go to the toilet and have a drink of port, and then we'd go back and dance a bit more.'

One night she and a girl she was friendly with were coming home together from a dance at New Earswick. It was about 12.30 a.m. – the dances finished at midnight – and they were walking home because there were no buses at that time of night. When they reached the end of Rose Street, they heard a commotion and saw a group of people singing and dancing in the middle of the street. Madge's friend had to carry on walking home – she lived in Burton Stone Lane a mile or so away – but never one to turn down the offer of a party, Madge joined in the singing and dancing with the group of people, who were celebrating George VI's coronation. One of Madge's neighbours had dragged his piano out into the street, and a lot of them were singing and dancing round the piano. Many of the other neighbours were standing on their steps to watch while their children were peeping out of their bedroom windows.

Among the revellers were six lads who had just arrived in York and had all been taken on at Rowntree's. With demand for Black Magic, Kit Kats and the other new Rowntree's brands still booming, the factory was short-staffed at the time and bringing men in from all over Yorkshire. A lady who lived a few doors down from Madge's house used to take in lodgers, and all six of them were living there. Among them were lads from Hull and Barnsley, and one called Bill Burrow, who came from the mining district of Castleford. He was only slightly taller than Madge, but his powerful chest and shoulders suggested that he had already had a year or two working underground in one of the numerous collieries in and around his home town, before seizing the chance of a less demanding way of earning a living.

Madge was really enjoying herself singing and dancing with them, until her mum (who was at her usual vantage point, standing on the doorstep chatting to the lady next door) spotted her and called out, 'Come on now, our Madge. It's time you were in bed.'

Madge really didn't want to go, but she knew better than to argue with her mum, so she went home, as meek as you like, said 'Night, night' to her mum, and made as if she was going upstairs to bed. Then, as soon as her mum wasn't looking, Madge slipped out of the back door, crept along the back lane and joined up again with the lads out in the street. A while later her mum came out again and spotted her, and said, 'I thought you were in bed. Get yourself home now.' But as

Madge got ready to do so, feet dragging and knowing that this time her mum would be keeping a very close eye on her, one of the lads, Bill Burrow, grabbed her arm and said, 'Where do you generally go dancing?'

Madge gave him an appraising look and then said, 'Well, usually we go to New Earswick or the Assembly Rooms.'

She said goodnight, then went home and up the stairs to her bedroom – she couldn't sneak out again with her mum on the prowl – but a few minutes later, Bill and the other lads all appeared in the back lane, having noted which house Madge had gone into. They perched on Parson's Wall opposite the back of the house, and were still singing away while Madge and Rose peered out of the window at them. 'I was dying to go out again,' Madge says, 'but I didn't dare because my mam would have scalped me if she'd caught me disobeying her again!'

On the Saturday night, Madge and her friend went dancing at the Assembly Rooms and there were the six boys, all dressed up in their best suits, waiting for them. Bill and Madge spent most of the evening dancing together and from then on they were courting. She had a choice of two suitors, because another lad was after her at the time as well, but she chose Bill and, as she now admits, it turned out to be completely the wrong choice.

Before long she and Bill were lovers, and not long after that she discovered she was pregnant. Illegitimacy – or 'getting into trouble', as it was known – was a very big deal in those days, and in many cases, if a 'shotgun wedding' could not be arranged, the birth would be hushed up. The unfortunate girl would often not only leave her job, but leave the area as well for a while and have her baby adopted before coming back. In other cases, to avoid the disgrace of having a bastard child in the family, the girl's mother would pretend that the new-born baby was an unexpected late addition to her own family, with the actual mother forced to maintain the pretence that her own baby was her sister or brother for years.

Madge kept her own pregnancy quiet as long as she dared, but her mum didn't miss much and one morning she stared at her daughter for a few minutes, her gaze travelling slowly down over the suspicion of a swelling around Madge's waist, and then said, 'Are you late, our Madge?'

Madge shot her a guilty look and then nodded. 'Yes, three months late.'

'So what are you going to do?'

'Well, get married,' Madge said. 'What else can I do?'

There were very few palatable alternatives. Back-street abortionists did exist and many desperate girls made use of them, sometimes at the cost of their ability to have children in the future, and sometimes even at the cost of their lives, but that idea never crossed Madge's mind, and nor did the thought of being a single mother. She was pregnant: Bill would have to make an 'honest woman' of her, and that was that.

However, her pregnancy could hardly have been worse timed, as Bill had now lost his job, partly through his own poor timekeeping and partly because it was still Rowntree's policy to bring in young workers as juniors when they were seventeen, and then sack them when they got to twenty-one and became entitled to the full adult wage. Bill was now twenty-one and he had been sacked. Madge and Bill had no money and no home to go to, yet whatever her own thoughts may have been about her daughter's pregnancy and Bill's suitability as a son-in-law – and she missed no opportunity to tell Madge that she thought Bill was 'a wrong 'un' – Madge's mum told her, 'You can live here and have the little front room and the little bedroom.'

6

Florence

Florence had only been working at Rowntree's for two years when war was declared in 1939. As a result, the box-makers had to move out of the Card Box Mill because the Army took it over as a supply depot, while other parts of the factory were also converted from their peacetime uses to produce munitions and other war materials. This went against every pacifist principle that Quakers held dear, and must have provoked some agonizing soul searching in the Rowntree family members, but whatever battles they might have fought privately with their consciences, they were realistic enough to know that if the Government required their factory for war work, it would be taken whether the family agreed or not.

The company instituted an allowances scheme to ensure that the families of employees on National Service did not suffer financial hardship, and Christmas gift parcels were not only sent to the men and women serving in the forces, but also to their families at home. When Alan Rathmell, who had worked on the production line making the first Kit Kats before the war and whose wife worked in the offices, first went missing in action and was then later reported to be a prisoner of war, Rowntree's made sure that his picture appeared in every issue of the monthly *Cocoa Works Magazine*, just to show his friends and family that he had not been forgotten. He still lives in York today.

Florence and her workmates were sent to Cream Packing on the top floor of the Cream Block and made boxes there for a while, but wartime restrictions meant that production of fancy boxes soon ceased altogether and the numbers of plain cardboard boxes coming off the lines were greatly reduced. To get to her new workplace, Florence entered the factory along an avenue of trees running from the main gates on Haxby Road. At the end, she went through a porch with oak double doors and a sundial above it, into the Cream Block, where the chocolate assortments were now made. Running parallel to the Haxby Road, it was a huge, six-storey, red-brick building with large rectangular windows and a frieze at roof level, painted a cream colour, that looked like the icing on a cake. That impression was strengthened by the row of flagpoles, like birthday candles, along the top, from which flew the Union flag and also the national flags of any distinguished foreign visitors to the factory that day. It was a brand-new building, constructed in 1936 to accommodate the extra machines and workers needed to cope with the phenomenal success of Black Magic and the other new brands.

Florence walked along the entrance passageway and onto the central corridor, which ran through the entire building from one side to the other. Originally an open space between two separate buildings, the corridor had exposed brickwork to either side and a high glazed and whitewashed roof overhead to protect it from the elements. There were hanging baskets at intervals, and Florence would pause to catch the scent of the flowers as she walked underneath. Further on, she took a flight of stairs with glazed decorative tiles on the walls that led up to the main production areas of the Cream Block, a series of cavernous, open rooms, punctuated by iron pillars and overhead girders, and extending over the five upper storeys of the building. As you climbed the stairs, the rich, sweet and slightly cloying smell of liquid chocolate grew stronger and stronger.

Like other food production companies, Rowntree's came under the direction of the Ministry of Food during the war, which imposed severe restrictions on manufacturers and a system of rationing for consumers. Cocoa beans remained reasonably plentiful throughout the war, but supplies of sugar and milk were drastically reduced, and although Rowntree's continued to produce thousands of tonnes of cocoa, chocolate and confectionery, much of it was 'vitaminized' and reserved for the forces, some for sale through NAAFI canteens, the remainder ordered by the War Office for direct supply to troops. This included 'Pacific and Jungle Chocolate', adapted to suit hot climates, that was issued to forces serving in tropical areas. Parts of the factory were also switched from making chocolate to the production of more basic foods. Rowntree's also made oatmeal blocks and fruit bars, and the Cream Packing department was turned over to the production of dried milk and the infamous dried eggs that those who lived through the war still remember with a shudder.

Under a system of switching food production between factories in different regions to minimize transport, Rowntree's had been put to work making jams and marmalade for Frank Cooper Ltd of Oxford, and in the summer of 1940 Florence even went 'strawberry plugging' at Hunstanton for sixteen weeks, picking strawberries and pulling the hulls out of them. The work was hard and her back would ache after a couple of hours, and by the end of the day she could hardly straighten up, but she loved the chance to be out in the fresh air, feeling the warm sun on her as she worked. Unlike the Rowntree's production lines, there was no one to tell her off if she helped herself to some of the goods she was handling, so she ate strawberries until she was sick of the sight of them. Once again, she and her fellow workers were being paid on piece rate by the weight of fruit that they picked, so once she had filled her buckets to the brim, she used to squeeze a few of the ripe strawberries in her hands and let the juices run into the buckets to make them weigh even more. The evenings in Hunstanton were like a return to her childhood in some ways, because she and the other girls were all in lodgings and there were so many of them and so few rooms that they had to sleep three to a bed. Even worse, one of the girls who Florence shared with snored louder than a German bomber passing overhead.

By the time the soft fruit was delivered to the factory, it was not always in the freshest condition. During the fruit season, the baskets and colanders of strawberries, raspberries and cherries were stacked high outside the Gum Block, and sometimes there would be a white, fur-like mould all over them, but when Florence called out to the men handling them one day, 'You don't really use those, do you?' they just said, 'Of course we do, we just put a hose on them to rinse all the fur off.'

Florence worked in the Cream Block for two years, but as soon as she was eighteen, the minimum age for work on munitions, she was transferred from box-making on the top floor of the Cream Block to fuse-filling in the Gum Block Extension on the Wigginton Road side of the site, where, despite the name, they had made Smarties in peacetime. Next to it was the Gum Block itself, where non-chocolate confectionery such as Fruit Gums, Fruit Pastilles, Beech Nut chewing gum and, later,

POLO mints were made. The Gum Block Extension was another brand-new building, constructed in 1937 to house the machinery for yet another of the new products created in the 1930s, albeit a product that had originally been produced as far back as the 1880s under the name Chocolate Dragees. The name was later changed to Chocolate Beans and in the 1930s they were relaunched as Smarties, and under that name became another huge success for the company, so much so that the Gum Block Extension, originally designed to be just two storeys high, had to be increased to five storeys to accommodate the extra production lines that were now needed.

The Gum Block Extension also had a unique roof. Among other things, the shells of Smarties were made from a mixture of flour and sugar, and they were coated by 'panning' them in giant revolving copper pans. The coating mixture was not weighed or measured; skilled male workers simply poured in liquid colour until, judging by eye and experience, they decided that the Smarties were the correct shade of red, yellow, orange, green and brown. The process involved some risk, since it threw flour dust into the air that even the most powerful extractors could not entirely remove, and fine flour particles suspended in the air are a notorious fire and explosion risk – one suggested cause of the Great Fire of London in 1666 was just such a flour dust explosion in the bakery in Pudding Lane where the fire began. So to reduce the risk of collateral damage to the surrounding buildings through explosion or the spread of fire, the roof of the Gum Block Extension was deliberately designed as a weak point, allowing explosive gases to vent upwards, rather than laterally into the surrounding buildings. As a result, when the Rowntree's factory was later adapted for wartime use, the Gum Block Extension was the obvious place to site the production of munitions, and the Smarties department became a fuse-filling factory known as County Industries Ltd, run by Ned Sparkes, leading to the long-running joke: 'You don't want sparks in a munitions factory.'

Florence was one of 850 women and sixty men employed in fuse-filling, and production continued round the clock, with the entire staff working alternate twelve-hour day and night shifts. Additional employees to carry out war work were recruited not just from York but from the rest of Britain and parts of the Empire as well, and European refugees from the Nazis were also employed. 'We had Polish people and Indian people coming to work there,' Dot Edwards recalls, 'men and women, and it was surprising how quick they got into it. They put up some Nissen huts up on Wigginton Road for them to live in, because most of them had nothing at all when they started, just the clothes they stood up in, but they were nice people to work with, they really were.'

The factory turned out 100,000 fuses and detonators a week, which were stored in an underground magazine, constructed by the cricket field on one of the sports grounds. The underground bunkers were covered with an artificial mound and double doors shielded by blast walls, and to a modern eye would have looked strangely like the underground home of the Tellytubbies, though their contents were far more sinister.

In 1938 all Rowntree's employees had been issued with a warning that the country might soon be at war, and had been given instructions about the safety procedures to be followed in the event of an air raid. The warning was sufficiently vivid for Florence to have nightmares about air raids that night, but it turned out to be twelve months premature, and the 'phoney war' of 1939–40 meant that it was the autumn of 1940 before

Rowntree's preparedness was tested in real air-raid conditions. The main air-raid shelters were built beneath the orchard near the Dining Block on the far side of Haxby Road, though there were also smaller ones under the Rose Lawn and on the Wigginton Road side of the factory, and the cellars of the larger factory buildings were also used as designated shelters. When the air-raid siren sounded, most of the workforce had to run across Haxby Road, or go through the underground tunnel and the Dining Block to reach the shelters in the orchard. As the girls hurried down the stairs and through the tunnel, there was none of the usual joking and laughter – some of them were white-faced with fear.

At first they were sent straight to the shelters whenever the air-raid sirens were sounded, but as this caused considerable disruption to production and many of the raids proved to be false alarms, a few aircraft spotters were trained in aircraft identification and then stationed on the roofs of the factory buildings to keep watch for German bombers. Only when approaching aircraft were actually sighted was the alarm raised and the employees allowed to leave their work stations and go to the shelters.

However, the aircraft spotting system was not without its flaws. When York was actually bombed, the alarm was not raised in time and some girls were still working inside the factory when the first bombs began to fall. There was no time for them to reach the main shelters and so they had to file down the stairs and sit in the changing rooms instead. Although most of the bombs fell nearer to the city centre, one bomb hit Rowntree Avenue, not far from the bunker where the detonators and fuses were stored; had a bomb hit that bunker, a large part of the factory would probably have been destroyed.

There were no deaths at the factory from the bombing, but one of Rowntree's air-raid wardens, Harry Hawley, died in an accident that would have been farcical had the outcome not been so tragic. Seeing a car approaching along Tang Hall Lane with its headlights full on, Harry shouted to the driver to dip his lights. He was ignored and the soldier accompanying him said, 'I'll stop him,' and drew his revolver, intending to fire a warning shot, but as he drew the weapon it accidentally discharged, hitting Harry, who later died of his wounds.

In addition to air-raid protection, a Local Defence Volunteers (Home Guard) company was formed from employees at the works, first aid classes were organized and many women joined the St John's Ambulance Brigade. On two occasions they even volunteered for duty in London to give the local ambulance staff, exhausted by the nightly carnage from the Blitz, a chance to rest and recuperate. The rest centre in the Dining Block was converted to a refuge for blitzed families, and a nursery was also established there to enable mothers with young children to carry out war work. The Rowntree's Joinery department manufactured cots and other equipment for the sixty children, from six months to five years old, who were looked after there while their mothers worked.

Florence also remembers Rowntree's employees taking collections of money and goods to help Londoners made homeless by the Blitz, and so much cash, clothing, furniture and household equipment was donated that a succession of pantechnicons was needed to transport it all to London. Twenty-six men employed in the Rowntree's Building department were also sent to London to help carry out repairs to Blitz-damaged houses.

Before Florence began work on the fuse-filling production line, she and all the other girls had to have a medical to check their general health and particularly their skin. Anyone who was suffering from a skin complaint or had shown themselves to be prone to such conditions in the past was not taken on, because the materials they would be handling were caustic and often toxic. The fear of invasion and 'Fifth Column' sabotage had also led Rowntree's to post security guards at the factory entrances and issue their employees with passes for the first time in the company's history.

Just inside the door Florence and her fellow workers had to pass through the doorkeeper's lobby, manned by a commissionaire wearing military uniform, where they had to turn out their pockets and surrender any cigarettes, lighters and matches. A succession of girls would tell him, 'You're wasting your time, love, I don't smoke,' but they were all searched anyway, every day. The commissionaire checked Florence's identity card – all the munitions workers had been issued with one – and searched her for contraband, not just concealed cigarettes and matches, but anything metallic that might cause a spark; the girls were not even allowed to take food into work with them, though that was more to prevent it being contaminated with TNT (trinitrotoluene), the explosive powder used in the fuses and detonators she was to make, than any risk of explosion. In common with the other women, Florence had to remove all jewellery, and anyone who was wearing a ring that they could not take off had to cover it with tape. As a further reminder, a sign hanging over the double doors to the changing rooms read: 'STOP! Have you handed in your CONTRABAND?'

After finally being waved through by the commissionaire, Florence went into the 'clean area' of the changing rooms, took off her clothes and hung them up in a kit bag, and put her shoes in a wire mesh basket under the bench. Dressed only in her underwear, she then stepped over a low wall a couple of feet high that divided the 'clean' section from the 'dirty' section of the area, where she put on her work wear: khaki, government-issue overalls and a khaki turban to cover her hair, and shoes with crêpe rubber soles – leather soles were thought more likely to create sparks through static or friction that might cause an explosion.

Her overalls had rubber buttons that had to be fastened right up to the neck, and were made of coarse serge, like soldiers' uniforms, which chafed against her neck. They were also deliberately made without pockets to make it even more difficult for workers to smuggle anything in. All that was permitted was the usual money bag on a string round their neck to hold the coins for their teas and meals, though none of the girls were allowed to eat or drink anything while working in the fuse production area as the toxic yellow TNT powder was like talc, so fine that it hung in the air and covered every surface. If Florence wanted a drink or to eat a snack during her tea break, she had to go to the cloakroom to do so.

Before she left the changing rooms to start work, she also had to put special 'make-up' – a face powder and a thick skin cream, like cold cream – all over the exposed skin of her hands, neck and face, to protect them as much as possible from the highly toxic TNT. Unlike the peacetime factory, where all the women would have a fringe showing under their turban, in the fuse-filling area everybody's hair had to be completely covered by their turban. There were showers and rows of sinks along one wall of the changing room for washing at the end of their shift, and a row of mirrors with posters above them. Like

Victorian 'cautionary tales', these forerunners of the modern health and safety notices told horrific stories, accompanied by lurid illustrations, of the terrible fate awaiting women who did not tuck their hair under their turbans, or who tried to smuggle in contraband items.

There was an ominous feeling about all these preparations, and as she and the other girls got ready for work, Florence found the silence oppressive at first, compared to their normal chatter and laughter. However, within a few weeks, what had seemed strange and slightly sinister had become familiar and routine, and the banter and laughter resumed.

Production was spread over three floors, and the workforce was mostly women, with a few men, usually those with medical complaints that excused them from active service, who did the heavier and less skilled jobs. The protective cream worn by men and women alike was only partially effective. 'It didn't do much good,' Florence recalls, 'because the TNT powder was really fine and, whatever protective measures we adopted, it still got absolutely everywhere.' Women working in munitions factories were given the nickname 'canaries' because the TNT powder that filled the air dyed their skin the same yellow hue. 'It was an orangey-yellow colour,' Florence recalls, 'and it turned everything it touched yellow: our face, our hair, our hands and arms, in fact all of our skin, even the soles of our feet went yellow. When you went out of the factory everyone would say, "Oh, I know where you work," because we were all yellow from head to foot and it wouldn't come off. We stood out like sore thumbs.'

That was an embarrassment to Florence at first, because not only did it look like she had jaundice, but she had to put up with jokes and comments from men she passed as she walked down the street, like, 'I didn't know Rowntree's were employing Chinese women now.' They were barely funny the first time, and grew ever more tedious with each repetition. However, in a strange way, her yellow skin colour was also a badge of honour, a visible sign of the important war work she was doing. She came to feel something like a surge of pride to be recognized as a munitions worker, and she also detected a new respect towards her, even from people she had known for years.

Florence worked for a while in the main magazine where they weighed out the TNT pellets and, she says, 'The powder there was awful. You had to wear a breathing mask over your mouth and nose as well as everything else, but you could still smell the sulphurous stink of it and the powder was so fine that it was just like dust.' No matter how careful she was about handling and pouring it, clouds of it hung in the air like fog all day long. The toxic TNT dust even seeped through the filters in her breathing mask and left her choking so badly that sometimes she had to fight down a feeling of panic as she struggled to get her breath. However, her stay in that section proved to be a brief one because after just a few days, she noticed a sore and itchy rash on her arms as she got ready for bed one night. The next day it was worse and by the end of the week it was covering her arms, her face, her back and torso. After the company doctor had examined her, she was moved out of the downstairs room where the TNT powder was worst, and sent upstairs to work on waterproofing the fuses, where conditions were a little better – but only a little.

Contact with the TNT powder caused a lot of women to suffer skin irritation. Like Florence, a number of them had to be transferred to different work after developing impetigo and similar complaints, and the other effects on their health could be even more serious. They were advised to drink milk rather than tea or coffee at their mid-shift break, presumably to put a lining in their stomachs that might prevent the absorption of some of the toxic constituents of TNT. People exposed to TNT over a prolonged period tended to experience anaemia and abnormal liver function, and an enlarged spleen from ingested or breathed TNT. Consumption of the powder also led to a person's urine being stained pink or red as the TNT was broken down within the body. The first time that Florence saw that, she panicked, thinking that she was suffering from internal bleeding. She spent a sleepless night worrying about it and was only reassured when she got to work the next morning and discovered that all the other women were complaining of the same problem. Some found it equally puzzling, if rather less disconcerting, that when they washed the yellow powder off their hands, the water they were using would turn red.

Summer heat made the working conditions even more intolerable. There was a total blackout, with blinds fitted or the windows painted black, and to keep the blackout the windows all had to stay closed at night, even in the hottest weather.

The fuses they were making were for twenty-five-pounder shells that were mostly destined for the campaign in the Western Desert in North Africa. The fuses came down the conveyors in wooden trays containing ten fuses, and all the parts to be fitted into them were in separate little recesses around the sides of the trays. As they moved along the conveyor, all those parts had to be fitted into the fuses. To minimize casualties in the event of accidental detonations, the girls all worked in separate cubicles, which made it difficult to talk to anyone other than their immediate neighbours, and they did their work inside steel boxes that had toughened glass windows to look through and two holes for their arms. Inside was a pipe like a red fire bucket, sealed at its bottom end and filled with sand to absorb most of the blast if a fuse detonated, and each girl had a brass set of scales – all the tools they used were made of brass because anything made of iron or steel might strike a spark and cause an explosion. Another of the canaries working on fuse-filling, Dot Edwards, recalls that she 'used to take this thing like a washer with a red side and a yellow side out of the fuse and put it on the scales. I used to have to scrape all this gunpowder in, until it was full, and then pass it on to the next girl who put black stuff into it and then passed it on again, to someone who'd crimp it, and so on.'

Florence and her workmates were surprisingly relaxed about working with fuses and detonators, because initially none of them seemed to realize the dangers of the work they were undertaking. Had they been told they were making bombs, they would no doubt have been much more nervous and circumspect, but perhaps fuses and detonators did not sound as perilous as bombs, even though both were just as capable of killing the person assembling them. Whatever the reason, there was a remarkably relaxed and happy-go-lucky atmosphere. Even when there was no music playing over the Tannoy to entertain them, the girls would sing anyway, belting out their favourite songs unaccompanied. One group of women called themselves 'The Cowgirls Union' because their favourite song was 'Ragtime Cowboy Joe' and they all used to sing along to it at the tops of their voices. During the Battle of Britain their songs were punctuated by news bulletins and there were big cheers from the girls whenever there was a report of a German aircraft being shot down. The girls all had to carry gas masks and do regular drills, including having to work at their benches or conveyor belts with their masks on. 'They made an awful noise when we put them on,' one of the workers, Marjorie Chapman, says, 'so we sat there making farting noises through our masks!'

Despite all the dangers, serious accidents were extremely rare. One did occur, however, when a woman working on the night shift blew off her fingers. The girls had to 'stab' the detonators – make three little marks in them with a sharp tool – and there was a safe and an unsafe side on which to do it. Unfortunately, probably through tiredness – they were working long shifts after all, one from half past seven in the morning until seven o'clock at night, and the other from eight o'clock at night until seven o'clock in the morning – the woman stabbed the wrong side and it exploded. One of her hands was inside the box when the detonator went off, and she lost her fingers as a result. The protective shield was also buckled in the blast, and it was then left in a prominent position in the department as a warning to the rest of them about what a moment's inattention or carelessness might lead to.

Madge Tillett, one of Florence's workmates who was working near the girl when the blast happened, remembers that 'Strangely enough, they sent us up to the next floor and told us to get on with our work, while they sent the girls from there home, even though they had not even seen the accident, but perhaps the theory was that it was like getting straight back on a bike if you've fallen off it. Maybe they thought that if they let us go home straight after the explosion, we might not have wanted to come back again. Crazy though it sounds – we were putting TNT in the fuses and detonators after all – until then I don't think I had fully realized how dangerous the work we were doing was.' If the authorities had hoped to keep news of the explosion secret, they had reckoned without the power of the rumour mill in a small city like York. Florence was interrogated by her parents about it, but all they could do, while her mother dabbed at the tears in her eyes with her handkerchief, was beg her to 'Please be careful.' Madge Tillett also remembers 'my poor old dad having a "ducky fit" because it got around that there'd been an explosion', which might have mutilated his daughter as well as the unfortunate girl.

There were only two other serious injuries in all the time Florence worked there. One occurred when a girl was using a drill and somehow allowed her hair to become caught in it. Her screams alerted her workmates, but by the time the drill had been stopped, the unfortunate girl had torn out a large patch of her hair and had an ugly wound on her scalp. Another girl was carrying some detonators and, through tiredness or inattention, she dropped them and lost part of her hand in the resulting explosion. Florence and the other girls were lucky not to hurt themselves as well, because they all made mistakes from time to time, 'but then, we were always tired out,' she says. 'We were only young, eighteen some of us, but we still had to do a twelve-hour shift.' Another of her workmates, Dot Edwards, made herself even more tired by staying out late in the evenings as well. 'I'd been to see *Gone With the Wind* about ten times,' she says, 'and sometimes I'd nod off at my box while I was filling fuses and drop one. If I'd struck my fuse on the red side instead of the yellow one, it would have gone off.'

There could easily have been another serious accident thanks to Florence's sister-in-law, who was, in Florence's words:

... a right one and could swear a bit, too. About one o'clock in the morning everyone used to get a bit drowsy – we weren't used to working nights – and one night my sister-in-law saw this, swore and said, 'I'll wake the buggers up.' So she got a paper bag, blew into it and then popped it with a loud bang! The charge-hand came rushing down with a face like thunder, shouting, 'Who did that?' and if anyone had told her, I think my sister-in-law would have been sacked on the spot, but no one said a word. The charge-hand reported us all to the manager, Mr Lambert, who was a Cockney, and he had us all in his office the next night. 'So you ain't done it, and you ain't done it, and you ain't done it,' he said, pointing at each of us in turn. 'Well somebody's bleedin' well done it.' But none of us would say anything and in the end he just sighed, shook his head and sent us back to work, but it was the last time my sister-in-law played a trick like that in there.

After she had been working upstairs where the fuses were made for a while, Florence was then put on 'flagging' – carrying the detonators to and from the magazine. They did it in pairs and took it in turns, one girl walking behind, wearing a long leather gauntlet that went up to her bicep and carrying a big leather Gladstone bag full of detonators, while the other girl walked in front of her, holding a red flag so that everybody knew to keep well clear of them, just as they used to do in front of cars in the very early days of motoring. Going up and down the stairs or along the corridors, the other workers were told always to keep to the left-hand side to leave plenty of room in case the 'flagger' – who was instructed always to keep to the opposite side – was coming up at the same time. In some ways, Florence found it more frightening to be the one walking in front with the flag than actually carrying the detonators. If she was holding the bag, at least she knew what was going on, whereas walking on ahead with the flag, whenever there was the least noise from behind her, she could feel the hairs rising on the back of her neck at the thought of what might be about to happen.

Florence and her workmate had to go through an underground passage to collect the detonators from the main magazine at the north of the factory site. The man in charge there, Charlie, a tall, genial man with a high forehead and a habit of talking out of the side of his mouth as if he was auditioning for a part in a gangster movie, would put the detonators in the bag in a little side room and then bring the bag out to the girls, and they would always spend a bit of time down there chatting to him before taking the detonators back.

Whenever the air-raid sirens sounded, the girls had to stop work, down tools and go to the shelters, blacking out the factory above ground as they went so as not to allow the least glimmer of light to give the German bombers a target to aim at. One night, the two girls had been down in the magazine for quite a while chatting to Charlie, and when they went back up, Florence with the red flag in front and her friend behind with the bag, they discovered that the whole factory was deserted and in total darkness. They came close to panic, thinking that the air-raid sirens must have gone off while they were gone, and, being underground, they had not heard them. They could not go blundering around the factory in the pitch darkness carrying a bag of detonators, so they did a hurried about-face, went back below ground and returned them to Charlie, and then sat chatting with him again, waiting for the all-clear to sound. 'I don't know if we'd have been quite as relaxed if we'd heard bombs start dropping round the factory that night,'

Florence says, 'because if one had hit the magazine, we'd probably all have been blown to kingdom come.'

No all-clear was sounded, but when they eventually risked another look above ground, they discovered that the factory was once more fully lit and fully staffed, with all the machines running. Only when one of their friends looked up and said, 'Where the hell have you been? You've missed your break,' did they realize that there had been no air-raid warning at all. They had been so busy chatting to Charlie that they had not noticed it was time for the 1.00 a.m. 'lunch' break. The factory had shut down for the hour-long break, and all the machines and lights had been turned off, so while Florence and her friend were huddled together with Charlie, waiting for the bombs to drop, everyone else was across the road in the Dining Block, eating their meal and wondering what had happened to them.

On other nights Florence and her workmates would be in the air-raid shelters together, packed cheek by jowl into the dimly lit, confined space, while they heard the sound of aircraft overhead and the crump of bombs detonating in the distance. Perhaps as a consequence of that claustrophobic feeling, Florence has had a fear of lifts and other enclosed spaces ever since, though she can still manage to crack a joke about it. 'I always tell my daughters to make sure I'm good and dead before they put the coffin lid on,' she says, 'because if I'm not, I'll die of fright anyway.'

Thousands of soldiers were stationed around York during the war, and an overlooker came round the factory one day and said to the girls working on fuse-filling: 'A lot of these soldiers are a long way from their own homes, and they've no one to wash for them and look after them. Would any of you be willing to take a soldier's washing home?' They all said 'Yes' and the overlookers then handed out a bundle of washing to each of them. The name on the bundle they gave to Florence showed that it belonged to a Corporal Davies. From then on, she brought the clean washing back every Monday and swapped it for a fresh bundle of dirty washing, and even though none of the girls had ever met any of the soldiers, the overlookers always made sure that they gave the same soldier's washing to the same girl every time.

'I didn't know anything about this Corporal Davies,' Florence says. 'I didn't know whether he was an old man, a young man, a married man, or what he was, but my mum had a soft streak and was obviously thinking about this unknown soldier, wondering who he was and imagining him sad and lonely and far from his family so, unknown to me, she had taken to putting little gifts for him in with the clean washing.' Every week Florence's mother put a packet of Woodbines for the soldier among his washed and pressed clothes, and sometimes a biscuit or two or a bit of home-made cake. That was a particularly generous gift, for rationing meant she was always short of butter, sugar and flour.

Clothing was rationed too, but whatever the shortages, Florence's older sister always seemed to manage to find the money and the coupons for a new pair of stockings. 'She used to buy these really expensive ones,' Florence recalls. 'Inca Sun they were, at four shillings and elevenpence a pair, so she must have been on good money. I couldn't afford that so I used to wait until she'd laddered them and thrown them out, and then I'd retrieve them from the bin and wear them myself – better a pair of laddered stockings than no stockings at all.'

After sending Corporal Davies small gifts for a few weeks, Florence's mother then put a note in with the clean washing one day. It read: 'If you want to come and spend a bit of time with a family here, you can come round one Sunday for a cup of tea, and if you don't want to come on your own, then bring a friend with you as well.' Florence's mum was not alone in sending notes to lonely soldiers; one woman working on the production line packing vitamin chocolate for the troops remembers that 'When the supervisors weren't looking, some of the girls used to put notes into the chocolates for the forces with their names and addresses on. I don't know if any of them ever got a reply!'

The next Sunday afternoon, Florence was in her room upstairs when she heard a knock at the door. Her mother opened it and Florence could hear men's voices that she didn't recognize, and then her mother shouted up the stairs, 'Flora, come down and see this young man you've been bringing the washing home for.' When she went downstairs there were two soldiers sitting in the living room, and Corporal Davies turned out to be a tall and very handsome man. He and Florence started chatting – he told her his name was Arthur and he came from Wolverhampton – and then after tea they went for a walk round the streets and through the park. She was very shy with him at first, but he soon put her at ease, telling her tales of his home town and the things the Army were putting them through before sending them off to war. He was a good listener too, plying her with questions about her work and what she liked to do in her spare time, and it was almost dusk by the time they came back to the house. Florence's mum took one look at her daughter's flushed face and sparkling eyes, and smiled to herself; the packets of Woodbines and the home-baking had been money well spent. From then on Florence and Arthur were courting.

A lot of other romances began at Rowntree's, sometimes with a workmate acting as Cupid. Beryl Thornton might never have met her husband had one of his workmates not taken a hand. Denis Woodcock came out of the Army at twenty-three after doing his National Service. He'd already done a seven-year full apprenticeship as a painter and decorator in York, and soon got a job in the Paint Shop at Rowntree's, one of more than fifty painters working there at the time. Usually they worked in pairs, but on a big job ten or twelve of them would come in together at a weekend to redecorate a large room. Denis was paired with a man called Johnny Holmes, who was an outgoing, larger-than-life character. They had been given the job of painting the office of Miss Billen, the formidable manager of the Cream Packing department where Beryl worked. They'd been in there a day or two and he was painting the inside of the window frame, when he glanced down into the yard and saw Beryl. He turned to Johnny and said, 'I like the look of that girl down there.'

'Which one?' Johnny said.

'That girl there with the black hair,' he said. The next minute, Johnny had put his brush down and was heading out of the room. 'Where are you going?' Denis said, but Johnny just said, 'It's all right, I'll be back in a moment,' and walked out of the door.

When Denis looked down into the yard again he saw Johnny come out of the building. He walked straight up to Beryl and said, 'My friend likes you.'

'So where is your friend then?' Beryl said.

Johnny pointed up at the office window. 'He's up there.'

As Beryl looked up she just caught a glimpse of Denis, who was so embarrassed that he ducked down out of sight. So she said to Johnny, 'Well, if he likes me, tell him to come and tell me himself, instead of sending his friend to do it for him.'

Johnny went back into the building and walked into the office with a big grin on his face.

'What have you done?' Denis said.

'Oh nothing,' Johnny said airily. 'I just told her you liked her and were keen on her.'

'Why did you do that?' Denis said, even more embarrassed, and then, after a pause, 'So what did she say?'

Johnny passed on the message, and a couple of minutes later, feeling a bit sheepish, Denis went outside, but by then Beryl had gone back in to work. He managed to find out who she was, though, and the next day he left a red apple on her workbench and waved to her through the window. 'I hadn't really noticed him before to be honest,' she says, 'but I wasn't going out with anyone at the time, so when he finally plucked up the courage, spoke to me and said, "Would you like to come out with me on Friday night?" I said, "Yes."'

They arranged to meet outside the Theatre Royal in Exhibition Square, but their first date wasn't exactly a conventional one. Denis had been planning to take her to the pictures, but he was a keen water polo player and the day before their first date, he was told that he had been picked for a tournament in Leeds. So when Beryl turned up and said, 'Where are we going then?' he said, 'I was going to take you to the pictures, but I'm sorry to say that I'm swimming in a competition tonight and I've got to get the team bus to Leeds. Would you come there with me instead?'

Beryl said she would, so their first date took place at Armley Baths in Leeds, with Denis in the pool and Beryl perched up in the spectators' gallery. Relationships have ended for less, and it was a miracle there was a second date after that, but Beryl liked him enough to give him a second chance, and that time, rather more conventionally, he took her dancing instead. They went dancing a lot after that, and were married in 1958.

Courtship was often a painfully slow, formal process in pre-war years, but the outbreak of war lent an added sense of urgency, and wartime shortages also led to some rather more unusual love tokens than the traditional flowers or chocolates. Madge Tillett's suitor played a trump card when he gave her a pair of almost unobtainable silk stockings. 'He'd got them from Iceland of all places,' Madge says, 'but stockings of any sort were as rare as hen's teeth then, and these were really good quality. So I thought to myself, "Well, he must be keen," so I got talking to him, we started going out, and that was it, we were married a few months later.'

Florence's courtship was almost as quick. She and Arthur had been 'stepping out together' for only three or four months when he was posted overseas. Almost all of the soldiers in his unit had been having their washing done by Rowntree's girls, and she was not the only one to have begun a relationship with a soldier. As a reflection of the close ties that had developed, the night before they left York, Rowntree's organized a party for the soldiers and their girlfriends in the Dining Block at the factory. Like all the girls, Florence had been privately imagining the farewell kisses and the promises and vows that she and her boyfriend would exchange before they parted – perhaps he would even propose! – but at the end of the evening there was not even a chance for them to say goodbye in private, because there was a heavy military police presence to deter any soldiers who might have been thinking of deserting and staying in York. So Arthur and Florence had to say their farewells within earshot and under the disapproving gaze of a heavy-set military policeman, and they parted with no declarations of undying love and certainly no proposal of marriage, just a brief kiss and Florence's promise to write regularly and to wait for him. She was not to see him again for almost five years.

In 1943, after Florence had been working on fuse-filling and red-flagging for two years and the company had produced almost eight million fuses, Rowntree's contract with the Government expired and was not renewed, but awarded to another factory instead. The girls all gathered to watch the very last fuse of all, number 7,809,579, come off the assembly line. A series of commemorative photographs was taken and the girls all 'sat around posing for the photographer', while Ned Sparkes filled the very last fuse.

Although they were all still on Rowntree's books, the company either wouldn't or couldn't take Florence and a lot of the other women back into the factory at first, so instead she had to go and work in Leeds for sixteen weeks, training to be a mechanical engineer. In peacetime, it would have been almost inconceivable that a woman would have trained as an engineer, but these were rapidly changing times and she was one of hundreds of women taking on highly skilled and physically demanding work that had previously been the sole province of men. In order to qualify, she had to make two gear rings from scratch to prove that she had mastered the necessary skills, machining them, filing them down and balancing them. They had to be perfect and it took her the full sixteen weeks to make them.

She travelled to Leeds by train every day, and continued to live at home so that she could save the costs of lodgings. So did Dot Edwards, who had been sent to a training school at the

Crown wallpaper factory in Leeds to train as a fitter for the Army and Air Force, and Joan Martin, who was sent to the Silver Cross pram factory in Guiseley near Leeds, which had been requisitioned by the Government to make parts for aircraft, including the Hurricane and Spitfire. Other girls were not so lucky. Madge Tillett was sent to Barnoldswick to work on aircraft repairs and had to stay in a hostel. 'It was all right really,' she says, 'except for one thing: there was never enough to eat. I used to work fourteen nights straight, so that I could get two days off and come home on the train to York, go to my mum's and get something to eat!'

When Florence came back to York, Rowntree's still did not have any work for her, so instead she went to work for the engineering firm of Cook, Troughton & Simms. Despite the opportunity to practise her new skills, she didn't enjoy it much, finding the work boring and the wages and conditions nowhere near as good as those at Rowntree's, so when trade began to pick up again and Rowntree's called her back, she didn't have to think twice. This time she went into Cream Packing. 'Thinking back to my interview before the war, I decided that they'd obviously lost the bit of paper that said "No Machine Work",' she says with a smile. She was packing the butterscotch chocolates and, being very fond of them, took the opportunity to help herself to one from time to time when the overlookers were not looking, but she ate so many that, she says, 'I got fed up of them after a while and stopped eating them – and I've never eaten them since!'

7

Eileen

Like so many other York girls, Eileen Morgan went straight to Rowntree's after leaving school when she was sixteen years old, in 1951. 'If you were growing up in York,' she says, 'when you left school, there were only two places you wanted to work. You either went to Rowntree's or you went to Terry's. A lot of people and a lot of families worked for one or the other, so if your granddad and your dad worked there, you went there too.'

Four young women of an earlier era had been so eager to work at Rowntree's that, either not wanting or not being able to afford rented accommodation, they got themselves a tent, pitched it in a friendly farmer's field at Pocklington, and then either walked or cycled the twenty-six-mile round trip into York every day to go to work. The tent proved a mixed blessing. The young women were so scared of earwigs – there was an old wives' tale that, as their name suggests, earwigs would crawl into your ears if you slept on the ground – that in an attempt to keep them at bay, they stuffed cotton wool in their ears before they lay down to sleep. The girls were also terrified of the wasps that plagued them on warm summer evenings, and at night they were frightened out of their wits by cows looming up out of the darkness and stumbling on their guy ropes or bumping into their tent. Despite all that, they lived in the tent through winter and summer, and kept up their marathon commute to work for twelve months in all, before finding more comfortable and conventional, if also more expensive, accommodation in a house in the city.

Eileen had no need of a tent, as she lived in a terraced house just off Burton Stone Lane, but her family background was very unusual. She was born in 1935 in her grandmother's house, where her father, Arthur, and mother, Doris, were living at the time. Her parents had known each other all their lives, having grown up in the same area, and they married young. Like so many couples in that era, they simply could not afford a place of their own at first, but when Eileen was still very small, her parents managed to save enough money to move to a house on Monk Stray on Malton Road. Eileen's dad worked at the Rowntree's factory loading cocoa beans into the grinding mills; it was hard physical work, but he was a tall and powerful figure and very fit. In addition to the heavy lifting he did at work, he had played rugby league for York in his younger days, and was a keen race-walker in his spare time.

Eileen's dad was a handsome man and, admits his daughter, 'He was cocky and even arrogant. I think he was "a word and a blow" sort of man; in fact I know he was,' she says, laughing, and he'd had a string of previous girlfriends before he met and settled down with Doris. 'He was quite a character,' Eileen says, 'and he used to say all sorts, though a lot of it wasn't fit for the ears of a little girl!' He enlisted in the Army as soon as war was declared, and his strength and fitness as well as his personal qualities saw him selected for the elite Commandos when they were formed in the wake of Dunkirk in June 1940. Eileen was only five when war broke out and her dad went away, and she has only the vaguest memories of him before the war, but she can clearly recall seeing him in his uniform boarding the train to go back to his unit after spending some wartime leave with them at home.

In 1944, Arthur's commando unit was involved in the fighting at Anzio. As special forces, they were operating behind enemy lines before the beachhead assault, and continued to take part in the fighting as the battle raged. It proved to be one of the bloodiest and most prolonged battles of the entire war. The twelve men in his unit posed for a group photograph before going into action – Eileen still has a copy – and the rest of them are standing there ramrod straight, legs together, as if they're on parade, whereas Eileen's dad is standing with one leg bent and his head tilted, looking straight into the camera with a quizzical smile on his face, taking it all in his stride. 'To me, that shows the arrogance he had,' she says, 'but the fact that he was so arrogant was probably what got him through it all.'

Eileen's father was one of only two men from that group who were still alive when the fighting was over, but he paid a terrible price for his survival. The battle was still raging when he was hit in the neck by a bullet fired by a German sniper, and because of the angle of entry, the bullet penetrated down through his neck and deep into his body. Badly wounded, he was picked up by the stretcher bearers and laid down next to some other casualties to await transport to a casualty clearing station. As he lay on the stretcher, helpless, thinking about his wife and daughter and wondering if he would ever see them again, he saw a German soldier rise from cover; he had probably been waiting until the casualties had all been gathered together before launching his attack. Arthur tried to shout a warning but it was lost in the noise of battle. He had time to study the German's features – he was blond-haired and looked to be no more than a boy – as, still unseen by anyone else, he drew back his arm and hurled a stick grenade. The last thing that Eileen's dad remembered seeing was that German's youthful face and blond hair, and the stick grenade turning end over end as it fell towards him.

It landed no more than a couple of yards from Arthur and exploded at once. A piece of shrapnel smashed into his knee-cap, badly wounding him, and other fragments of the grenade ripped into his face. He passed out, and when he came round it was to a world of pain and utter darkness, for the explosion and the shrapnel had blinded him. His right eye had been completely torn out by a shard of flying metal and his right eardrum was perforated. His left eye had also been badly damaged, his knee had been shattered and he had several other wounds including the bullet hole in his neck. His wounds were so bad that after he had been taken to hospital in Naples, he was given just twenty-four hours to live, but he was a strong man, with an even stronger will to live, and he pulled through. The doctor who examined him told him that he should try to get himself to the United States, because it was the only place where surgeons had the skills, the equipment and the facilities to have a chance of saving the sight in his remaining eye, but the wound then turned gangrenous and in the end the left eye had to be removed as well.

When he was well enough, Eileen's dad was taken back to England – his ship was bombed on the way, but although damaged, it did not sink – and he was then treated at the American Red Cross hospital at Fishponds in Bristol. Eileen's mother took her to visit him there. Eileen was just nine years old then and barely remembered her father, and it was a terribly traumatic visit because, she says, 'He looked simply horrendous. His wounded leg was still in plaster, his hair had grown long, there were scars all over his face and scalp, and to allow his wounds to continue to heal and to keep his eye sockets open until he could be fitted with glass eyes, he had two pieces of blank pink plastic in the sockets, which made him look even more alien and alarming to me.'

They kept him at Fishponds for nine months, mainly, according to Arthur, 'to cheer the Yanks up' who were also being treated there. He was well positioned to cheer them up because with his leg still in plaster from groin to ankle, his wheelchair had been fitted with a solid wooden platform jutting out parallel to the ground, on which his leg rested while he was wheeling himself around. This gave him the perfect opportunity to provide a much-appreciated service to his British and American friends. Alcohol was of course banned from the ward, but just outside the hospital gates there was a pub with a 'beer off' – an off-licence. Had any of the hospital doctors had time to consider the matter, they might have paused to wonder why Arthur's wheelchair always seemed so much harder to manoeuvre after his regular excursions for 'a breath of fresh air'. Even more curious, his leg, while still encased in plaster and draped with a hospital blanket, seemed to have swollen to two or three times its previous size. Had they pursued him to the ward, the mystery would have been solved at once, because accompanied by much muffled laughter and clinking of glass, the blanket was peeled back to reveal a line of beer bottles, nose to tail the length of the wooden platform on either side of his leg. The contents were consumed every evening, adding greatly to the morale and well-being of the assembled company, and the next day Arthur would set off for another of his wheelchair constitutionals, with the empties neatly arranged down the sides of his leg beneath the blanket, ready to be swapped for full ones.

No doubt to the disappointment of the wounded soldiers he left behind who would have to find another way to get their beer, Eileen's dad was eventually transferred to Stoke Mandeville. Although his leg was healing, he remained seriously ill and his doctors still hadn't found the sniper's bullet that was lodged somewhere inside him and that was making him so ill. One day, his nurse told him that a General was coming to make an inspection of the ward and that he had to tidy his bedside locker. As he reached over to start doing so, he froze in agony, locked into that position and unable to move. When doctors examined him, they found the cause was the sniper's bullet, which had passed right down through his neck and his torso, before becoming lodged in his ribs. As he stretched out, the bullet must have shifted position slightly and trapped a nerve.

With the bullet at last removed, Arthur continued his slow recovery and when his doctors judged that he was strong enough, he was sent to complete his demobilization from the Army and then came home to York. Eileen says:

> *I can remember really well the day he came home. I was ten years old then and Mum and I went to York station together to meet his train. I can even remember exactly where we were sitting as we waited for Dad's train to arrive. In those days as you went into the station, on the platform where there are now tables and chairs for a café, back then there was a circular, wrap-around seat with a wrought-iron pillar in the middle. We sat there waiting for him to come through the barrier, as you had to in those days – it wasn't open as it is now. All the fears*

I'd had when I first saw him in hospital had now disappeared. I knew who he was now. I'd visited him many times since then at Fishponds and at Stoke Mandeville, and I'd got used to him and the way he was. I was just looking forward to seeing him.

Joe Corrigan, whose family ran Corrigan's Funfair at Scarborough, had also been blinded in the war, and had been in hospital at Stoke Mandeville with Eileen's dad and demobilized with him. When Eileen went to see her dad at Stoke Mandeville, she saw Joe Corrigan's family coming in and bringing him all sorts of different kinds of fruit that were virtually unobtainable in Britain in wartime – either they had been raiding the Rowntree's hot house for exotic fruits or they had some strong connections in the black market. As Arthur and Joe were both York men, the two of them had been sent home together. Eileen spotted them a fair way off, with her dad towering over Joe, who was only a little fellow.

As they came through the barrier Eileen saw her mum's expression change. A moment before they had both been happy and excited, chattering about what it would be like to see him and what they would do that evening to celebrate, but as soon as she saw him, she was absolutely furious – not with Arthur, but with the Army. Both Arthur and Joe had just been demobbed, and when they'd handed in their uniforms and army kit, and signed the last of the endless army forms, they were supposed to have been issued with civilian clothes: their 'demob suit', as it was known. Both of them had indeed been sent home wearing double-breasted suits, but instead of a white or striped shirt, dark tie and black shoes, like everyone else who was being demobbed, they had been kitted out with khaki shirts to which white collars had been attached, they were still wearing the red ties from the hospital and they had scuffed army boots instead of shoes. They looked more like tramps than returning war heroes and, Eileen says, 'Mum was blazing with anger about it because she felt, rightly, that it demeaned them. You just weren't demobbed like that, and the clear implication was that because these two men were blind, the army clerks had decided that because they couldn't see what they were wearing, it didn't matter what strange combination of clothes they were given.' It blighted what should have been a joyful homecoming.

After a brief spell at home, Eileen's dad then went to St Dunstan's in Brighton, a charity that helped blind ex-servicemen to come to terms with their disability and learn new skills to aid them in coping with civilian life. After being evaluated there, Arthur was sent to the St Dunstan's training school at Church Stretton in Wales to start learning Braille. 'He never did the standard Braille because his hands and fingers were too chunky,' Eileen says, 'so he did what was called "Moon Braille" – circles and lines instead of little dots.' He also learned to type so he could try to earn his living as a typist but, she says, 'Dad simply couldn't stand it. He was an active man and hated sitting at a typewriter, and the money he could earn from it was also really poor. There was no pension or other benefits and the pay was only one pound, two shillings and sixpence a week.' Of that modest sum, Eileen's dad sent the pound home to his wife and kept only half a crown as spending money for himself.

Eileen still wonders why he even attempted typing:

He could have trained to run a corner shop instead, like a small newsagent or a tobacconist, or he could have trained as a physiotherapist, or done plenty of other things – St Dunstan's offered all kinds of training and support to help blind people back into work, and he was still only thirty-one years old – but all he wanted to do was go back to Rowntree's. I suppose it was what he knew and he felt safe in that environment. So in the end he just came home; I don't even know whether he came on his own or whether someone brought him, but he just turned up on the doorstep one day and said he couldn't stand it any more. Mum and I were shocked to see him standing there. He did bring his typewriter with him and kept it at home, and I can remember the sound of him tapping away on the keyboard occasionally, but he rarely used it and of course when I got to sixteen years old and started working in the offices at Rowntree's, I was the one who had to do the typing if any was needed and he just did the dictating!

Rowntree's had been helping Doris and Eileen financially while Arthur was in hospital and at St Dunstan's, and Philip Rowntree now came to see him and told him that if he returned to Rowntree's and completed retraining, Philip would personally guarantee that Arthur would be given a suitable job. 'They would have given him an easy job to do, I think,' Eileen says, 'but no, although it was a heavy job, he wanted to do the job he'd been doing before the war, back among the men that he knew, splitting sacks and pouring cocoa beans down the chute into the grinding mills. So that is what he did. He took up his old job again and kept doing it for the next twenty-five years.'

The cocoa beans he handled were grown in Ghana and Nigeria and brought by huge cargo ships to Hull docks. Transferred to barges, they were then carried up the Humber, the Ouse and into the Foss Lock, from where they were discharged into the Rowntree's bonded warehouses lining the waterfront. It was a popular run for the bargees because they were often given bags of chocolate misshapes as a perk of the job. The cocoa beans were stored in the warehouses by the river until they were needed, then taken to the factory and raised on the hoist that ran from the ground floor to the top floor of the Elect Block in the northeast corner of the factory site. It was known as 'The Gables', although, confusingly, the same name was given to the top floor of almost every one of the score of different buildings on the factory site. The hoist was for products only, and off-limits to all employees unless they could produce a note from the company doctor to say they were too badly injured or infirm to use the stairs.

Eileen's father did not have to climb flights of stairs every morning, because he worked on the fourth floor and there was a long wooden ramp leading up to it, so he only had to climb a relatively short flight of stairs and could then use the ramp to reach his workplace. He did his day's work on a raised platform near the hoist. A man called Taff Limbert used to take the ten-stone (sixty-four-kilo) sacks of cocoa beans from the hoist, one at a time, wheel them over to Arthur and rest them against his leg so that he knew exactly where they were. Arthur would take hold of them, slit them open with his knife, lift and twist the sack in one movement, then pour the beans down the chute into the mills where they were ground, and he performed the arduous task with such dexterity that he was the equal of any of his sighted comrades. 'He was a remarkable man and became quite famous around the factory,' Eileen says. 'The tour guides showing visitors around the site always used to make a point of taking them to see my dad at work.'

The cocoa beans that Arthur poured down the chute into the grinding mills underwent a series of processes as they passed down through the floors of the building. The crushed beans were first hand-sorted to remove foreign material such as dirt and stones, then roasted and winnowed – passed through drums where giant fans blew the husks away. The beans were then ground down again, first into cocoa 'nibs' and then into the creamy paste known as 'cocoa liquor'. Cocoa powder and cocoa butter were produced as by-products of this complex process.

The cocoa liquor was then transported to the Melangeur Block at the southeastern corner of the factory site, between the railway lines and the Wigginton Road. There the cocoa liquor was mixed with sugar, vanilla and some of the cocoa butter, and 'conched' – stirred continuously to allow the volatiles, the vinegary acids contained within the chocolate liquor, to rise to the surface and evaporate, creating a distinctive, sharply acidic smell that cut the rich aroma of chocolate over that corner of the factory. The longer the chocolate was conched, the smoother and better tasting it was. The chocolate for the Black Magic assortments was conched for two days – 'two long days' according to the advertising copy – allowing almost all of the volatiles to evaporate and leaving a rich, high-quality chocolate behind.

The Melangeur Block produced a continual assault on the senses. Pushed by men dripping with sweat in the hot, humid atmosphere, steel containers like the 'coal tubs' used in coal mines rumbled across the floor between the ranks of huge, clanking machines, their paddles moving endlessly to and fro as they conched the chocolate. Some found the constant heavy aroma of chocolate in the air – so rich that it was tasted as much as smelled – enticing, but others thought it was overpowering and a few found it nauseating. Still others failed to notice it at all, as if their sense of smell had been so overwhelmed that it had simply ceased to function.

The hot liquid chocolate produced in the Melangeur Block was sent to all the different departments, including the Cream Block where the chocolate assortments were made, and the Cake Block (chocolate blocks were known as 'cake') in the centre of the factory site, near the offices, where chocolate bars like Aeros and Kit Kats were produced. Originally the liquid chocolate was carried in huge tubs, but later it was pumped under pressure through a network of insulated pipes, like some strange forerunner of Willy Wonka's chocolate factory. Another network of pipes running throughout the factory, like the steam heating pipes that run beneath the streets of Manhattan, carried steam generated by the boiler house to provide heat for melting the chocolate and for various other processes; it also warmed the radiators throughout the factory. There was even enough spare capacity to heat the water in the Yearsley swimming pool on the far side of the Haxby Road via a pipe laid beneath the road. It was supplied as a goodwill gesture, with the City of York only being charged a nominal sum for it.

Eileen's mother, Doris, had worked at Rowntree's on the night shift, making munitions throughout the war, and with her father away fighting for his country, Eileen's granddad used to look after her while her mum was at work or sleeping during the day. After Arthur came home, Doris stopped work and in late 1946 she gave birth to a son, a little brother for Eileen, but he lived for only five hours before he died:

Mum lost three children altogether. I was the firstborn, then she had a stillbirth, and on the night of the York Blitz in April 1942 she lost a baby boy as well, and then there was the little one after the war. She should never have had children really. She had a very rare blood group, Rhesus B Negative, which I and the rest of my family have all got, but they didn't know what it was then. Rhesus Negative wasn't discovered until 1948 and she was already gone then. When you have a child now, you are given an injection straight away to prevent antibodies that would damage the next baby, and I've been lucky because I've never made any antibodies anyway, but it cost my mum three children. My little brother was only two and a half pounds when he was born, but he was lovely, and I don't know if my mum ever really recovered from the shock of losing him. I don't think Dad did either. It was the only time I ever saw my father cry, and I've never, ever seen a man cry like that again. He was absolutely heartbroken. My mum died two years later, in January 1948, when I was only twelve. Had she been living today, the doctors would almost certainly have saved her life. She probably had toxicaemia and pre-eclampsia, but she shouldn't have died. Had she been sent to hospital earlier, she would probably have survived. It hit my dad hard; in fact, I think losing my mum hit him even harder than losing his eyesight.

As soon as St Dunstan's heard about Doris's death, one of their visitors, 'a big, tall lady' called Miss Pierce, came and took Eileen out with her for two days, just to get her away from the house and spare her at least some of the upset and sadness. 'Miss Pierce took me round with her to all the houses she was visiting,' Eileen says, 'and we went for a drive out into the country in her car and she took me for tea and cake, both of which were very big treats for me, indeed for anyone at the end of the war, but that was the sort of thing St Dunstan's did. They didn't just care for the blind people, they looked after their families too.'

When Eileen's mum died, the family were living at Tang Hall, on Carter Avenue, about a mile east of the city centre, and it was quite a distance from the factory, so they needed to make it easier for her dad to get to work. 'My auntie, Dad's youngest sister, stepped in then and even gave up her own job to come and live with us and help out,' Eileen says, 'but we just had to move, there was no two ways about it, we had to get him nearer to the factory. He couldn't have got to work otherwise, because he couldn't go on the bus on his own.' So in May of that year they moved to Tennyson Avenue, just off Burton Stone Lane, a few hundred yards west of the factory, on the far side of the mainline railway tracks.

About a year later, Arthur remarried. He met Eileen's future stepmother, Alice, at Dunollie, the Cocoa Works Rest Home established by Rowntree's in Scarborough. At the end of the war, the Rowntree's Board of Directors had a substantial sum left over from the wartime hardship fund they had established for employees on National Service and their families, and from which Eileen's family had benefited. Rather than simply distributing it through the profit-sharing scheme, the directors opted to use the remaining money to establish a rest home instead, where employees in need of convalescence from illness or injury, or who had undergone a period of stress or a bereavement, could apply to have two weeks' rest and recuperation at no cost to themselves, well away from their work and family commitments.

Dunollie, a large detached house set in two acres of grounds on Filey Road, near the South Cliff in Scarborough, was purchased and converted to provide accommodation for thirty-three people, including the staff. It had spectacular views towards the castle and out over the harbour, and was lavishly appointed, with a stone-pillared entrance opening onto a beautiful oak-panelled hall with a minstrels' gallery. There were marble fireplaces, intricate plasterwork, a library, a billiards room with cedarwood panelling and twenty-five bedrooms. The aim was that Dunollie should have 'the atmosphere of a guest house rather than a convalescent home, and accommodate employees of either sex and of any age'. In line with that description, just like the holidaymakers in the town's boarding houses, residents of Dunollie were banished from the house during the day and had to go for a walk round the Italian Gardens, or stroll along the promenade or the pier until late afternoon.

Although some of the residents were convalescing or in mourning, others had simply gone there for a rest and, freed from the grinding routine of their daily work, many were more than ready for a bit of fun. Eileen's friends Sue and Maggie went to Dunollie to recuperate after they had both been ill. It was Mischief Night while they were there, a once-strong northern tradition that involved playing pranks on people the night before Bonfire Night, but which has now largely fallen into disuse as the American Halloween has taken over kids' imaginations. Sue and Maggie had exchanged a bit of banter with two men who were also staying at Dunollie, and when the men went off to the pub, Sue and her friend borrowed a needle and thread from the nurse, went up to the men's room and sewed up the cuffs of their pyjama jackets and trousers. After the men had come back from the pub, well refreshed, Sue and Maggie listened outside their door, stifling their laughter as they heard the commotion when the men discovered the trick that had been played on them. An hour or so later, when the men's loud snores showed that they had fallen into a drunken sleep, Sue and Maggie tiptoed back into their room and, while the men slept on in blissful ignorance, the two women swapped over the two sets of false teeth that were steeping in glasses on the bedside tables. When they came down in the morning, both of them had put in the wrong false teeth and spent most of breakfast grumbling to each other about how 'My teeth just don't seem quite right somehow.' Although they eventually realized their mistake, they assumed it was their own drunken error from the night before, and never discovered the trick Sue and Maggie had played on them.

However, resting employees were not supposed to enjoy themselves too much while in Scarborough. There was an eleven o'clock curfew at night to stop those who had been enjoying their own brand of recuperation in Scarborough's pubs from staying out too late and disturbing the other occupants of the house.

Rowntree's had also sent Eileen's dad to Dunollie to help him recover after suffering some kind of nervous breakdown in the aftermath of Doris's death. While he was staying at Dunollie he met Alice, who also worked at Rowntree's making Smarties, though Arthur had never met her there; with so many thousands of employees, it was impossible to get to know more than a tiny proportion of the people who worked at the factory. Alice had had complications following an operation and had been sent to Dunollie to recuperate, and the two of them got talking and spent most of the rest of their time there together. They kept in touch after they came back to York, and Alice then began coming round to the house regularly to take Arthur out for a drink. Eventually, a year or so later, they got married.

'She was younger than Dad,' Eileen says, 'lovely and very kind, and we all got on with her really well. She was only twenty-seven when they married, nine years younger than him, and she took on a blind man with a fourteen-year-old stroppy daughter – which I was in those days – and she was good for him, there's no doubt about that. He was not an easy man to live with, I think, but Alice was a wonderful wife to him. She absolutely adored him and was totally devoted to him.'

After the marriage, Alice stopped working at Rowntree's, because she felt she wanted to take care of Arthur and be free to take him to work in the mornings and to bring him back at night. She used to walk with him along the street and up onto the railway bridge every morning, where one of his mates from work would meet them and take Arthur in to work. Alice would then go back up to the bridge at 5.30 p.m. and meet him again after his day's work.

Despite his disability, Eileen's dad continued to do all the things he used to do when he could see. Before the war he used to enter the walking races at the Rowntree's sports days and races run by the local working men's club. 'When he came back blind,' Eileen says, 'we all thought that he would never be able to race-walk again, but Dad had a very different opinion about that. Every Whit Monday the club organized a big walking race called "The Clarence Walk", held through the streets of York, and after the war, they had a trophy made, a really nice one about eighteen inches high, and named it "The Arthur Morgan Trophy" in his honour, never imagining that he would ever race for it.'

However, despite his blindness and the continuing pain from his war wounds, Arthur was determined that he was going to enter the 1950 race and he began training in secret. His plan was to start from the bottom of Malton Road and walk all the way to the Hopgrove (near what is now the York outer ring road) and back, about the same distance as the actual race. Eileen's Uncle Bill – Arthur's brother-in-law – was to ride shotgun, pedalling his bike alongside. When Eileen saw them getting ready to go out, she ran to get her own bike out of the back yard. 'Can I come too?' she said as she wheeled it into the street.

Her dad's expression showed that he did not think much of the idea. 'You won't be able to keep up,' he said.

'I will, I will. Ple-e-e-ease,' she said, as she saw him wavering.

'All right then, but if you fall behind, you'll have to go straight home.'

She watched, puzzled, as Bill fastened a dog collar tight around the bicep of her father's right arm and clipped a lead to it. He then mounted his bike, holding the other end of the lead in his hand. They set off up the street, an odd procession with Arthur striding out, Bill riding alongside him, and Eileen bringing up the rear, her legs pedalling furiously to keep up with them. They made unsteady progress at first, with Arthur veering from left to right, stumbling into the gutter at one point, and at another almost bumping into the bike, as Bill issued a stream of commands – 'Left a bit … Now come right a little … You're too close to the kerb …' – but gradually they grew more confident in each other, and by the time they were halfway to the Hopgrove, Bill, still acting as navigator, did not need to say a word or even glance in Arthur's direction. Still holding the dog lead, Bill concentrated on steering a straight line with his bike, while Arthur focused on the pressure of the lead on his bicep. If he felt it beginning to go taut, he knew he was walking too much to the left, and if he felt it slacken, he knew he was going too much to the right, and that was how he kept on track and could keep to a dead straight course, even while walking flat out.

Although her legs were aching long before they reached the Hopgrove and turned for the homeward leg, Eileen did not utter a word of complaint and she kept pedalling along behind them all the way back. She was stiff as a board when she got up for school the next morning, but when they got ready to go out again that night, she was once more sitting on her bike, ready to follow them.

As far as possible, Eileen's father did his training for the race in secret and did not hand in his entry form until the last possible moment. As usual the local bookmakers were taking bets on the race. Off-course bookmaking was illegal then, but the police usually overlooked it. If you asked anyone around the town in those days, they would almost certainly be able to point out the nearest bookies to you, usually in a backstreet building with frosted glass windows or the blinds pulled down, a pall of cigarette smoke hanging over it and a surprisingly large number of men coming and going through its door.

Despite Arthur's attempts to keep his training regime secret, word inevitably began to get around. Neighbours saw him setting off and coming back, dripping with sweat, an hour or so later, and put two and two together, and after he handed in his entry form at the club, the secretary was telling everyone he knew. When people heard Arthur was entering the race, they began putting bets on him to win. At first the bookies offered generous odds against him, perhaps scarcely believing that people would be stupid enough to risk their money by betting on a blind man with a patched-up kneecap from a war wound, and certain in any case that he could not win. However, so many punters took the odds, including large numbers of Arthur's workmates at Rowntree's, that the bookies stood to lose a fortune if Arthur won – he even had a big bet on himself – so they set out to do everything they could to stop him winning.

The race took place over a six-mile course through the streets of York, starting at the working men's club, passing along Clarence Street, Gillygate and Bootham, and finishing at the old Clifton Hospital. The streets along the course were absolutely packed with people, and Eileen can still remember the deafening noise of them shouting and cheering. Among the crowd were judges making sure that the walkers were all heeling and toeing, and that none of them were cheating by breaking into a run. There were also a few of the bookies' henchmen scattered through the crowd, who shouted, howled and whistled whenever her father came within range, trying to put him off and disrupt his communications with his brother-in-law. When that failed, they jostled Bill on his bike, causing him to swerve dangerously close to Arthur and nearly sending him over the handlebars at one point – but Arthur kept striding on, steadily moving clear of the field. In desperation, the bookies' men even got someone to let a dog loose in front of Arthur, in the hope that he would fall over it, but although he stumbled, he recovered himself and kept going. Despite everything they did to try to stop him, he eventually won the race by a distance. 'I was cheering and shouting myself hoarse as I saw him coming towards the finish line,' Eileen says. 'But he just walked in, as if it was all part and parcel of the day, a bit of a stroll to work up an appetite for lunch. Now we've got the Paralympics and all that, so we're used to disabled people doing things,' she says, 'but in his day it was a novelty; disabled people just didn't do that sort of thing then. When he won the Clarence Walk, his own walk for the Morgan Cup, it even made the *Daily Mirror* – my son still has the photograph that the *Mirror* took of the three of us: my dad, Uncle Bill on the bike and me on my little pushbike next to them.'

Eileen's dad was not the only big winner that day. There was a well-known man around York called Joe Miller, who owned a number of fish and chip shops. He was a big gambler, too. After the race, he came into the changing room, walked up to Eileen's dad and pressed a note into his hand and said, 'Have a drink with me and from now on every time you do that, that's what you'll get.' Arthur thought it must be a ten-shilling note or something, but when he showed it to Bill, he said, 'Do you know what he's just given you? That's a twenty-pound note you've got there.' Twenty pounds was an absolute fortune then, the equivalent of well over £500 today. However, Arthur didn't keep the money; together with his own winnings from the bookmakers and his prize money from the race, he donated it to St Dunstan's in gratitude for all the help they had given him. In addition, all the proceeds from the concert held at the working men's club that night were given to St Dunstan's. Eileen was not there; at fourteen years old she was too young to be allowed in the club, even on such a special night for her father, and while he celebrated with Alice, Bill and his friends, Eileen was at home with her grandmother as usual.

'He won the walking race at the Rowntree's Sports Day on the bumpy grass field at the Haxby Road sports ground about three times as well,' Eileen recalls, 'and every time he won it he got a suitcase as his prize – we hadn't room to stack them all!

I remember there was another blind man at Rowntree's who was a really good swimmer and, like my dad, he won a lot of races. He used to swim breaststroke and they'd always put him in the lane next to the side of the pool, so he could just brush the side with his fingers on each stroke and keep himself on course.'

8

Madge

Madge was twenty years old and seven months pregnant when she and Bill got married. It was the day after Remembrance Day, 12 November 1938. The wedding reception was a very homespun affair, back at her mum and dad's house with a few home-made sandwiches and cakes. The very next morning, Madge went into labour and her baby, a little boy, was born two months premature in the front room of her parents' house. It was a difficult birth and although he was alive and perfectly formed, the baby was in a very frail condition.

Immediately after the birth, the midwife who had delivered him had a muttered conversation with Madge's mother. Exhausted from the birth, Madge did not hear what was said and was too weak to intervene, but she formed the impression that 'the midwife never really seemed to bother with the baby after that'.

Madge had given up her job to have the baby, and with no money and a husband also out of work, her immediate prospects were less than bright. The midwife and Madge's mother may have reached the conclusion that, on top of all that, an ailing, premature baby to look after might have been too much for the family to cope with, but whatever the reason, after living for just five hours, her son died. 'In a way it was a good thing,' she says now, a faraway look in her eye, 'because we had no money and nowhere to go but that little room,' but there were many times in the years ahead when she fell silent, staring into the fire, and thought about the son she had lost and what might have been. She went on to have three wonderful daughters, but there was never to be another son.

Miscarriages, stillbirths and early deaths are tragic in any era, but they were far more common then, in the days before the National Health Service. Women were less well nourished and much harder worked, and the high cost of calling in a doctor meant that many women would often shut their eyes to warning symptoms until it was too late. Muriel, who began working at Rowntree's not long after Madge, lost three children in a row:

> *We were trying for a family, but first I had a miscarriage and then I had two stillbirths, both boys. After that we decided to adopt. My doctor wasn't really in favour of it, because he said there was nothing physically wrong with me and I could have kept trying for a child of my own, but I just couldn't bear the thought of going through all that again. So we adopted a girl, when she was a month old. I never met her parents, I just didn't want to, so my auntie and uncle went and picked her up from Leeds instead. When we went to court for the adoption, they told us that when she was old enough to understand, we should tell her that she was adopted – 'better for her to hear it from you than to be told by someone else', they told us. So when she was about seven years old, I told her a little story about where she had come from. I said that we got her from a home for children who didn't have a mummy or daddy, and I told her about my two little boys who'd died at birth. After*

> *I told her, she was crying and crying. I was still crying myself when my husband came home from work, and I said to him, 'I hope I haven't done the wrong thing, because she's so upset.' As I was settling her down to sleep that night, she was still crying and I said to her, 'But you are happy with us, aren't you?' And she said, 'Yes, but I'm crying for your little boys.'*

Madge had only a few days to recover from her own tragic loss before she went back to work in her old job at Rowntree's. There was no option but to do so, for her wage was the only money that she and her new husband were bringing in. She and Bill carried on living with her parents for a couple more months, but he was still out of work and making little effort to find any, and finally Madge's father, who was, she says, 'very keen on working', gave her an ultimatum: 'He'll have to go. He isn't trying to get a job, he's just staying in bed. You can stay, but he'll have to go.'

When she told Bill, he said, 'Well, what are you going to do about it?'

She said, 'I'm married and you're my husband, I'm coming with you.'

He went out to find them a place to live and met a couple who offered them a room for eight shillings a week – and that was all it was: one room in a decrepit slum house in Union Terrace that also housed several other families. Madge and Bill had a little coal fire on which she used to boil a kettle, their bed, a second-hand table and two chairs, and a rickety old wardrobe for their clothes – not that they had many – all in that one room. There was a sink with a cold tap at the end of the hall, shared with the other families, and in the yard at the back there was an outside toilet that they also had to share, not just with everyone in their house, but with the occupants of three other houses as well. Going outside to use it almost invariably meant joining a queue.

They had so little money that Madge found it hard to put anything by to save for things, and anyway, if she'd had any savings at home, her husband would almost certainly have spent them on drink or gambling, because he had already shown himself prone to both of those vices. However, there was a savings club at Madge's work. It wasn't run by Rowntree's, it was just done between the women themselves and run by one of her workmates. They used to put in twelve pennies – one shilling – each over the course of the week, and after twenty weeks they then had a pound that they could spend on whatever they wanted. 'It sounds like nothing now,' she says, 'but back then it was a small fortune.' Madge used her first pound to buy a washing tub, a rubbing board (a ridged board – the washboard used by 1950s skiffle groups – on which washing could be scrubbed), a posser (a hand-operated tool with a long wooden handle and a perforated copper dome at the bottom that was used to agitate the washing in the tub), a scrubbing brush for doing the floors, a floorcloth, a clothes line and three dozen pegs. When she told her sister Rose, she said, 'That'll do for a wedding present, then!'

There were few laughs at home for Madge. It was a miserable existence, and not just because of their living conditions. They did not have a happy marriage at all, and her husband was, in her words, 'a bit of a rum one' to say the least. He was not a good husband to Madge and he was not a good father to their children when they arrived. Although he was not tall, no more than five foot five and only a little taller than Madge herself, he was very broad-shouldered and powerful. Madge says:

I was quite strong myself, but he could outdo me. I had more than a few bumps from him over the years, but then, he was a bad 'un. Before I married him, my mother had said to me, 'Get rid of him,' but unfortunately I didn't listen. He was all right up until we got married, but it all changed after that. He was a devil for 'acting on' – picking an argument over nothing – and he wouldn't give in. I had a mind of my own and I wouldn't be told, so no wonder I suffered. He used to go mad, and maybe he didn't realize how much he was hurting me, but I had black eyes, a broken nose and bruises everywhere, but still I kept on with him. I didn't have a choice. I couldn't leave him. I had no money and anyway, I was really frightened of him. He used to say to me, 'I'll do you in, if you leave me.'

Among the handful of possessions that they had taken with them when they moved out of Madge's family house was a beautiful clock that she had won in a baking competition just before she left Park Grove School. Madge had been chosen to represent her school and had to bake a sponge cake with custard. It turned out perfectly, but the competition was open to girls from all the schools in the area and even when they got down to the final half-dozen competitors, she still did not imagine for a moment that she might win. However, 'Everybody else had made the custard very sweet,' she says, 'and I was the only one who hadn't put any extra sugar in. The judges said to me, "You can always add more sugar, but you can't take it out," and they gave me the first prize. The whole school gathered in the big hall for the presentation. It was quite a do. The Lady Mayoress came and presented me with my prize, and I remember looking out and seeing Mam and our Linda watching me.'

Madge's prize was a carriage clock made from heavy brass with glass side panels that allowed you to see the movement ticking away. It was inscribed 'York Gas Company 15th Annual Cookery Competition for Elementary Schoolgirls, 17 June 1932'. Her dad was so proud that he told Madge, 'I'm going to put it on my bedside cabinet, so it's the first thing I see in the morning when I wake up.' All the time she lived at home, her dad kept it on his bedside cabinet, and Madge was going to leave it for him when she moved out, but Bill insisted that they took it with them. When she next saw her mum, she told Madge, 'Your dad's heartbroken that you've taken that clock.' So Madge said, 'Tell him I'll bring it back for him.'

'I had a basket,' she says, 'that was the fashion then, and I tried to smuggle the clock out of the house in the basket with a cloth draped over it, but my husband spotted me and said, "What have you got there? I know what you're trying to do. Get it put back." And he made me put it back on the mantelpiece. I was frightened of him, so I had to do what he said.'

Even now, Madge never uses Bill's name, always referring to him as 'my husband', a reflection of the deep psychological scars of that long, abusive relationship she endured. As she says now, 'To know lovely chaps like Peter Luger, and then to marry one like I did … but then I wouldn't have had three lovely daughters if I hadn't, would I? So a very good thing came out of a bad one.' Madge had been desperately unhappy almost from the moment they were married, but they were never to divorce; people just didn't then, the way they do today. It was not just Bill's threats to her, chilling though they were; there was virtually no help for women wanting to leave their husbands then, no women's refuges or social security payments, very little childcare, and what little there was was very expensive. If you had no money, there was little prospect of getting any, particularly if your children were too small to leave at home on their own while you went to work, always assuming you could find any work.

Like the majority of firms in that era, Rowntree's would not consider married women for full-time employment; as soon as a female employee got married, she was obliged to leave her job. If that seems overbearing and paternalistic to modern eyes, the company could at least offer a coherent rationale for the policy. In an era largely devoid of 'ready meals' and modern labour-saving devices, the work of raising children, cooking, cleaning, washing and keeping a house was unrelenting, and Rowntree's management believed it was fairer on a married woman, as well as on her children, if she did not have to combine a full-time job at the factory with another full-time job at home. They also believed that married women might be taking jobs from those who did not have a husband to support them or, even worse, from men who had families to support. However, whether Rowntree's directors should have been making such decisions, rather than allowing the women to make them for themselves, was another matter altogether.

Many women workers at Rowntree's understood the rationale behind the policy, even if they did not always agree with it. 'Life was hard then at work and at home,' says Muriel, one of Madge's workmates. 'At work it was all heavy, old-fashioned machinery and a lot of lifting and carrying, and at home there were no labour-saving things like there are now. I used to be down on my hands and knees in the backyard trying to get the oil stains out of my husband's overalls by scrubbing them on the grate over the drain. Mind you, I've never had a washing machine; even today – and I'm eighty-six – I still wash everything by hand.'

Those women who disagreed with Rowntree's policy adopted their own pragmatic response to it by concealing their marriages from the company and all but a handful of trusted friends, and continued to work there as 'single women', at least until they became pregnant.

Even if they had no children, married women would still have struggled to make ends meet if they left their husbands. Madge had no money and no job, so leaving Bill and setting up on her own somewhere else, especially once she had children, was never going to be an option. She had made her bed, as they used to say then, and she just had to lie in it.

Madge's parents were desperately worried about her, but powerless to intervene, and the whole family also had to deal with a double tragedy. Madge's sister, Marian, a quiet, kindly girl with never a bad word for anybody, was only twenty-three when she was diagnosed with meningitis. Doctors told her parents that even if she survived, she had already suffered irreparable brain damage, but in the event she died.

Not long after that, Madge's brother, Richard, died in equally tragic circumstances. A handsome man and a very smart dresser, with a beautiful camel-hair overcoat, he was much older than Madge, but very fond of his little sister. When Madge was in her teens he would sometimes take her to the Empire cinema as a treat, and as they walked down the street, Madge can still recall swelling with pride as she watched all the girls' heads swivelling when they caught sight of her handsome brother. He married a London girl and when war broke out he was working in a fruit and vegetable shop in Croydon while awaiting his call-up for the Army. When the first fire-bomb raid on London began, he went out of the shop without a helmet, and when a bomb struck a nearby building a beam fell on him. Before ambulance crews could reach him, looters had stripped him of everything: his wallet, his shoes, his identity card and even the cufflinks from his shirt. His frantic wife knew only that he had not come home that night, and she began touring hospitals in the area, showing his photograph to people, hoping against hope that he was safe somewhere, injured and unrecognized. When she eventually reached the hospital where he had been taken, one of the staff recognized him as a patient from the photograph, but by then Richard had died of his injuries and his wife could only go to the morgue to identify his body.

Such tragedies put Madge's own sufferings into perspective, but they did not make her life any easier to bear. She and Bill continued to live in that one room for almost two years. By then, war had broken out, and with a labour shortage as more and more men enlisted or were called up, Bill had at last found work back at Rowntree's. Young, fit and strong, he should have joined the Army himself, and 'I wish he had done really,' Madge says, 'because it would have done him good, but he got out of it. He said he had a bad heart, but I don't know that he really did.' Bill Burrow never did join up, and though there was a strong suspicion that he was 'swinging the lead', his claims of poor health were never put to the test and he continued to work at Rowntree's right through the war.

With the coming of war and the need for every pair of hands to be put to work, Rowntree's relaxed its rules a little, and though married women were still not permitted to work full time, there were increased opportunities for them to work part time or as casual workers, and from then on, women employees, including married women in casual or part-time employment, formed an ever more significant proportion of the workforce.

When married women rejoined the company, they were segregated from the single girls and worked in teams with other married women. They were sometimes seen as a 'bad influence' on the young, single girls, who were presumed – by Rowntree's management at least – to be innocent and virginal young maidens. But, contrary to the belief of many of the women, their segregation was not only because the married women might prove to be a dangerous, corrupting influence upon them, with their often bawdy banter about themselves and their husbands, and the quality, or lack of it, of their sex lives. Some girls from sheltered backgrounds did find working with the married women an eye-opening and sometimes intimidating experience, and new girls were often the butt of most of the banter and practical jokes. Some even went home and cried themselves to sleep after their first few days at work, but most soon adapted and in time came to value the camaraderie with the other women. Rowntree's actual reason for segregating the married from the single women was on the more humdrum but practical grounds that married women who had spent some time away from the factory bringing up their children would no longer be able to keep up with the speed that the single girls could maintain on the production line. In their own interests and to prevent rows and disputes breaking out with those who felt they were losing money because of the slowness of their workmates, the married women were allowed to work together at their own pace.

There were inevitable disagreements between individuals at Rowntree's, but there were few splits between whole groups. One of the few sources of potential tension was between the women with husbands in well-paid jobs, who worked part time just for 'pin money' to buy luxuries – a minority – and those who worked out of absolute necessity. The difference was summed up in the comment that could often be heard around the factory: 'We work for need; you work for greed.'

Madge was now able to go back to work, but even with two wages coming in, she and her husband were still existing on just twenty-eight shillings a week between them. Bill smoked, so he kept two shillings a week pocket money for his cigarettes, and after the rent was paid they had just eighteen shillings on which to live, and much of that was spent by Bill on drink and gambling. They had even less money when Madge fell pregnant again and once more had to give up work.

Her first daughter, Fay, was born in 1940 in that cramped room in Union Terrace, but soon afterwards they had the chance to rent a little two-up, two-down house in Townend Street in the Groves, a slum district just outside the walls on the north side of the city. Her two other daughters, Hazel and Lynne, were born there over the next few years. The rent – five shillings and ninepence halfpenny a week – was lower than they had been paying for their one room in Union Terrace, but it accurately reflected the very poor condition of the house. Like many inner-city districts of York, such rows of cramped terraces had been constructed by nineteenth-century jerry-builders to cash in on the surge in demand for housing fuelled by the booming populations of Britain's industrial towns and cities.

The houses were built from the cheapest materials. The brick floors were laid directly onto the bare earth and so were always damp, there were flimsy internal partition walls, and there was usually only a single course of bricks separating each house from its neighbour. The ventilation, insulation and soundproofing were all inadequate, with arguments or raised voices in one house echoing through the neighbouring houses. There was usually no interior plumbing and sometimes there was not even an inside tap, and no damp course, so that mildew and rising damp were always a problem. In a low-lying city like York there was the added risk of flooding, which could occur at any time of the year.

Madge's house was damp and decaying, with rotting window frames and black mould on some of the walls. There was no electric light and no lights at all in the bedrooms or the kitchen, just one gas mantle in the front room. If they needed light elsewhere in the house, they had to use candles. The three toilets in the yard at the back were shared between five houses, but it was at least a house of their own, and after two years in one cramped room in a shared house, that was good enough for Madge. 'It's marvellous how you manage if you have to, isn't it?' she says. 'Well, you have to, I suppose, don't you?'

The houses in Townend Street had already been condemned before they moved in and were set to be demolished, but with the war breaking out, they were left standing and Madge and Bill ended up living there for nine years. There was no bathroom, of course, just the standard tin bath that hung on a hook on the wall outside in the yard, and Madge would put it in front of the fire to wash her children. They had a fire oven, but coal was so dear – two shillings and elevenpence a bag – and money so tight that Madge would often buy 'six-pennorth' of cinders instead. First thing in the morning, in the bitter winter weather and often when she was pregnant, she would wheel her empty pram down to the coal yard near the River Foss and queue outside the big gates, waiting for the yard to open. If you were late getting there, often there were no cinders left. She remembers standing there for half an hour on a day so bitter that her arms had gone white and numb from her elbows to her fingertips, and her hands were so cold that she could not even grip the handle of the pram. When she was at last let in, the coal man filled up the pram with cinders and then she had to push it back up the hill again.

All the clothes, sheets and nappies had to be washed by hand, and as her husband had to wear all-whites for his work, there was never any shortage of washing to be done. Madge didn't get a washing machine until many years later, and even then it was second-hand – she paid five shillings for it – but after all those years of hand-washing everything, she thought it was wonderful. 'Those were the days!' she says now, with a laugh. 'A lot now don't realize how tough life was back then.'

There was an air-raid shelter in the yard, but when the great air raid on York took place in April 1942, Madge did not have time to get to the shelter. She was pregnant with her second daughter, Hazel, and her eldest, Fay, was still only little – there was just a year and ten months between them. The sirens went and then the bombs started falling, so Madge got under the table with Fay and they just sat there, listening to the sound of aircraft overhead, the whistle of the bombs falling and the crump of explosions. The noise of bomb blasts got louder and louder, and then they were dropping all around them. It sounded as though the bombs were falling in the street in front of them and then in the yard behind, and Madge really thought her time had come. In fact, they weren't quite that close, but one did fall just along the street, and Park Grove School diagonally across the street in front of the house was hit as well.

Madge and her sisters had always thought their mum would be the first of their parents to die, both because of her size and because she had had a series of operations and was often in terrible pain, but she was a strong woman and lived to a ripe old age. Instead, Madge's dad was the first to go, dying of a stroke not long after Fay was born. In the cruel way that even the closest families can sometimes manage, one or two of her siblings implied to Madge that she was to blame for his death because her father had been so worried about her living with her abusive, drunken husband that the stress had caused the stroke that killed him. It was another private burden for her to carry, another blow to her self-esteem.

Madge and Bill were still living in the same house at the end of the war, but after she gave birth to her youngest daughter, Lynne, in 1949, there were then two adults and three children living in a small, damp and crumbling two-up, two-down. Before the war there had been plenty of families in much more overcrowded conditions than that – the house she'd grown up in wasn't much bigger and had ten children in it – but the new Labour Government was committed to eradicating overcrowding and slum housing, and Madge and her family were given a new council house. Their old one was demolished under the slum clearance programme, though strangely enough, a couple of houses were left standing at the end of Townend Street and are still there today, even though the rest of the street was knocked down.

Madge had gone back to work at Rowntree's after Fay and Hazel were born, but had stopped working again when she was pregnant with Lynne. Not long after she was born, one of the supervisors came to see Madge and said, 'We've got a special order for some fancy boxes, enough work for a month or two, would you like to come back?' She jumped at the chance, went back for two months, and ended up working in the Card Box Mill for over twenty years. More and more of the Card Box Mill's production was of plainer boxes like Black Magic and Dairy Box, but there was still a demand for more expensive, hand-made or hand-finished boxes, for Valentine's Day, Easter or Christmas presents, and occasionally deluxe boxes were made for special orders like the ones covered in golden silk that Queen Elizabeth the Queen Mother used to order by the dozen as Christmas gifts. Madge and her workmates often wondered whether the Queen Mother actually paid for them or if she was presented with them as Rowntree's Christmas gift to her.

Every year, when Madge received her profit share bonus at Easter or Whitsuntide, she used to buy her girls a new dress or buy the material to make them one. She claims that she's 'no good at knitting from a pattern', but she used to knit pullovers and matching cardigans with complex patterns for her girls. Hazel still remembers an outfit her mum made for her with a cream skirt, sweater and cardigan with a pattern of yellow ducks chasing each other round the bottom of it. With her two eldest girls being close together in age, Madge often dressed them in similar outfits, but that did not always work out for the best, and the girls once had a prolonged, furious argument over who would wear the cream and who would have to wear the beige version of a beautiful flowered dress with ribbons to tie at the side.

Although Madge tried to hide her bruises and shield her daughters from the worst of her husband's violence, in later years the two eldest girls, Fay and Hazel, told her things that showed that they had always known what a brute and a bully he could be. Either because Madge no longer argued with him, or because he had mellowed with the passing years, or just because he was older and weaker, he had become less violent towards her by the time their youngest daughter was born.

The only real respite Madge had from her work at the factory and at home, and the demands of her husband, were the times she spent at her mum and dad's house with the children, when, if only for a few hours, she could enjoy something of the warm family atmosphere of her childhood. There were also occasional street parties, like the one to celebrate the coronation of Queen Elizabeth in 1953. Tables were laid in Rose Street from end to end, and all the houses were decked out with Union flags, paper garlands and bunting – though none were as beautifully decorated as Madge's mum's house, where her paper flowers were once more framing the door. The children had running races on the back field while the adults drank and ate, or gathered for a singsong around the piano that had been pushed out into the street, and, like many other people in Britain, Madge watched television for the very first time, crowding with a group of neighbours into one of their front parlours to watch the coronation ceremony on a set that had been bought or rented for the occasion.

Madge also had two brief stays at the Cocoa Works Rest Home, Dunollie, in Scarborough. Most of her workmates had been there to recover from illness, operations or bereavements, and one day Madge said to one of the supervisors, 'All these girls are going to Dunollie and I've never had the chance to go.' The supervisor said to her, 'You're too healthy, that's why! But would you like to go?'

Madge said that she would love to and the supervisor promptly arranged it for her. Much to Bill's audibly expressed disgust, Madge went off without him and spent a week at

Dunollie, and then, later on, when she had been in hospital for an operation, Rowntree's sent her back there for another week's rest and recuperation. Then it was back to her life with Bill. Helped by the greater financial security guaranteed by the post-war Labour Government's social reforms, women of the next generation no longer risked destitution if they left their husband, and divorce no longer seemed inconceivable, but for Madge, fear of her husband and the needs of her children meant that there could be no diversion from the path she had chosen when she married Bill Burrow. For her it really would be 'until death do us part'.

9

Dorothy

Dorothy Birch was born in Heslington Road in York in 1936, a damp, low-lying area of the city where the autumn mists seemed to hang over the area for days on end. She was still only a baby when the family home and the whole of their street were condemned under the slum clearance programme. They were crumbling terraced houses, in a desperate state of repair and overrun with vermin, so the family was moved to Clifton, where they were building new houses. 'I have a picture of me sitting on my auntie's knee,' she says, 'and in the background you can see them still building the houses behind us, so they must have been moving people in as fast as they could, even while they were still building the rest.'

Her mother died suddenly in 1938 when Dorothy was just two years old, and she has no memories of her at all. Her father, James, worked shifts at Rowntree's in the Melangeur department, and even though Dorothy cannot have been more than three at the time, she can clearly remember waiting for him and seeing him coming down the road on his way home from work – it is her earliest memory. She was still only three when war broke out and her dad had to go off to war, leaving behind Dorothy and her sister, who was five years older, and hoping that their grandmother – her dad's mother – would be able to look after them.

For the next six years they were brought up by their grandmother. 'We were fortunate,' Dorothy says, 'because she and the rest of the family all rallied round and helped each other to look after us.' A lot of their clothing was hand-me-downs or second-hand, but if they needed shoes, their grandmother made sure they always got new ones, not second-hand, though they were usually plimsolls, which were all their grandmother could afford.

Her grandparents' house was small, with 'a right houseful of people living in it', Dorothy says. 'We were sleeping three and four to a bed, though my grandmother and granddad had a room to themselves. I was only little and I slept in the middle of our bed with my big sister on one side and my cousin on the other. We shared that room and that bed for years and as I got squashed between the two bigger girls or got woken when they snored or tossed and turned, I used to dream of having a room of my own one day.'

There was never a time when Dorothy's grandmother and granddad didn't have a house full of kids. Even when some of their own children grew up and moved away, there were already grandchildren to take their place. Of their own children, their son Arthur, Dorothy's uncle, was in the Army, serving in the Black Watch regiment, and he had married and was living away, but his brother still lived at Dorothy's grandmother's with his wife and children. Dorothy and her sister were also permanent residents, and after the war there was their dad, too, because when he came home, he moved in as well.

The house was always crowded and noisy and the only time the children had to themselves was when they were outside.

Dorothy and her sister played rounders, hopscotch and other games for hours with the other kids in the streets; 'Even the grown-ups used to come out and join in with us sometimes,' she says, chuckling at the memory. They would also often go over to Clifton, where there was a disused aerodrome, and they would play in the fields behind it for hours. 'We'd be jumping over the becks,' Dorothy says, 'and damming them with mud and stones, trying to make little pools and waterfalls; nobody used to bother us up there.'

At weekends and in the school holidays, those days seemed endless and carefree, but with so many people in the house to care for, the children were all expected to work for their keep and to do their chores before they went out to play or to school. 'Every day my grandmother would give each of us children a job to do before we went to school in the morning, and again before we went out to play after school or at weekends,' Dorothy recalls, 'and there was no question of postponing it or not doing it; when Grandma said "Jump", that's what you did. If she wanted meat from the butchers in Clifton – and it was a long walk from our house – or a "penny duck", a bit like a faggot, for my grandfather's lunch, she'd send me off to get it before I set off for school in the morning. If I complained, she'd just say, "If you're late for school, it's your own fault, you should have got up earlier. Now you go there first and get that meat before you go to school."' There was a specific day for each job around the house – washing day, ironing day, baking day, cleaning day and so on – and with no washing machine, no vacuum cleaner, nor anything else to make life easier, the jobs took all day.

Her grandmother was very strict with the children. 'At the time, we always used to think she was hard,' Dorothy says, 'because she thought nothing of giving you a good smack, but looking back I can see that she must have had it hard herself, bringing her own children up and then having to do it all again with her children's children as well, and always being so short of money that she never had two coppers to rub together. She must have got quite frustrated at times.'

Dorothy's grandmother was no less strict when it came to illness. 'You weren't mollycoddled in those days,' Dorothy says. 'If you had a cold or something like that, you just had to get on with it. If I said to my grandmother, "I've got a cold," she'd just say, "Well, you can still get up and go to work." I've been a bit like that with my own children, but I don't think I was quite as strict!'

Some families would try to avoid calling in the doctor in any circumstances, because in the era before the National Health Service, a doctor's bill was not cheap. However, certain infectious diseases like measles had to be registered with a doctor, and with a serious illness, however short of money the family might have been, it would reach a point where the doctor had to be called in, though some exercised discretion when treating patients from the poorer parts of York. Sometimes a bill would be heavily reduced or waived altogether if the family had fallen on hard times. 'I remember my dad telling me that when my mother was ill and in an awful lot of pain,' Dorothy says, 'he had to pay for her medication and it was an awful lot of money for him to find on his wages, but in the end the doctor kept bringing it for her and not charging for it at all. So doctors weren't just out for the money, there was a lot of kindness, too.'

Dorothy was still only young during the war years, and does not have too many clear memories of the bombing or the impact of rationing, but 'I can remember that there were no sweets,' she says, 'and to make the butter ration go a bit further,

I can see my grandma now taking the cream off the top of the milk, putting it in a little jar and shaking it until she got a little piece of butter out of it.' There was never any spare money and Christmas and birthdays were nothing like they are for kids now, though she is sure that she and her sister were just as excited on Christmas Eve as her own grandchildren are today. The two girls would hang up their stocking on Christmas Eve and they might get one present in it, if they were lucky. There would be an apple or an orange and maybe a few nuts in the bottom, and that might be it for them until the next Christmas. 'I would have loved a doll,' Dorothy says, 'but I never had one right through my childhood, not even a second-hand one, there just wasn't the money to spare.'

Things became even harder for Dorothy's grandmother when her husband died. He had worked in the goods yards at the railway station all his life, except when he was fighting in the First World War. When war broke out again in 1939, it reduced him to near despair; the 'war to end war' that he had fought had merely led to another one, twenty years later. When the Germans bombed York in April 1942, the railway station was badly damaged and the stables where the horses were kept were set on fire. Dorothy's granddad often worked with the horses and absolutely loved them. Although they were short of money and had little food to spare with wartime rationing, he was always sneaking out of the house with a few carrots or a couple of sugar lumps in his pocket, to feed to his favourite horses as treats. He was at work when the incendiary bombs hit the station and the stables caught fire. He could smell the stench of singeing horsehair as the wall of flames moved closer, and he and another man made frantic attempts to get the horses – big work horses, like shire horses – to safety, but they were terrified by the explosions, the smoke and the flames, and were running around, rearing up and lashing out with their hooves, and impossible to control. No matter what her granddad and the other man did, they could not get the horses out of the blazing stables and goods yard, and in the end every one of the horses at the station died. 'He must have seen some awful sights in his time, especially when he was a soldier during the Great War, but losing the horses really, really got to my granddad,' Dorothy says. 'He was never the same man at all after that.'

York Minster escaped serious damage in the raid, but the city's ancient Guildhall was set on fire and left a ruin, and Rowntree's original factory at Tanners Moat, just off North Street, also fell victim to the German bombs. Used as a warehouse since production had been moved to the Haxby Road site almost fifty years before, it was packed full of sugar, and burned with a ferocious intensity. Firemen were still damping down the smouldering ruins two days after the raid.

Families whose wives, mothers or daughters were working on the night shift at Rowntree's on the night of the raid faced a long, anxious wait until they came home. One of them, Joan Drake, remembers that because of the bomb damage and the hordes of people out in the streets seeking news of friends and family, it took her a lot longer than usual to cycle home along Dodsworth Avenue. 'I vividly remember,' she says, 'my sister and her husband waiting anxiously, looking out for me in Burnholme Avenue, and when I got there, I got the biggest hug of my life.'

The war had further strengthened the already strong community feeling among those who worked at, or even just lived near, the factory. Joan Drake benefited from that when the chain broke on her bike as she was cycling along Dodsworth

Avenue to work the next day. A man she did not even know offered to lend her his own bike and repair hers for her while she was at work. Joan had a moment of blind panic when she came out of work that night and, confronted by hundreds of bikes in the bike racks, could not remember what the one she had borrowed looked like, but fortunately there was a vaguely familiar-looking bike in her normal space in the rack, which turned out to be the right one, and when she reached Dodsworth Avenue, there was the man waiting for her with her own, fully repaired bike. 'I've often looked back on how trusting we were even of complete strangers in those days,' Dorothy says, 'and thought to myself that it was perhaps a bit naive. Maybe we were lucky, but I can't ever recall someone being taken advantage of and I think perhaps people were just kinder and more honest back then.'

Dorothy's father had been in the Royal Artillery during the war, serving with the 70th West Riding Field Regiment. They went to France as part of the British Expeditionary Force (BEF), and while the remnants of the BEF were being evacuated from Dunkirk, leaving almost all of their equipment behind, James Birch and his comrades fought their way to Cherbourg and were evacuated from there with all their guns and equipment intact. He later fought with the big guns in Tunisia, Italy and Greece, where he suffered a serious wound to his arm. With the rest of his regiment, he was awarded the freedom of the City of Bradford when he came home at the end of the war, and Dorothy has vivid memories of going to see the ceremony in September 1945.

The city, 'the wool capital of the world' as its citizens liked to call it, made a vivid impression on her. As their train breasted a hill and rattled down towards the city in the valley bottom, the sky seemed to darken into twilight even though it was the middle of the morning, and as she stared, fascinated, out of the train window, it seemed to sprawl to the horizon with its forest of smoke-belching mill chimneys piercing the skyline, each adding their contribution to the pall of smoke that hung over the city.

As they came out of the station, Dorothy had never seen such traffic or heard such noise. In the cobbled street behind the station, intrigued but more than a little frightened and clinging tightly to her grandmother's hand, she peered into the yard of a textile mill, and even from the great iron gates she could hear the thunder of their battalions of looms, while the sweating men manhandling great bales of wool towards a hoist were shouting to make themselves heard above the din. It was a windless autumn day and as they walked from the station to the town hall square where the ceremony was to take place, a rain of tiny smuts and soot fell from the skies like winter snowflakes. The majestic buildings they passed were all of stone, but so smoke-blackened that they could have been carved from coal. A brass band played as the soldiers, immaculate in their dress uniforms, marched into the square and formed up in front of the town hall steps, and Dorothy, breathless with excitement, scanned the ranks of faces, searching for her father. None of the faces looked familiar and she was almost in tears when in the end her grandmother had to say, 'That's your dad,' and pointed him out to her. 'I didn't recognize him at all,' Dorothy says, 'but then I hadn't seen him for six years and I was only three when he went away.'

Her dad moved in with them at his mother's, leading to a fresh reshuffle of the sleeping arrangements as he took one of the bedrooms and the children were squeezed even tighter into the remaining rooms. He slipped straight back into the routine of the house and returned to work at Rowntree's almost as if the war had never happened, but the six years he had been away had created a gulf between him and his younger daughter that was never to be completely closed. 'I was never really able to sit down and talk to him,' Dorothy says. 'I knew he was my dad, of course, but there wasn't that closeness between us that there was between him and my sister, but then she'd been that much older and she had had a lot more contact with him before he'd gone away to war.'

By her fourteenth birthday, in 1950, Dorothy was a tall, slim and beautiful young girl with a ready smile, and she was even more eye-catching because she wore her hair in an unusually short style for that era, while her friends all wore their hair long. 'I've had short hair all my life and I've never had it long,' she says, smiling at the memory. 'I got into the habit when I was young because my grandmother would never let me grow it long. With all those children in the house, I think she was frightened of us getting nits, because they were around then just as they are now, and I suppose it was just easier for her and one less thing to worry about if we all kept our hair short.'

Like Madge and Florence, there was no question of Dorothy continuing her education beyond the legal requirements, and she left school as soon as she was old enough. She left at the end of July and, along with a friend of hers, went straight to Rowntree's for a job. They passed the medical and all the tests they were given and were both taken on. When she came home and told her dad that she had got a job at Rowntree's, he snorted and said, 'I'll give you a month.' He must have thought she would be too scatter-brained and too impatient to stay the course, 'But I lasted a fair bit longer than a month,' she says, 'twenty-six years in total, not counting the time I had off to have my children.'

On her first day, as she walked into work, she passed stacks of baskets and crates of fresh fruit waiting to be taken into the Gum Block. 'The smell of fruit when I went into work in the morning was wonderful,' she says. 'They had every kind of fruit you could think of there, ready for the Fruit Gums and Pastilles being made.' She blicked-in at the time clock and, wearing her white overalls, started in the Nut Room, inside the Almond Block, where all the nuts were processed for the different chocolate blocks and assortments, and where they also made marzipan. There was also a Raisin Room where the dried fruits were sorted; girls working there had to sort seventy pounds of raisins an hour. The charge-hands would check batches at random and if they found more than three of the tiny raisin stalks, the whole seventy-pound batch would be rejected and the unfortunate girl would have worked an hour for nothing.

Dorothy was put on sorting different nuts – almonds, hazelnuts, Brazil nuts – for different parts of the factory. 'When I started work for the first time and went into the room I'd been allocated to,' she says, 'I just stood there, open-mouthed. There were all these people rushing about, the machines and conveyors were clanking and rumbling, everything was happening at top speed and the noise was absolutely deafening; I think that's why we all talk so loud even now, because you had to shout over the noise of the machines. On that first day, I just stood there looking round and thinking, "Goodness me, how am I ever going to be able to do this?"'

The Nut Room was a fearsomely hot place in which to work, because it was directly above the Hot Room, which, as the name suggests, was so fiercely hot that there were signs on the door warning those with pacemakers, high blood pressure or other ailments not to enter. The men who worked in there were permanently drenched with sweat and drank pint after pint of water in their break times to replace the fluids they had lost. In winter they would work all day in conditions like the jungles some of them had fought in during the war, but then emerge, sweat-soaked, at night, into what might be a snowstorm or several degrees of frost. Given that, it was scarcely surprising that the men who worked in the Hot Room averaged more days off work with ill health than any other group of workers in the factory.

The heat in the Hot Room was necessary to melt chocolate that had solidified inside the pipes or machines when production had been halted. Whenever that occurred, the only solution was either to fire a steam-driven 'pig' – a steel cylinder slightly smaller in diameter than the pipe – through the pipes to clear them, or else dismantle the sections of pipe, separate them and take them to the Hot Room to melt the chocolate. The pipes or machine parts were then hosed clean with scalding hot water in the adjoining Wet Room that was tiled from floor to ceiling.

There were two overlookers in the Nut Room, one man and one woman, and, says Dorothy, 'If they saw us with any make-up on at all, they'd make us go and wash it off before we started work. I didn't wear it at work anyway. I didn't think it was good for my skin in that hot, humid atmosphere, and my grandmother definitely would not have approved. My dad didn't like me using it either, except for a little bit if I was going out. Later on, when I was a bit older, I used to get pancake make-up that was sold in a stick but again, I'd never wear it to work, only when I was going out.'

One of Dorothy's first jobs in the Nut Room was to sort blanched almonds. There was a large stainless steel hopper where the nuts were steamed, and then a man brought them to Dorothy's work station in a tub and tipped them onto the table for her and the other girls to sort. They had to work their way through them, taking out all the skins and picking out the bits of shell, and then they were put into huge ovens to be dried. There was another room where the nuts were roasted, and if she was sent in there to sort them, she used to come out covered from head to foot in brown dust from the effects of the roasting process. 'It was heavy work,' she says, 'because we were only small – I was seven stone wet through then – but I loved it.'

There were also what were known as 'pan almonds', which all had to be a certain size, so Dorothy and her workmates had to sort them and grade them by size. 'We used to like that,' she says, 'because if you got onto those pan almonds, you earned your money fairly easily, and we were often set to work on them on a Friday, so it made for what we called an easy day.'

They also had a break from their normal working routine when they went over the road to do their Day Continuation classes. Dorothy still has a scar on her hand from her attempts to master woodwork. 'It was nice to get a change from the conveyor belts,' she says, 'and we all had a laugh, but while some of the ladies who did it before us used to make wardrobes and all sorts of things, I couldn't even make a table, to be honest.

'Every Friday when we got paid, they used to come round with your pay packet and a tin for charity and you'd put a penny in, and they'd go round all the machines for people to put money in. That was a very Rowntree's thing to do.' Wages had risen since Madge and Florence started at Rowntree's, and

Dorothy was paid one pound ten shillings a week. She had to give it all to her grandma who would keep most of it for her board, but give her five shillings back to spend on herself. 'I had to put half of it into my uncle's mail order catalogue every week to buy clothes,' she says, 'and I could easily spend the rest. There was never anything spare.'

Even though Dorothy was now mature enough to have a full-time job and go to the cinema or dancing at night, her grandmother would still always give her an extra job around the house that she had to do before she could go out. 'Mind you,' she says, 'I didn't go dancing or anything much when I lived at my grandmother's, because she and my dad were very strict, though I was very shy anyway. For all that I worked at Rowntree's among all those people there, I hated going to youth club or something and walking into a room with all the people there. Even when I had grown up and was getting married, when I was going out with my husband, if we were going to the pub or something, I'd walk in his shoes! My sister could walk into a pub on her own and have a drink; I could never have done that. I couldn't walk into a crowded room, it was torture for me. It was all right if I was the first there, I didn't mind people coming in after that, but I couldn't bear it the other way round. Even now, I don't like doing things by myself.'

Whether partly as a result of her own troubled childhood – having lost her mother at such an early age and then seen her father away at war for most of her childhood – Dorothy valued her family above everything else and was never happier than when she was surrounded by family members, a feeling that has persisted to the present day. When she went out, although pubs were firmly off her itinerary, she loved the cinema and used to go regularly with her friends:

We used to get all dressed up. I never liked the big, circular skirts, so I always used to wear the straight pencil skirts, and it was interesting getting on the back of a motorbike in one of those! I'd put on as much make-up as I thought my grandmother would let me get away with, and my friends and I would go to the pictures two or three times a week – the programme changed on Monday and Thursday and there was a different one on Sunday as well. It was always a laugh because there used to be two films on and in the interval between them, when the organ played and the ice-cream girls came round, everyone would get up and parade around. We'd all have a good look around and see who was there and what was going on. We didn't want to miss anything. It used to make me smile when I'd see girls who had been sitting with one boy before the interval, settling down with a different boy as the lights went down again.

The film was not always the main attraction, and sometimes she did not even bother checking to see what picture was showing:

If you were in the back row, it didn't really matter what film was on. All you had to do then was watch out for the ushers coming round and shining torches along the row to make sure you weren't up to anything your mother wouldn't like! We'd go to the Clifton Cinema sometimes, just because if you went upstairs, there used to be double seats in the back row up there, which were even better. There were at least a dozen cinemas in York and we went to them all at one time or another, though to be honest, some of them were pretty terrible. There was a real fleapit on Clarence Street called

The Grand, and it was anything but grand. It was a real dump and you were never going to see a film if you went there because the seat-backs were so high you could barely see over them to look at the screen.

There were also film shows every lunchtime in the Joseph Rowntree Theatre next door to the Dining Block at the factory, but given the staunch Quaker morality of the Rowntrees, there was not much likelihood of any heavy breathing being tolerated in the back row. One of Dorothy's workmates, Beryl, remembers that:

After you'd had your dinner in the Dining Block from about 12.30 to 12.45 or thereabouts, they had a film in the cinema that you could go and watch. They were short films, most often a serial, something like Flash Gordon, *which you could watch over a few days, and you had to go the following day just to see what happened next. But sometimes they'd show a feature film and you'd watch it over four or five days, broken up into twenty-minute sections. It always seemed to stop at a lovely part and you had to wait until the next day to see what happened next. If they'd ever shown a really long film like* Gone With the Wind, *it would have taken the best part of a fortnight to watch.*

There was a billiards room as well, where employees could go and play a frame or two of snooker or a game of billiards at lunchtime or after work, and Rowntree's pensioners used to come in and play there as well. There was also a film show every Monday evening after work. The girls could go home, have their tea and change, and then come back to the factory.

They would watch a film in the theatre from seven until nine, and then go into the lecture hall next door and dance to records until ten o'clock, when the dancing ended in time for everyone to catch the last buses home.

Although many of the old Rowntree's traditions were still being observed when Dorothy began work there, the Rowntree family's control of the company that bore their name had been progressively diluted ever since Joseph Junior's death in 1925. His son, Seebohm, had succeeded him, but he lived in Buckinghamshire, and while he remained in nominal charge, his work on political and social reform preoccupied him and left room for others to manoeuvre to supplant or succeed him.

Among them was George Harris, one of the architects of the new brands and new business philosophy that had transformed the company in the 1930s. Whatever his qualities as a visionary marketeer, Harris was a divisive, abrasive character with a strong anti-Semitic streak, but his significant contribution to the company had led him to lobby for and then demand a place on the board. To give added weight to his campaign, he spuriously claimed to have been offered a place on the board of Marks & Spencer, adding, 'But I've turned it down because, frankly, I don't think I could spend the rest of my working life working with Jews.' Seebohm then wrote to his fellow directors, conceding Harris's talents but urging them to reject him because of his 'Hitlerite tendencies'. Seebohm's views prevailed at the time, but when he retired in 1941, Harris became his successor, the first non-Rowntree to chair the company.

Despite his high public profile, like his fellow directors, Harris was an almost invisible presence around the factory. Dorothy never saw him in her department, and sometimes she would read a story about him in the paper and think how strange it was that, even though she spent every working day within a few yards of him, people who read the local paper knew as much about him as she did.

Harris remained as chairman for eleven years, but his behaviour became increasingly eccentric and arrogant, and the final straw came in 1952 after Harris was issued with a parking ticket in the centre of York. Having harangued the policeman who had issued the ticket, saying, 'Don't you know who I am?' and telling him that a man of such importance to the city should have been exempt from the parking restrictions applied to mere mortals, Harris then announced that he was going to contest the ticket in court and conduct his own defence. Nothing could have been further from the traditional Rowntree's virtues of dignity, humility and service to the community, and his fellow directors resolved to remove him from the board without delay. As he arrived for work one morning, Harris was confronted in the car park by the directors, flanked by Rowntree's security men. He was presented with a unanimous vote of no confidence and a resignation letter for him to sign. Only when he had done so was he allowed into the building, and then only to clear his desk. It was a less than glorious end to the career of a man who had helped to rebuild Rowntree's fortunes and launched some of its most iconic brands.

The fall of Harris did not lead to the Rowntree family retaking control of the company that bore their name, and Seebohm Rowntree's son Peter became the last family member to serve on the Rowntree's board of directors. It was now purely a business, controlled by shareholders and directors who were motivated by the balance sheet and not by the combination of the profit motive and the zeal for social reform and philanthropy that had marked the Rowntree family years.

10

Florence

Florence and Arthur, the young soldier she had been stepping out with, wrote to each other all the time he was away, and at the war's end, as soon as he was demobbed in 1946, he contacted her and they resumed their relationship. It was a long-distance one at first, because he was working near his home in Wolverhampton, and after the years he had been away at war the long wait was almost unendurable for Florence, but early the following year, he at last came back and moved in with her family. Just before he arrived, in the depths of one of the coldest winters of the century, with York's rivers frozen solid from bank to bank, snow piled high along every street and icicles like stalactites hanging from the gutters, Florence's father died in bizarre and tragic circumstances. 'My mum had told me that he used to cut his toenails with a piece of broken glass,' she says. 'It sounds bizarre but she swore it was true, and one time when he was doing it, he cut his toe quite badly with the glass. He didn't get it treated; he hated making a fuss about anything and he never had time off work or went to the doctor, no matter how ill he felt.' Florence's father was far from alone in that attitude, and often it was less from fear of doctors than the cost involved.

The Labour Government elected in a landslide victory in the 'Khaki Election' of 1946 that saw Winston Churchill ousted, had pledged itself to slay the 'five giants: want, disease, squalor, ignorance and idleness' that had blighted life for so many in pre-war Britain. One of the most significant results of that pledge, the National Health Service, offering free medical treatment to the entire population, came into existence on 5 July 1948. It lifted a huge burden from the poor, eliminating the constant background fear of the financial consequences of illness and disease that troubled even the most robustly healthy families, but the NHS came too late to save Florence's father. The wound to his foot became infected and, left untreated, it then became gangrenous. Eventually a doctor was called in, but by then the only treatment he could offer was the amputation of the leg in a last-ditch effort to save Florence's father's life. The leg was duly amputated but the gangrene had spread too far by then and he died not long afterwards, in January 1947.

Florence and Arthur delayed their wedding for a period of mourning for her father, but they were married in October of that year. For many women marriage not only marked a farewell to single life but also to Rowntree's as well, thanks to the company's continuing policy of refusing to allow married women to work full time. Florence, however, had no intention of stopping work, for her husband's wage alone would not have been enough to support them. Even though the Rowntree's rules meant that she would now only be allowed to work part time, even half her former pay was better than none at all.

When women workers got married, the company always gave brides-to-be the privilege of being able to entertain their friends and workmates with a celebration party in the Dining Block. They brought presents and were served cake and tea, and speeches were made, but they also took the chance to play practical jokes on the bride-to-be. Many a prospective bride left the canteen to find the arms of her coat had been stitched up, or her pockets filled with cocoa powder, and one woman was tied to one of the pillars in the canteen while her friends made her face up like a clown.

Even without the excuse of an impending wedding, workers at Rowntree's, like those in most factories, played endless practical jokes on each other. One woman who was leaving the Kit Kat department to join the cleaning staff was grabbed by the men working in her section. They trussed her up with parcel tape so she couldn't move a muscle and then placed her on a steel trolley and wheeled her into the Wet Room, where they cleaned the chocolate containers that they used. They filled one of the big sinks with water, sat her in it, and then poured gallons of liquid waste chocolate all over her. Another woman, Kath Webster, recalls how she and some of the other girls took their revenge on an unpleasant, overbearing overlooker. 'We got some fudge chocolate,' she says, 'mixed it all up and shaped it to look like a pile of dog poo and left it in the middle of the aisle. When the overlooker came by, she went mental. In fact she went mental twice, the first time when she thought it was dog poo and she was tearing her hair out trying to work out how a dog had got into the building undetected, and then she went crazy a second time when she realized how we'd tricked her.'

One of the most alarming, though ultimately harmless, pranks was perpetrated on a young apprentice during the summer shut-down for the factory's annual holiday. It was a time when the entire factory site was deserted, save for the caretakers, nightwatchmen and the teams carrying out the annual maintenance and deep cleaning of the silent machines and empty rooms. The unfortunate apprentice had been detailed to help the team unblocking sections of pipe partly blocked by chocolate that had set, by sending a 'pig' through it. The apprentice was stationed beneath the open end of an overhead pipe, which had been disconnected from the next section, and was told to stand there, stock still, holding a galvanized bucket above his head, covering the end of the pipe, ready to catch the pig when it emerged.

All was quiet for a moment, and then the pipe began to shake and he heard a rattling sound. There was a jet of steam and a spray of semi-liquid chocolate and then what sounded like a gunshot. Driven through the pipe by steam under extremely high pressure, the pig emerged from the pipe at such a velocity that it punched a hole straight through the bottom of the bucket, went through the window beyond it and even smashed through the window of the next block as well, before coming to a halt against the far wall. The apprentice toppled over backwards, still holding his bucket, but though frightened out of his wits, he was physically unhurt. Had any of the perpetrators of that prank been caught by the management they would probably have been sacked on the spot, but as it was, the broken windows were hastily replaced, the apprentice kept quiet about it, and both he and the rest of his workmates lived to fight another day.

Florence's friends were much gentler with her, contenting themselves with pinning balloons all over her coat and giving her an armful of small gifts for the wedding. Florence and Arthur were married at Heworth Church, but they had the reception at her home, because, she says, 'we didn't have the money for anything fancier'. She even borrowed her wedding dress from a friend at Rowntree's. It was velvet and had been folded up in a cardboard box for some time so she had to hang it up to steam in the bathroom to get all the creases out of it. 'We didn't even have a wedding cake,' she says, 'because we couldn't afford it, so we had a few sandwiches and buns my mother made. My sister tried to help by making custard to go with them, but she burned it!' Even though the war had ended, rationing was still in force, so they had to do without custard because there was no sugar with which to make any more.

Rowntree's had traditionally given women employees a china tea set when they got married – a tray, a dozen cups and saucers, two bread and butter plates, a cream jug and a sugar basin – but Florence's wedding came a little too late, because the company had stopped that particular tradition shortly before. However, they did give her a set of cutlery; it saw heavy duty over the years and now, sixty-five years later, she is down to the last two knives.

Florence and Arthur went to Morecambe for their honeymoon. They stayed in a bed-and-breakfast guest house which cost them eleven ponds eleven shillings for the week; she still has the receipt among her family photographs and souvenirs. When they came home, they lived with her mother at first; back then most couples lived with one or other of their parents when they got married, because there weren't many who could afford their own house straight away. Two of her sisters had married and moved away by then, so there was a little more room in the family house than previously, but when their daughters Carol and Beryl were born there, all four of them had to share the same bedroom. They saved every penny they could for a place of their own, but even though their names had been on the waiting list for a council house from the day they got engaged, they simply had to wait until their turn came, and with slum clearance, bomb damage and six wartime years when virtually no new houses were built, not to mention the post-war baby boom, there was no shortage of other people competing for what housing there was.

In the end they had to wait for over five years, because their eldest daughter, Carol, was already four years old by the time Florence and Arthur were finally offered a council house of their own. The one that they were allocated was at Acomb, which was a long way out of town on the far side of York from the factory, and that made it difficult for them to get to work. However, if they had turned it down they might have had to wait another five years, so they took it and then began looking for someone living closer to the city centre who might be interested in a swap. Eventually they traded their council house at Acomb for a two-bedroom prefab in Foss Way. It was not a like-for-like swap; the prefab was a definite step down on the housing ladder, but it was at least more solidly constructed than many of that era, and it did have a bathroom, though there were no other mod cons, and certainly no fridge or washing machine. Florence had to scrub the washing on the wooden table every week and then put it in the boiler to wash.

Apart from its close proximity to their work, the house in Foss Way had one other significant advantage: it was just across the road from her mother's house. Florence had three children by then, the two girls and a boy, Malcolm, born seven years after Beryl. With money always tight in the household, Florence went back to work at Rowntree's within six months of the birth of each one, though from then on she only ever worked part time. Fortunately one of Florence's sisters did not go out to work; she had always stayed at home to help their mother, so she looked after the kids who were not at school when Florence was out at work.

The economy had been booming throughout the 1950s – as one dour Yorkshire industrialist later commented: 'If your business couldn't turn a profit in the 1950s, there was something seriously wrong with you' – and rapidly rising wages were now allowing many working-class families to live at a level above mere subsistence for the first time in their lives. The average annual wage in 1940 of about £200 had more than doubled by 1950, and doubled again by 1960. Five-day working, pioneered by Rowntree's in 1919, was now almost universal, and paid holidays, which had been restricted to one week a year for most pre-war workers, had been increased to two or three weeks a year, greatly increasing leisure time for working families. In line with the rising incomes and increased time off, a wealth of new 'luxury' and 'lifestyle' products were introduced to satisfy demand from a new class of mass consumers, for whom shopping was ceasing to be merely a matter of necessity and becoming a pastime instead. Rowntree's own modest contribution to the trend was a new luxury product, After Eight, the first 'thin mints'.

Florence had been put to work in Cream Packing when she went back part time, and in 1962, when After Eights were first introduced, she was put on the production line for them. Some of the women put the chocolates into their little individual waxed paper envelopes, while Florence's job was to put them into the boxes, but she did not last long on that. 'There had to be exactly twenty-six mints in each box and you had a little clicker – a hand-tally machine – that you clicked to make sure you put the right number in the box, but I was always too busy talking and kept losing track of how many I'd put in. Every time I checked, there was a different number on my clicker than there was in the box, so in the end I said, "Oh, I think I'll go on day work instead," [taking all the materials round to the other women], so I could do day work and chat to them to my heart's content, while they put the After Eights in the boxes.'

Although most of the boxes Rowntree's used were now mass-produced by machine, unique ones, like those that Madge had hand-made, were still made for Easter, Christmas and other special occasions. Deluxe 'red box' editions of After Eight were also made, packed in a beautiful padded box and including sugared almonds and other confectionery, but no thin mints. One of the packers remembers Rowntree's putting a man on night security while they were being produced to stop pilfering of the sugared almonds and the other expensive items. However, they did not prove popular and the red box edition was discontinued.

Florence's husband Arthur had never worked at Rowntree's, and instead had a series of jobs working as a book-keeper at offices in and around York. Florence says:

> *He had a real good head for figures, not like me, I was a real dunce! But at least I have a sense of humour to make up for it, whereas Arthur would sit through the funniest joke you ever heard and never even crack a smile. Not that he was grumpy, he was anything but that, but he just didn't get the joke. I said to him many a time, 'Arthur, you've no sense of humour.' He'd always deny it but it was absolutely true. He'd been training to be a chartered accountant before the war, but Hitler put an end to that and afterwards Arthur had to settle for office work and book-keeping, though he kept moving to different jobs because he was always trying to better himself.*

It was the same with houses. Once we'd scraped enough money together to buy our first house, a tiny little terrace, he was always on the lookout for a slightly better house in a slightly better area, or one that we could improve and then sell on, and every time he found one, we would be on the move again. We moved so many times, twelve at least, that I lost count in the end. We'd just get everything ready, the house decorated, the garden planted and tidied and all, and then he'd come in and say, 'Right, we're moving,' and we'd be off again. It got so it felt like it was hardly worth unpacking the suitcases!

He was trying to better himself all the time and it wasn't easy because the office work he did was not that well paid and he didn't have a pension scheme or anything. He was a grafter though, he used to work all day long and then he'd come home and do book-keeping in the evening, just to try and make a little extra money. I don't think he ever got the rewards he deserved and his work was hard. I remember one time when he was working at Micklegate Motors, a salesman came in with an adding machine. It was nineteen pounds but it would have made his work so much easier and quicker. However, he had to tell the salesman, 'I can't make a decision on it. I'll have to ask my boss, Mr Eric, and let you know tomorrow.' But when he asked his boss if they could buy it, Mr Eric just said, 'No, old man, it makes the brain lazy,' and he wouldn't buy it for him, so Arthur had to keep slogging away, keeping the books the old-fashioned way, with brain power, pen and ink.

Arthur was as meticulous with the household accounts as he was with his book-keeping. He had a green box with compartments for all their household expenses: rent, rates, gas, electricity, the weekly food bill, clothes and shoes for the children, and there were also sections for holidays, Christmas and birthdays. Every week when he had been paid his wages, and even after he had retired and had his pension, Arthur would sit down and carefully divide his money between the compartments. By the time he had finished, there would be very little left over, but although they lived a simple life, rarely went out and had few, if any, luxuries, they never went hungry, were never in debt and always managed to have a few days' holiday every year.

Many of Florence's friends would go back to the same place and the same boarding house for their holidays year after year, but within the limits of their budget, she and Arthur used to like to ring the changes, and over the years they went to almost every east coast resort, from Scarborough as far south as Great Yarmouth. Another time they borrowed a car and went to the Lake District, but the car broke down and they found themselves standing on the forecourt of a garage counting out the cash that would have been their holiday money to pay for the cost of the repairs. They had to cut their holiday short because they had run out of cash, but while they were waiting for the car to be repaired, they took Malcolm to a stream across the road from the garage and sat on the bank while he threw stones into the water to make a splash or skimmed flat pebbles across the surface. He loved doing that so much that as they were driving home later that day, he turned to his mother and said, 'That was the best holiday we've ever had.'

11

Dorothy

In 1952, the same year that George Harris had been forced to resign, Dorothy reached her sixteenth birthday. She had been working at the factory for two years by then and was judged to be ready for a transfer to the Cream Block, where hundreds of girls and women were employed. They made the different-flavoured centres, covered them with chocolate, hand-piped or hand-marked distinguishing patterns onto them, placed the different centres into the correct compartments of the boxes, wrapped them in Cellophane and then packed them into the 'outers' that usually contained a dozen boxes.

Dorothy was put to work in Enrobing, the part of the production line where the centres of the chocolates were enrobed (covered) with chocolate. All the different chocolates for the Black Magic assortments, twelve in each box, were produced in the Cream Block, but there was no single continuous production line. Within the huge iron-pillared rooms, a series of areas were sectioned off from each other, where different centres were produced before they were all brought together in Enrobing and Cream Packing, where the boxes were filled, wrapped and despatched.

Dorothy and the other girls had to undergo a 'pin inspection' once a week. The overlookers would say, 'Come to the end, ladies,' and they would line up all the girls at the end of the machines and then check their overalls, including their lapels for what they used to call 'foreign substances': pins, hair clips or anything else that might drop in the chocolate. The Rowntree's rules about what workers could and could not wear were even more strictly enforced in the Machine Room, and the girls were checked for pins, brooches, earrings or even pearl buttons. Wedding rings were permitted, but they could not wear a ring with a diamond in – not that any of the girls could afford one – in case it came out of its mounting and fell into a chocolate, though unless they broke a tooth on one, it's hard to imagine too many customers complaining if they found a diamond instead of a soft centre in their Black Magic assortment.

Even too heavy a perfume was forbidden, because that could affect the taste of the chocolate. 'We all knew that they didn't even like you wearing make-up,' Dorothy says, 'but even so, there were the odd few girls who wore it to work. I remember one girl in Enrobing who came in with full make-up on every day, like a doll really, and with her hair done up and her turban tied in a special way as well, but she was very much the exception. Strict as they were with the rest of us, the overlookers never told her to wash it off; I don't know how she got away with it, but somehow she did. Over the years, things got a lot less strict anyway, and by the 1960s and 1970s you'd see girls coming in wearing full make-up and all sorts of strange outfits under their overalls.'

Smoking was also banned in the factory. That did not bother Dorothy as she was a non-smoker, but some of her workmates found ways to smoke a crafty cigarette from time to time. One of them, Sue Mizzi, says:

There were four of us and we were all about sixteen or seventeen, and what we used to do – they can't sack me for owning up to it now, can they? – was to go and smoke in the toilets at dinner time. I'd go in the toilet, climb on the seat and open the window and a couple of girls would keep watch while I had a cig out of the window, and then we'd swap over. Every now and then someone would say, 'Look out, the overlooker's coming,' and then we'd be throwing the cigarette out of the window, and fanning the air with our hands or a towel to try and get rid of the smell. And the overlooker would come in and say, 'Is someone smoking?' and we'd all be looking like butter wouldn't melt in our mouths and going, 'Oh no, there's no one smoking here.' I think that's why in later years they decided to have smoking rooms at Rowntree's; they couldn't stop it, so they decided to control where it happened.

Near the end of the production line there was an x-ray machine, like a primitive version of a modern airport security scanner. A versatile worker like Dorothy was regularly moved to different roles within the department, and she worked for a time with a small team of women operating the machine. She had never been in hospital nor had an x-ray, so it was the first time she had ever seen an x-ray machine and she was astonished at what it could reveal. She was itching to take an x-ray of herself, just to see what she looked like on the inside, but that would have required her to be on both sides of the screen at once, so she had to content herself with examining the chocolates instead.

She had to take all the bars out of one of the outers, chosen at random, and put them through the machine. The x-ray pictures came up on a big screen and she had to check them to make sure that there were no foreign bodies in the chocolates. She and the other women who operated the machine were amazed at the things that they found stuck to the underside of chocolate bars or buried deep within them, including bits of metal, buttons and sometimes an odd coin on payday when the girls had been sorting out their wages. Every so often the overlookers would come round, brandishing a chocolate that contained something that most definitely should not have been there, though it was not always the girls' fault. It was not unknown for a small part of one of the machines to break or come loose and fall off. 'If you weren't careful,' Dorothy says, laughing at the thought, 'you might get a bolt as well as a nut in your chocolate!'

Even stranger and less pleasant things could have been found in chocolate in the nineteenth century, though an x-ray machine would not have detected them. Unscrupulous food and drink manufacturers routinely substituted ingredients with cheaper ones to bulk up their products, and added flavourings and colourings that were at best questionable and sometimes harmful or even poisonous.

Tea and coffee merchants sold 'tea' made from the dried leaves of other plants, or bought spent tea leaves and coffee grounds from hotels and coffee shops and adulterated them. Used tea leaves might be boiled with sheep dung and ferrous sulphate, and then coloured with Prussian blue, turmeric, verdigris, tannin or carbon black. Used coffee grounds were revived by mixing them with roasted and ground carrots, beans, turnips, chicory or acorns, further bulked with sand and coloured with red lead or 'black jack' (burned sugar). Cocoa was bulked with wheat flour, arrowroot, Indian corn (maize), sago, potato flour, tapioca or chicory, and coloured with red ochre, Venetian red or various compounds of iron. Ground glass was sometimes added to sugar, and unscrupulous confectioners used irritant or poisonous ingredients to produce the vividly coloured sweets that attracted children. Yellow sweets were coloured with gamboge, a gum that was a violent irritant and purgative; red sweets could be dyed with vermilion or red lead; white sweets might contain china clay, and green sweets could be coloured with verdigris or copper arsenite. The sweet wrappers were also dyed with the same poisonous materials. Despite repeated legislation, the use of poisonous additives in food and drink manufacture was not finally outlawed until 1899.

Given this unsavoury background, it was not surprising that Quakers like the Rowntrees, seen as people of integrity and strong morality even by those who did not share their religion, should be more trusted to supply wholesome food and confectionery than their venal competitors. If even Quakers were not always above bulking or flavouring their cocoa – potato starch, flour, sago and treacle were ingredients in Cadbury's cocoa in 1861, and Rowntree's used flour, sago and arrowroot – they could at least be relied upon to stop short of using poisonous ingredients.

By Dorothy's day, the principle concern of the overlookers in the Cream Packing department was not poison but dirt. At the start of every working day, she and the other girls had to wash their hands and nails and then present them for inspection to make sure they were clean. Any girl who had dirty nails would be sent to clean them at once and warned that any repetition would lead to suspension or worse. The factory nurses also used to come round at intervals and inspect the girls' hands, arms and nails, and if they found any sort of skin complaint, the unfortunate girl would be taken straight off the production line and sent to the sick bay for treatment. The overlookers were so strict on cleanliness and hygiene that girls were not allowed to go to work without wearing 'proper stockings', and no sandals or bare feet were allowed. One of Dorothy's workmates, Beryl, recalls, 'They'd also ask you intensely personal, quite embarrassing questions like: "When was your last period?"' Being rather shy about such matters, Dorothy never even asked why they wanted to know.

Whether such questions were designed to identify girls who were pregnant or for some health-related reason, with a working population of several thousand girls and women of child-bearing age, it would have been surprising if unwanted pregnancies had not been a regular occurrence. 'It was a more innocent age then,' Dorothy says. 'You were brought up quite naive really, and you certainly weren't told the facts of life or anything like you are today.' Given that naivety and the lack of effective contraception, it was inevitable that some young girls at Rowntree's 'got into trouble', but although they might have been censured by the self-appointed moral guardians outside the factory walls, their fellow workers usually had nothing but sympathy for them. 'If girls did get into trouble,' Dorothy says, 'people were generally supportive. It was just what went on and we knew that it could happen to anybody in any family. There was a feeling of "There but for the grace of God …"'

After a brief spell of enrobing, Dorothy was next put on 'setting' – putting the centres into the Black Magic assortments. She and the other girls had to place the centres onto waxed paper bases, and they then passed through the enrober to be dressed with a covering of liquid chocolate. The enrobed chocolates then passed along the line to the pipers, who used piping bags to hand-decorate chocolate swirls onto the top of each chocolate, or the markers, who used a tool like a thin wire fork to mark their surface, giving each chocolate its own identifying mark. The finished chocolates were then cooled, and some would be left to mature for a few days, before they were returned to the line for 'cupping' – putting the chocolates into separate compartments, originally frilled paper cups but later vacuum-formed from a single sheet, of the Black Magic box. The work was not as delicate as it might sound and newcomers on cupping always got sore fingers from the constant friction of the paper cups into which they put the chocolates. It took a few weeks of toughening up their fingers before they became accustomed to the work.

After the box had been packed with chocolates, another girl would give their surface a good polish with a soft brush to remove any finger marks, and then she closed the lid and put the completed boxes on the conveyor. When they first started work, Dorothy and the other new girls in Cream Packing had to leave their boxes open so they could be checked by the overlookers before being sealed, and the end of their unofficial apprenticeship was signalled when the overlooker told them that from then on they could close the box lids as they completed them. The boxes were check-weighed, sealed, wrapped in Cellophane and placed in the outers – large cardboard boxes that held a dozen individual boxes. A man with a trolley or a bogey would come and take them down to the landing stage for packing and despatch, originally by rail, but in later years by lorry.

The production processes were often complex and some of the work was highly skilled, but Dorothy learned to do all the different jobs on all the different machines – and there were twenty-one of them in all – from setting the centres at one end of the line to enrobing and piping at the other, and she used to fill in for any of the women who needed to 'spend a penny' outside break times, because the work stations had to be manned every minute of the day as the machines never stopped running. However, like all machines, they did occasionally break down and a group of mechanics were always on call if they were needed. At such times, rather than standing idle, Dorothy and her workmates were sent to make the cartons for Dairy Box or Black Magic, while the engineers repaired the machine.

New girls were usually put to work for half a day on one of the different centres, to see if they could keep up with the pace of the other women. 'They showed you how to do it a couple of times and then you just had to get on with it and have a go,' Dorothy says. 'When I first went on there, the line was going and the belt was moving, and it was all happening so fast. There was one bar, a little hazelnut log thing called "Speed" that we did as a makeweight in Dairy Box, and it was well named because it used to go that fast that I was thinking, "Oh, my God!" I was staring down at the belt, almost hypnotized by these ranks of chocolates marching past me on the belt, and I started to fall behind. I was feeling really dizzy staring at the chocolates and I thought, "This is not good," and began to panic.'

Dorothy had been warned that new girls sometimes turned dizzy and fainted at the belt, and had to be taken to one side and told to stare at something that was not moving until they recovered, but she had forgotten the warning until one of the other girls caught sight of her and said, 'Dorothy! Just look up.

Look at the wall, look at the wall, don't look at the belt.' When she did what they said, she began to feel less dizzy straight away, and as she began to pack the chocolates almost automatically, rather than thinking too much about what she was doing, she found she could do it and keep pace with the speed of the belt. Her workmates helped her through it and within a couple of weeks she was 'into it and as blasé as anybody else about it'.

The girls had no say about where they worked within the room. The overlookers sent them to wherever they were wanted that day, and Dorothy just looked at a sheet pinned to the wall near the entrance doors when she arrived in the morning to find out where she was working. 'They'd say, "You're on machine number so-and-so today,"' she says, 'so we moved round. You weren't on the same machine all the time, but I never found the work monotonous anyway, there were always different people to chat to.' If she was still shy in unfamiliar surroundings, Dorothy now felt right at home among the girls in Cream Packing. She had a mischievous sense of humour and an infectious laugh and she really enjoyed herself at work, sometimes more than she should have done, at least as far as one overlooker was concerned. 'There was a very strict overlooker in there, very strict on your behaviour as well as your work, but we were young girls, so we liked to have a laugh, and we were often in trouble and getting told off for larking about when we should have been working.'

There were six machines upstairs, another six downstairs and then four more in another, smaller room. Dorothy says, 'We never liked to go in there because the overlookers in there were awful. One of them was only tiny but she was a fiery little thing. We used to say, "Oh, please don't send us in there with her."' However, one of Dorothy's workmates, Elsie Scaife, who worked in Enrobing piping chocolates, had a way of controlling even the most belligerent overlooker. Elsie's sideline was telling fortunes by reading tea leaves, and the girls she worked with would even bring their tea cups back into the factory after their lunch break, so that Elsie could read their tea leaves for them. They would have to pack Elsie's line of chocolates as well as their own while she told their fortunes, but all of them thought it was well worth it.

One day the overlooker in charge noticed what was going on and called Elsie into her office. She tore her off a strip and told her, 'You can't be reading tea leaves on the company's time.' Elsie mumbled an apology and then turned to leave. 'Wait a minute,' the overlooker said, 'I haven't said you can go yet. Now, sit down and tell me what you can see in this,' and she passed her tea cup over to Elsie. With one eye on her own future prospects, Elsie found herself able to predict great things and much impending happiness for the overlooker.

The older women in Cream Packing were less easily intimidated by the overlookers than the juniors, and some were not even fazed by the strict Rowntree's rules about not eating the chocolates. 'There were chocolates going along the conveyor in front of you all day,' Dorothy says, 'but you weren't supposed to eat any of them; you daren't touch a chocolate when the charge-hands or overlookers were around. If you did and got caught, they jumped on you, definitely, though you could eat one if you were a bit sneaky about it. It didn't bother me that much anyway because I'd never been a big chocolate lover; there was an odd one I liked, especially the Black Magic – my favourites were the Orange Point or the Montelimar – but I never ate a lot, even before I went to work at Rowntree's.'

Dorothy would go to elaborate lengths to sneak a chocolate from the conveyor belt when the overlookers and charge-hands were distracted or away from their posts, but some of the senior packers scarcely bothered to conceal what they were doing. One of them, 'one of the old school' who had been working there for years, had just helped herself to a chocolate and her jaws were still moving when an overlooker walked by, caught sight of her and said, 'Are you eating a chocolate?' The packer just looked at her and said, 'Yes. Why, do you want one?' and offered her the tray of soft centres she was packing into boxes. Stunned by this barefaced cheek and at a loss as to what to do about it, the overlooker turned several shades of red and finally hurried off without another word, with the packer's laughter echoing in her ears.

Another woman was even more enterprising. 'I'm telling tales out of school,' she says, 'but I and a couple of my friends preferred pastilles to chocolates, so by prior arrangement with some ladies from the Gum department who preferred chocolates to pastilles, we used to go to the toilets at the same time. We'd take a few chocolates with us and they'd bring some pastilles and we'd swap with them. Mind you, you soon got fed up of them if you ate a lot, so we never ate that many. It was risky too, because they could search you coming in and going out, and if they caught you, they could suspend you or sack you.'

There was always a powerful, heady aroma of liquid chocolate in the Cream Packing room and some of the girls couldn't bear the smell of it. One of them found it sickening after a while, but it never put Dorothy off. 'I think when you were amongst it you got so used to it that you almost didn't notice it,' she says, 'but when you came out, your clothes really smelled of it. My grandma always said she could smell it on me as soon as I got home.'

After setting the chocolates, she next learned how to pipe (squeezing the swirls onto the top of the Black Magic chocolates with a piping bag). There were 'light pipers' who added an identifying flourish to some of the Black Magic range, including the Cherry Cups, and 'heavy pipers' who worked on the Chocolate Whipped Cream Walnuts, surrounding the nut with a piped chocolate swirl, like a miniature helter-skelter.

Dorothy is left-handed but she was forced to learn to pipe right-handed, because space was so tight alongside the conveyor belt and the pipers sat so close together that, had there been right-handed and left-handed girls next to each other, they would have been forever getting in each other's way and bumping into each other. Dorothy was sent to the back of the enrobing machine to learn piping, practising on the uncovered chocolates until she could do it. 'I can remember being really upset about it,' she says. 'I wasn't used to using my right hand and I made a real mess of it to start with, but I didn't want to be moved out of there because the women I worked with there were brilliant, so I persevered until I could do it right.' Gradually she was able to match the skill and the speed of the others, and there was a real pride in the work they did. 'I look at a box of chocolates now,' she says, 'and I think to myself that they're nowhere near as nicely presented as when they were hand-piped.'

One of the juniors was given the job of keeping the pipers supplied with piping bags of warm chocolate, each new bag thrust into their hands as the previous one was emptied. The junior did nothing else but refill the piping bags when they ran out because the machines were running all the time, non-stop.

Dorothy can remember working till nine o'clock at night sometimes. She was paid overtime – known at Rowntree's as 'extended hours' – for the extra hours she worked, but there was no choice about whether to work or not, and the extra hours sometimes made an already long day almost unbearable.

In the periods from September to December, and February to March or April every year, preparing for and dealing with the Christmas and Easter rushes, Dorothy worked until seven or eight o'clock almost every evening, and if she did not want to work the extended hours she had to produce a doctor's note to say why she was unable to do so. She and her workmates were allowed just half an hour for tea at the end of their normal day's work, which was not enough time to go home. If they knew they would be doing overtime in advance, most of them brought in packed meals to eat, but if the company wanted them to work overtime and had not warned them the day before, they issued tickets that the girls could take over to the Dining Block and exchange for a free meal. However, the food they were given was neither as filling nor as appetizing as the lunches served in the dining hall. One woman remembers that she and her workmates were given a saucer of chips and some beetroot for their evening meal on more than one occasion, and if they wanted bread and butter with it, to bulk it up a little, they had to remember to bring their own to work with them.

The pipers would give the juniors a very hard time if they were too slow to fill their piping bags or messy about how they did it. 'There was one team of women in particular,' Dorothy recalls, 'a married women's team, and they were monkeys to us, they really were. You had to go to the back of the machine and fill their piping bags up with chocolate – the liquid chocolate was running all the time – and if you got any chocolate at all on the outside of their piping bag, they used to go absolutely spare, but despite that, I thoroughly enjoyed my time there; I absolutely loved it.'

The community of women employees spent so much time together that they got to know each other almost as well as they knew their own families, and Dorothy could discuss problems with her workmates that she would never have dared to talk about at home. 'We used to talk about all sorts of everyday things that were going on around us,' she says; 'problems with our families, money worries, falling out with boyfriends, everything. The majority of them, especially the married ones, would help you if they could. You could talk things over, often more with them than you could at home. I mean, I couldn't have told my grandmother much about what was going on in my life! Though, having said that, she was still a really good grandmother and she was lovely and kind to me.'

Although television was now more widely available, few of the production line workers could afford a set. Most went regularly to the pictures, and as they worked on the production line Dorothy and her friends would tell each other about the films they had just seen and describe the plots and the characters. 'When I was on with the pipers or the markers,' Dorothy says, 'if you got in with the right crowd and one of them had been to the pictures the night before, they'd tell you the whole story of the film they'd been to see while you were working. In return, as we were all on piecework, we would all do a bit of extra work to keep up the output of the girl who was telling the story, so she wouldn't lose any money. After that the music would come on over the Tannoy and we'd all have a sing together;

old-fashioned songs like "My Gal's a Yorkshire Gal" and "Pal of My Cradle Days". As long as the work was getting done, they didn't mind you singing and talking as much as you wanted.'

When the chocolates left the pipers, they went through one cooler and then there was a girl on what was called 'halfway', who took them off that conveyor belt and put them through a second cooler. It was the job that Dorothy liked least. 'Sometimes the chocolates would get stuck to the conveyor belt,' she says, 'and there were these little wires stuck in the belt. If you weren't careful, they'd catch your fingers as you were trying to get the chocolate off, and if you cut yourself on those it didn't half sting. Or sometimes it went too far and you'd have to stop the machine or you'd tell the operator "Missed one sheet!" because otherwise they'd come through stuck on the belt and that was another mess to be cleaned up.'

Every so often there was a hand inspection by the overlookers, though on these occasions they were less concerned about how clean the girls' hands were than how hot they were. If someone's hands were too warm when they were piping, the heat would affect the chocolate, and when it got too warm, by the time it got to the end of the line and started to cool down again, it would have gone white, so it all had to be stripped off. The overlookers used to come along and say, 'Change your bag,' and the pipers would all start again with a fresh piping bag.

Sometimes it was not just the pipers' hands that were too warm. In very hot weather, the entire Cream Packing staff would sometimes be sent home because the chocolate would get too warm and turn white or even start melting out of shape. One of Dorothy's fellow pipers, Sue Mizzi, still remembers gazing wistfully out of the window on a hot day, watching kids in Haxby Road heading for the swimming pool or the banks of the river, while she willed the mercury in the thermometer to rise a couple of degrees higher. She kept muttering to her friend every few minutes, 'What's the temperature? Are we there yet?' At the start of the lunch break at 12.30 p.m. they would hesitate, hoping that the overlooker would come round to tell them not to come back in the afternoon, but often they'd be disappointed and would have to turn up again at 1.30 p.m., ready for the afternoon shift, only then to be told, 'It's too hot, go home.' However, if there was a prolonged hot spell, the company would try to claw back at least some of the lost production by bringing the start of the day shift forward to 6.00 a.m. instead of 7.30 a.m. Work would begin in the cool of the early morning and continue until around lunchtime when, if necessary, the girls would once more be sent home as the temperature again began to climb too high.

In summertime, kids used to cool off with a swim in the Ouse or York's other river, the Foss, and in the 1800s a 100-yard stretch of the bed of the Foss had even been laid with flagstones and enclosed with wire netting at either end to create an open-air swimming pool known as 'Yearsley Bath'. However, tragedies were not unknown when inexperienced swimmers went out of their depth, got into difficulties in the strong current, or became tangled in underwater debris or vegetation, and in the early years of the new century there had been an incident when a young boy drowned. The boy's father, Jack Crosby, worked for the Rowntree's Fire Brigade and he was determined to do all he could to avert such tragedies in the future.

He was helped by another member of the Fire Brigade, Wilf Woodcock, who was one of the best swimmers in York, a winner of the annual York River Swim, which was held between the site of the modern Clifton Bridge on the River Ouse and Blue Bridge a mile and three-quarters away. Wilf had once used his river swimming ability to save a young man's life. He happened to be pedalling his bike along the bank of the river near Clifton Ferry when he saw a young man on the far bank slip and fall in. The young man could not swim and would have drowned had Wilf not dived in, swum across the river and rescued him.

One immediate consequence of such incidents was the Rowntree company's decision to construct the Yearsley swimming pool so that the children of employees and of York people generally could swim in safety. Completed in 1909, the Yearsley swimming pool was at once donated by Rowntree's to the City of York. Lifeguards were permanently on duty and a sign on the diving board warning 'Fancy diving prohibited' offered further reassurance to hesitant swimmers. However, in summer kids continued to swim in York's twin rivers, and in an attempt to ensure that no other parents would have to endure the heartbreak of seeing their child drown, Wilf and Jack put together a squad of men from the Rowntree's Fire Brigade to teach all the local kids to swim.

In his own time and at his own expense, Wilf trained to be a lifeguard, winning a gold award. He then brought the rest of the Fire Brigade members up to the same standard, and they went on to teach as many children as possible how to swim and how to lifesave, too. Over the years several children who got into trouble swimming in the Ouse and the Foss, and who would otherwise have drowned, were rescued by people trained by the men of the Rowntree's Fire Brigade.

12

Eileen

Eileen left school on the day she reached her sixteenth birthday. 'I'd always been considered a bright pupil at school,' she says, 'but I left without even taking my O levels, mainly because I had a bit of a bee in my bonnet about the headmistress. I hated her, absolutely detested her, and that feeling only got stronger when she made me serve her dinner to her every day for a year. That was a punishment after I had asked her if I could leave school because all my friends were older than me and they had all already left. She said, "No," so I said, "Right, the very day that I pass my sixteenth birthday, I'll be walking out of school." So I did, stupid though it was, when I look back now.'

She immediately joined her father at Rowntree's. It was 1951, and a good time to be starting work. The Festival of Britain that same year signalled the start of a revival in British morale and the beginning of a decade-long boom in the economy after the long years of austerity that Britons had endured during the war and for years after it. Aged sixteen, Eileen could not even remember a time when rationing had not been in force in Britain. It had been imposed soon after the outbreak of war, when she was just five, and although rationing of bread, potatoes, eggs and petrol had now been abolished, ration coupons were still required for sweets, sugar and meat until 1954.

Despite her lack of O levels, Eileen had had a good education at a York grammar school, but at the time she gave little if any thought to possible alternative careers, having always assumed that she would start work at Rowntree's straight from school. The offices at the factory were seen as *the* place to work at the time, because they paid the best wages in York – two pounds twelve shillings and sixpence a week, which was much higher than shop work and a very good wage for a young girl in those days (equivalent to about £200 a week today). And just in case Eileen was harbouring any different thoughts, as soon as she left school, her dad said to her, 'You get yourself to Rowntree's offices.'

'You had to have a grammar school education to work in the offices,' Eileen says, 'and you had to pass quite a strict exam to get in as well.' The exams had been devised by the latest generation of the industrial psychologists that Rowntree's had been employing since the 1920s to advise on recruitment strategies, assess the potential of interviewees and, in line with the industrial psychologists' mantra of 'a place for everyone and everyone in their place', to steer them to the most suitable part of the factory for their particular skills.

Girls interviewed for office jobs underwent a much more searching examination than those applying for work on the factory floor, after which they were unofficially graded 'A', 'B', 'C', 'D' or 'E'. The industrial psychologists also patronisingly and offensively – if sometimes accurately – categorized less able women into types, which included 'muddler' and 'careless'. 'A's would be offered work in the office without hesitation, and often 'B's would be employed there too, but 'A's and 'B's were unlikely ever to be offered work on the production line, since the industrial psychologists subscribed to the theory that the more intelligent candidates would have a short attention span and would soon become bored by production line work and either quit or, even worse, stay and make trouble. By the same token, even if their formal education had been limited, the more intelligent applicants for production line jobs might find themselves steered towards office jobs instead. Production line jobs were reserved for 'C's but, if there was a labour shortage, then 'D's were often hired as well, sometimes over the strenuous objections of the industrial psychologists. That happened in the mid to late 1930s when demand for Black Magic really took off, but the rate of subsequent sackings of unsuitable employees also rose sharply to as much as 20 per cent, no doubt to the private satisfaction of the industrial psychologists who had advised against employing them in the first place. 'E's were regarded as hopeless cases, too clumsy and unintelligent to be trusted with even the most basic production line work, and they were invariably shown the door.

Eileen must have been graded 'A' because she was told at once that she had qualified to join the Rowntree's office staff. The factory was a huge, sprawling place, but Eileen and the other new office girls soon got to know it as well, if not better, than most of the long-term employees, as they were put in the Post Office Messengers department to start with and given the task of taking messages round to all the different departments, so they soon got the feel of the layout.

'Not all the departments had telephones,' Eileen says, 'and of course there were no emails or anything like that then, so a lot of the orders and messages went by typed or handwritten letters and memos that were delivered by the messengers – and it wasn't just me; there were half a dozen of us taking messages round.' The girls were taught the routes and accompanied the first few times they did them, but after that they were on their own and, like the postmen and postwomen out in the real world, they were expected to deliver the mail, come hail or rain, sleet or snow, storm or tempest.

There were three different routes and the messengers did one route every hour. In between deliveries they sorted their mail, just like the workers in a general post office, and then went out to do another round. The first route was the office route, on which Eileen set off with her bag of letters and went to the Cream Packing department offices and all the other offices around the factory, ending at the Wigginton Road office block. Constructed in 1896, it was one of the first buildings in the area with electric lighting, and had something of the look of an auditorium or a chapel, the latter impression reinforced by a beautiful stained-glass east window featuring the white rose of York. The junior office employees worked in a large semi-open area on the ground floor, overlooked by a circular gallery that opened onto the offices of the directors and senior managers. Perhaps in tribute to the potential for office feuds on the ground floor, under the gazes of spectators on the gallery above, it soon acquired the nickname of the 'Bear Pit'. Underneath the ground-floor offices, and even lower on the works pecking order, were the cellar offices and storerooms of the 'understairs staff' – the cleaners and caretakers. To the north of the Bear Pit, and connected to it at first-floor level by a red-brick bridge, was another five-storey office building, and beneath it was the landing stage, the underground terminus of the Rowntree's railway sidings where raw materials and supplies were unloaded and finished goods shipped out.

The second route was the factory route, going round all the different confectionery production departments, and the third route was the outside route. On the latter Eileen walked down the Gum Corridor, and then went out to the Saw Mills, the Card Box Mills, the Power Plant, the Sugar Plant and the Elect Block. 'As I went by there,' she says, 'I always looked up towards the top of the hoist, where I knew my dad would be working, but I could never see him there, he was too high up.' She went on to deliver the letters to the plumbers, joiners, electricians and decorators and all the other tradesmen, and after that she was always glad of the chance to sit down for a few minutes while she sorted the next batch of letters and memos back at the post room, because it was a very long walk right around that circuit.

She was outside most of the time and it could be miserable in bad weather, although even when the sun was shining, the outside route could be something of an ordeal for her. She was a beautiful girl, with shoulder-length dark, straight hair, and very slim, weighing only about seven stone at the time, and attracted a lot of attention as she delivered the mail. She could have found walking round the sprawling factory site intimidating, but she took it all in her stride. 'You were on your own as you went through the routes,' she says, 'and on two of them you didn't really see many people. You were usually just going to the edge of the rooms or the outside of the buildings where the mailboxes were, so you were always on the edge of what was going on. People used to shout at me and sometimes wolf whistle, but I just used to keep walking and tried not to take any notice, though I was probably blushing like mad.'

In winter, she would sometimes complete her round of the outside route without seeing more than a handful of people, but in summer the factory was a hive of activity. Every summer teams of painters would strip down the iron railings around the site, clean off any rust and repaint them in the Rowntree's dark blue livery. The three flagpoles on the roof of the Cream Block and the cream frieze around the top of the building were repainted and the giant ten-foot-high letters of the 'Rowntree's Cocoa Elect' sign on the face of the top storey of the Elect Block were also refurbished. Visible for miles around, they were formed from highly glazed bricks, which stood out vividly against the cream painted brickwork. One summer morning, as Eileen walked underneath and looked up towards where her dad was working as usual near the hoist, she stopped to watch as a man on a plank cradle, slung between two ropes, washed down and polished the lettering until it gleamed, and then began repainting the bricks around it to throw the sign into even sharper relief.

The factory route began in the corridors of the Cream Block and, like most of the factory, it was always immaculate. As soon as Eileen stepped through the doors, she could smell polish and often fresh paint, mingling with the delicious aromas of chocolate and roasting nuts. There were carefully tended baskets of flowers hanging on chains from the high ceilings in the corridors, and in every reception area and office there were vases of fresh cut flowers that were renewed or replaced on a daily basis by the Estates department. One London worker, visiting Rowntree's in 1934, said that it was 'impossible to conceive an industrial establishment more varied in its processes or more cheerful in its appearance than Rowntree's. The rooms and corridors, overhung with baskets and foliage, provided a startling contrast to the depressing aspect of our East End factories.' Even when the company was on the verge of bankruptcy in the early 1930s, the Estates department still provided cut flowers at the same lavish rate.

The factory route was her favourite one, she says, 'because some of the girls used to throw chocolates into my bag as I walked past and I used to take them back and share them out with the other girls.' However, that was not without its risks, because there used to be a factory detective in those days called 'Peddler Palmer', and it was not because he rode a bike. He was a huge man who had acquired his nickname because, despite his job, if even half the rumours about him were true, he was one of the biggest crooks in the place. One day Eileen had just walked through the Machine Room where they made and packed the chocolate assortments, and she was coming down the stairs with some chocolates in her mail bag when she bumped into Peddler Palmer. Taking chocolates was a sackable offence and she was terrified that he was going to search her. Her guilt must have been written all over her face, but luckily he let her pass and she got away with it, though her heart was still beating wildly when she got back to the post room.

It was something of an education for her to see all the different processes that were involved in making Rowntree's products. The areas where the confectionery was produced were as clean and hygienic as they could be made in that era, but some of the other parts of the factory, such as the Mould Shop where the tinsmiths worked, were 'like something out of Dickens'. There were drop-stamping machines clanking and banging as they pressed out the moulds, tinsmiths trimming off the excess metal; others were soldering the parts together, with soldering irons glowing red hot, and everywhere there were clouds of smoke and the stench of hot solder. It was a side of the factory that people did not really think about or see; as well as the sweets and chocolates, and the fancy boxes with ribbons and tassels, there was heavy industry there, too.

One of the tinsmiths, Horace Woodcock, was always inventing things and coming up with ideas on how to do things better. Rowntree's had a suggestion scheme, where employees could fill in a form with their suggestion and if the company wanted to make use of it, they'd offer a sum of money as a reward for the idea. When they were launched in the 1930s, Smarties were made on moulds that pressed out half the shape, with a flat bottom, and then the two were brought together to make the finished shape. Horace had the bright idea of designing two sets of flexible moulds, fitted to two rollers that would press out the complete shape in one operation, doubling the rate at which the factory could produce them. He put his suggestion to Rowntree's, and having evaluated it they offered him sixty pounds for his idea, which was an awful lot of money in those days – the equivalent of about £1,200 today – but Horace held out and said, 'But I'm giving you an idea that will double your production. It ought to be worth more than that.' They then called him into the office and offered him double the money: £120. Even that didn't seem like a lot of money to him, but after thinking it over, he accepted. In fact, a Dutch company was already beginning to manufacture a machine that worked on similar lines, and in the end Rowntree's made no use of Horace's invention and bought one of the Dutch machines instead, so as it turned out, he did pretty well for himself.

After about six months, new office girls were considered to have served their unofficial apprenticeship and were allocated to an office in one of the departments. Eileen was sent to the sales office on the fourth floor of the Wigginton Road block (a building that no longer exists, for it was demolished in 2009).

She worked in the offices there until 1952, but then, chafing at the prospect of totting up accounts and ledgers in the same room with the same people, in the town where she had grown up, for the rest of her working life, and eager to see at least a little bit more of the world, she resigned.

Eileen had made up her mind to join the forces and would have liked to have joined the WRENs (the Women's Royal Naval Service), not because seafaring was in her blood, but mainly because she liked the uniform! However she needed O levels for that and, thanks to marching out of school on her sixteenth birthday, she did not have any. She knew that she did not want to join the Army and, with the WRENs ruled out, that only left the RAF, so as one of her friends had joined the RAF a year before, she decided to follow suit.

Ironically perhaps, having left one job totting up accounts and ledgers, she found herself doing another, working in the Pay Accounts department on an RAF base in Wiltshire, but it was where her skills and experience lay. 'I joined Pay Accounts because I was good at maths,' she says, 'it was my top subject. After I had taken the entrance test for the RAF at the recruiting office in Leeds, the wing commander called me into her office and said, "Has anyone told you what this test is about?" I said, "No, why?" "Because you got 98 per cent," she said. "And we've never, ever had a woman score so highly."

'I said, "Actually, it was the same kind of test that I took when I went to work at Rowntree's, so I'd already had a bit of practice!" Although the IQ tests were not identical, there were similarities in the kinds of questions asked. It must run in the family because when my son, Alan, took his test on joining the RAF, he scored 100 per cent.' To this day, Eileen is a very modest woman and although she shows an obvious and understandable pride at her son's achievement, all she will say about her own outstanding performance is: 'I don't remember feeling particularly pleased with myself at doing well in the tests. I was just grateful to have passed. I think I said, "Thank God I got in."'

Those serving in the RAF came from all over the country, but when she was off duty and exploring some of the villages around the base, Eileen sometimes felt as if she was a foreigner in her own land. Her Yorkshire accent and dialect words like 'snicket' (a narrow path) and 'ginnel' (a passageway between two buildings) proved as impenetrable to the natives as their Wiltshire burr did to her, and she found shopkeepers speaking ... very ... slowly ... to ... her ... as if she was a particularly backward child, rather than an adult who just happened to come from a different part of the country. Nor was there always the warmth and friendliness she had been used to in her home town. Some locals were very friendly, but others often seemed startled if she spoke to them, and would sometimes scuttle away without even replying. She was a little homesick at first, but her work kept her occupied and she soon made friends on the base and settled into service life.

While in Wiltshire she met her first husband, who was also serving in the RAF, and after their marriage in 1954 she moved to Sussex with him and had two sons, Chris, born in 1954, and Alan in 1957. Eileen is tight-lipped about that time in her life – it was not a happy relationship and in 1961, after seven years together, the marriage ended in divorce. She returned to York after that and went back to work at Rowntree's. Soon afterwards she met her second husband, though he did not work at Rowntree's, but as a printer at a local firm. They were married in 1966.

At this time, Eileen's dad was still living in York and still working at the factory. He kept doing that heavy physical work right up until he was fifty-five, when he had what was either a heart attack or a very severe attack of angina. At that point a visitor from St Dunstan's came to see him and said to him, 'Come on, Arthur, that's enough now,' and eventually persuaded him to retire.

Arthur and Alice stayed together for the rest of his life and he never let his blindness slow him down or stop him from doing the things he wanted to do, whether it was at work or in his time off. He loved his racing and his rugby league and he used to go to 'Glorious Goodwood' and Brighton races every year – he liked to go to Sussex once a year to revisit St Dunstan's, and, says Eileen, he and Alice, 'went there seventeen years on the trot'. When he went to Goodwood, he would stand near the rails, and although he could not see the horses, he could feel the thunder of their hooves through the turf, hear the commentary over the Tannoy and the roar of the crowd, and he could describe the race afterwards so vividly that you would have sworn that he had watched it.

He used to 'watch' the racing on the television every week, listening to the commentary and picturing the race in his head. One Saturday he was sitting on the sofa, having just switched the television off after listening to a race, when there was a knock at the door. A local child had gone missing and the police were going from house to house in the street asking everyone if they'd seen or heard anything. Eileen's dad invited them in, and one of them asked him, 'Where were you at three o'clock last Saturday?'

'I was here, watching the racing on the TV,' Arthur said. 'I do it every Saturday.'

The policeman did a double-take. 'But you're blind,' he said, as if he was Hercule Poirot, catching out a master criminal in a lie.

'That's right,' Arthur said, 'but I still watch the racing on TV,' and he rattled off a description of the race he had just heard, as if it was being run in front of his eyes. The policeman didn't say anything else, he just thanked him and left.

Eileen's dad also loved to go down to Wembley with his mates for the rugby league cup final every year, and he was treasurer of York Rugby League club as well. He played dominoes in the pub with his mates, and he could even play darts; Eileen has photographs of him doing so. She says:

He didn't let his handicap stop him from doing anything. And I never once heard him complain or say, 'Why me?' Although once, when I asked him if he often thought about what it had been like when he could see, there was a catch in his voice as he said, 'There isn't a day when I don't wish I could have my sight back just for an hour,' so that, just once, he could see his wife, his son-in-law and his grandchildren, and see again the places around York that he had known so well. Strangely enough, even though he'd never seen them, when I once said to my dad, 'What do you think the two boys look like, Dad?' he described them to me almost perfectly, but the opposite way around. When he told me what he thought Chris looked like, he could have been describing Alan, and when he talked about Alan he was drawing a near perfect picture of Chris.

In the early 1960s Eileen's dad suffered a real blow to his confidence when there was a break-in at his house. He was in his fifties by then and he and Alice had gone out for the evening to a presentation dinner in the dining hall at Rowntree's, where Arthur and a few other employees were given awards to commemorate their twenty-five-year service for Rowntree's. As he and Alice were leaving the house, all dressed up in their best outfits, they passed a scruffy-looking young man. Alice did not recognize him, and though it was unusual to see a stranger in a street where everyone knew everyone else, she thought nothing more of it at the time.

However, he must have noticed them coming out of the house, realized from their clothes that they were going to be out for the evening, and had then gone round to the back of the house and broken in by smashing the bathroom window. He trashed the house and stole jewellery and other valuables. 'He took my mum's engagement ring and Alice's ring,' Eileen says, 'though he didn't dare take my dad's watch – a Braille watch would have been too easy to trace, I suppose – and he knew my dad was blind, because he'd tipped his spare glass eyes out onto the bed while he was searching their room, but it made no difference, he robbed them anyway. They had a coin meter for the electric and he had broken into the meter and stolen the money from that as well.'

When Arthur and Alice got back and put the key in the lock, they could not open the front door because the thief had dropped the latch to stop anyone disturbing him. When they went round to the back, Alice saw that the back door was wide open and realized at once what had happened. They did not know whether there was anyone still in the house, so Arthur sent Alice upstairs to check while he stood at the bottom of the stairs, blocking the way and saying in a loud voice, 'If anyone's here, they're going to have to get past me if they want to get out,' but the house was empty. The thief had got what he wanted and gone.

'I don't think my dad ever really recovered from that burglary,' Eileen says. 'It wasn't so much the money and the possessions they had lost, as the knowledge of how vulnerable he now was, and I think it was the first time he'd ever felt that way. He was getting older and he knew now that he wasn't safe even in his own home. It really did make a big difference to him and the way he was.' It was a growing worry for Eileen and Alice as from then on, Eileen's once fiercely independent father became increasingly dependent upon them.

When Eileen had started working at Rowntree's again, she had only wanted to work part time, and as a result she had no option but to go into the factory because there was no part-time work in the offices. Perhaps a little to her surprise, she found that she loved working on the line and 'did everything', including packing Dairy Box, Black Magic, After Eight mints and Smarties. She had to pack a certain number of boxes an hour to earn her money, keeping up with the rate that had been set for the job; if she fell behind she risked being first 'clock watched' and then sacked if she did not improve. Eileen had no trouble keeping up and even 'made the rate' on one line – being timed by the 'time and motion' man to set the rate that everyone else would have to achieve. As another packer, Muriel, notes with a wry smile, 'When the timekeepers used to come with their stopwatches and clipboards, to set the rate for the job, the machines never stopped when they were around and nor did we!'

Eileen worked in the factory until 1967, when she left to have her third child and only daughter, Karen. It was the 'summer of love', but although hippies were beginning to appear on the streets of York, and the hair of male workers at Rowntree's – now tucked under hairnets – was beginning to lengthen, the all-pervading aroma at the factory remained chocolate, not marijuana. In any case, 'flower power' largely passed Eileen by; she was too busy earning a living and having her children. Soon after giving birth to Karen, Eileen went back to Rowntree's and carried on working the 'twilight shift' in the evenings – a shift specially introduced to aid married women with young children – until just before the birth of her third son Stephen in 1969. After he was born, she went back to Rowntree's again and carried on working there until 1980, but this time she worked as a cleaner because, she says, 'I was getting older then and I couldn't keep up to speed on the line. I was a supervisor, a charge-hand and a shop steward as well, so I did everything really.'

Eileen's children have maintained the family's military tradition. Although her daughter Karen did not join the forces herself – she is a bank manager – she did the next best thing and married an RAF officer, while both of Eileen's elder sons followed in her footsteps and joined the RAF and became career officers. Chris was a flight lieutenant, Specialist Aircrew, and Alan was a wing commander.

When Alan was in line for promotion to squadron leader, one of the things he had to do was make a presentation to a roomful of officers, including some very senior ones. Alan chose to do his presentation on the Battle of Anzio. Around the time of Remembrance Sunday a few years previously, there had been an article in *The Press*, the York newspaper, about men who had been wounded in the war. It was illustrated by a photo of Eileen's dad going into his garden shed, where he used to do joinery. Alan decided to use that photograph and, Eileen says, 'He asked Dad to tell him about Anzio, because as a rule Dad didn't talk about the war at all, but he told Alan about it.'

When Alan did his presentation, he put up the photograph and said, 'This is my granddad, he fought at Anzio.' He went on to describe the battle and then, at the end, he showed the picture of Arthur again and said, 'But what of Granddad?' and then he signalled for all the lights in the lecture room to be switched off. After leaving his audience sitting in darkness for a few seconds, he said, 'Ever since Anzio, this is all my granddad has seen for the last fifty years.' The presentation obviously had a considerable impact on the audience because for weeks afterwards, Eileen says, 'People were coming up to him and telling him that they'd heard about the presentation he'd given. Chris even heard about it and he was serving at an entirely different base, at Brize Norton.'

Arthur and Alice had been married for fifty-two years when he died in 2001. 'In all, he had lived for fifty-seven years totally blind,' Eileen says, 'so he never saw Alice's face, nor my husband's, nor our children – his grandchildren – but Dad was a happy man and he never let his blindness get him down.' Eileen was sixty-five when he died, and her dad was eighty-seven, but even then, she says, 'I never, ever answered him back. You just didn't do it. If I said, "I don't think you're right, Dad," he'd just say, "I know I'm right." And I'd end up saying, "Well, maybe you are, Dad." You'd go around it somehow, because you just didn't argue with him. It was worse in his younger days because he really did have an awful temper then, and he went through a stage when he first came home after the war when I think he really couldn't handle being blind and that came out in his temper, but, despite that, he was a remarkable man and I loved him dearly.'

When Arthur died, a St Dunstan's visitor came and talked to Alice, Eileen and the family, and offered the organization's help, and she was there at the funeral, too. The collection taken at Arthur's funeral was donated to St Dunstan's (now called Blind Veterans UK) and Eileen supports and fundraises for them to this day, in gratitude for the help that the charity gave to her father and his family all those years ago. 'They were so good to him,' she says, 'and they are a wonderful, wonderful organization.'

At the time of Arthur's death, Alice was already suffering from the onset of Alzheimer's and, Eileen says, 'Alice just couldn't cope with it. I wanted her to come and stay with me but she wouldn't do it and stayed in their house. It was only fifty yards away round the corner from me and I used to go in and see her two or three times a day, but she died only fifteen weeks after my dad. I think she just couldn't live without him. You hear of people dying of a broken heart and I think that's what killed her.'

13

Maureen

Maureen Graham started work at Rowntree's on her fifteenth birthday in April 1959, and it was, she says, 'the longest day of my life. It was awful. I was a skinny little thing, the overall was far too big for me, the turban practically covered my eyes so I couldn't see what I was doing, and even worse, I was wearing a pair of white ankle socks.' As she joined the jostling crowds of women making their way into work that morning, she realized that there were about 6,000 women at the factory and 5,999 of them, from the youngest girls to the women approaching retirement, were all wearing stockings. The only one in the entire workforce who was wearing ankle socks was Maureen. She was a shy girl, who had grown up in a small farming village fifteen miles outside York, and the ways of the 'big city' were new to her. 'I was a country lass and didn't know any different,' she says. She never wore ankle socks again, going bare legged until she could afford to buy a pair of stockings herself. They were expensive and easily laddered, but there were several shops then where you could get damaged stockings mended invisibly.

Maureen had been allocated to Smartie Packing and the overlooker there set her to work packing tubes of Smarties into outers with two older girls in charge of her. Maureen was completely overawed and intimidated by them and was all fingers and thumbs as she struggled to put the tubes into the boxes at anything approaching the speed of the experienced girls alongside her. After struggling for a couple of hours, desperate for a brief respite, she asked the senior girls if they would mind if she went to the toilet. That was normally forbidden outside the official break times, but they told her to 'go ahead and take your time about it'. However, Maureen suspects that it was more an act of desperation than kindness and still shudders at the memory. 'To be honest,' she says, 'I think they were glad to be rid of me, because I was so slow and clumsy to start with that I must have been holding them up and costing them money. It was all so new to me, it was physically hard work and it was a very long day for someone who, after all, was still just a kid and fresh out of school.'

When they got to the official break time, there was always a rush for the toilets. The rules had not changed over the years; girls were still not allowed food on their work tables, so if they wanted something to eat at break time, they either had to eat it sitting on the floor or they had to go downstairs to the room where they kept their coats. Then, as soon as they had finished eating, they had to dash to the toilets and be back in time to start work as soon as the machines started running again, or risk falling behind with their work.

Maureen absolutely hated the work and the factory at first. She had actually wanted to be a nurse but her mother wouldn't let her apply. When Maureen asked her why, she said, 'Because you're too squeamish. You won't make a nurse. You'll get married and have babies.' Maureen has always regretted and resented that, and later felt more than a tinge of understandable anger that while her mother refused to allow her to train as a nurse, she gave her blessing to Maureen's youngest sister to do so. Now, as Maureen says, 'I'm on my own and I could do with a job that pays a bit of money,' her regret at that missed opportunity is still strong, though she consoles herself with the thought that 'I think I've had a better life than my youngest sister despite that – well, certainly a more colourful one anyway!'

Alone in her room, Maureen cried herself to sleep that first night, and if she could have found a way to avoid going back to work the next day, she would have grabbed it with both hands. 'I'd lived a very sheltered life as a country girl with very strict parents,' she says. 'I'd been raised to say my prayers each night, never to tell lies and to go to Sunday School every Sunday. I was brought up really straight-laced, I couldn't even talk to boys, and I was still only a child, just fifteen years old. People now wouldn't think of sending children off to work at that age, they wouldn't let them do more than a Saturday job, but things were different then and I had no choice but to get on with it.'

She was skilled enough with a needle and thread to take in her overalls and turban so that they fitted her better, and she donated her ankle socks to her younger sister Shirley, who was to undergo the same 'ankle sock trauma' when she started work at Rowntree's eighteen months later. Either Maureen had forgotten to warn her, or perhaps she wanted her younger sister to suffer like she had!

At half past seven the next morning, Maureen was back at her work station and, as she got used to it, the work slowly became easier. However, what had already been a traumatic introduction to the world of work became even more so when the excitement of receiving her first ever wage packet – two pounds seventeen shillings and sixpence (forty-four pounds today) for her forty-four hour week – rapidly turned to despair when, as she left the factory that night, she realized she had lost her wage packet somewhere in the maze of corridors and buildings. She retraced her steps but could not see it anywhere, and when she reported the loss to the wages office, she received sympathy but no offers of compensation. Distraught and still in floods of tears at having undergone that bruising first week for nothing, she was sitting on a bench in the entrance lobby when a woman from the wages office hurried down the corridor towards her holding a brown paper packet in her hand. 'You're in luck,' she said. 'Someone found it and handed it in.' Maureen was so relieved and elated that she could almost have kissed her.

Maureen was born in 1944, while the Second World War was still raging. Her parents both served in the war, her father fighting with one of the Scottish regiments, while her mother was a WREN, and like so many other children then, she had been looked after by her grandparents while her parents were away. The oldest of five children, three girls and two boys, Maureen lived with her parents in a three-bedroom terraced council house in a little village called Hayton, three miles outside Pocklington. It was an idyllic childhood, for their house was surrounded by open country, and Maureen and her brothers and sisters would be out playing in the fields and woods from dawn to dusk, searching for birds' nests, looking for frogs and newts in the streams and muddy drainage ditches, and foraging for wild strawberries, gooseberries, blackberries, rosehips and sloes in their seasons. At weekends, as soon as the sun was up she would take a basket and pick mushrooms in the pasture and the fringes of the woods. When she got back, her mum or grandmother would check them carefully to make sure she had not picked any toadstools and then fry the mushrooms up for their breakfast.

The children had a pet dog with the unlikely canine name of Roger. It was a pure-bred collie and might have been a valuable sheep dog, but the farmer who had bred it had fired a shotgun near it when he was training the dog and had frightened it so much that it became useless as a working dog. The farmer might well have used his next cartridge on the dog, but Maureen's uncle, who worked at the farm, offered to take it off the farmer's hands. His mother, Maureen's grandmother, had the dog for a while, but 'my granny got bored with him', she says. 'She got bored with everything after a while and things she got bored with often finished up in a hole in the garden.' So her grandchildren inherited the dog. They kept Roger for years and took him to York with them when they moved there some years later.

The children were very much thrown on their own resources when they played in the house or outside, but Maureen cannot remember ever feeling bored as a child. She was a voracious reader, even though in that small village, miles from the nearest library and with no money to buy books, she could never get enough reading material. She spent a lot of her time drawing pictures, playing cards with her brothers and sisters, and making up games that they could play. The family didn't own a television until Maureen had grown up and gone to work at Rowntree's, and even then she barely watched television until after she got married.

Although the family was poor, they always managed to scrape enough money together to pay for a holiday every year.

Maureen's mum had never been on holiday when she was growing up and she was determined that her children would not miss out in the same way. One year they were going to have to cancel the holiday because, with three weeks to go, they just did not have enough money to cover the cost, but Maureen's dad had entered a competition in one of the newspapers. 'The first prize was a radiogram and it was something we kids would have loved,' Maureen says, 'because we used to have to smuggle the family radio upstairs, plug it into the light and hide under the blankets with it to listen to Radio Luxembourg. If mum and dad had had a radiogram, they could have listened to it and we could have had the other radio all to ourselves. However, Dad didn't win that radiogram but he did win fifty pounds in cash instead and that was enough to save our holiday, though to be honest we'd have preferred to have stayed home and won the radiogram instead!'

After she left school and started work, in order to get to the Rowntree's factory every day, Maureen had to cycle to Pocklington, catch a bus into York and then another bus out to the factory. That not only extended her already long working day by another two hours, but as winter arrived and the weather deteriorated, she could no longer even be certain of getting to work on time. Rowntree's insisted on punctuality from all their employees and there were severe financial penalties for lateness. Workers who were even slightly late for the 7.30 a.m. start still found that the factory doors had been shut and they would lose their entire morning's pay. Faced with that prospect, Maureen had no option but to move into digs, renting a bedsit in a house just over the railway bridge from the factory, and from then on she only went back to the family home at Hayton at weekends.

Her room was on the top floor and the smell of boiled cabbage always seemed to drift up the stairs from the family's ground-floor kitchen. Maureen had just the one room, with cracked lino on the floor, a small fireplace, a bed, a tiny table in an alcove and two hard chairs. With no wardrobe space, she had to keep her spare clothes in her suitcase under the bed, not that she owned many clothes. There was a bathroom on the floor below, but if she wanted to take a bath she had to pre-book it with her landlord and pay an extra sum for the hot water she used.

She had lived in the country all her life until then and didn't know a single soul in York, so it was a miserable, lonely existence at first. There was very little tourism in York in those days, and it was an insular, provincial city with a reputation for being an unfriendly sort of place, compared to the warmth of towns and cities elsewhere in Yorkshire. To an outsider like Maureen, it seemed as if everybody was related to everybody else or knew everybody else, and had grouped themselves into cliques of which she was no part.

However, she slowly began to make some friends in the Smarties department and from then on, instead of dreading it, she actually started looking forward to going to work, though she still absolutely hated living in digs. It cost her ten shillings a week to be a lodger in an upstairs room in somebody else's house, and though in theory she was free to use the kitchen, in practice she had to pass through the family's living room to reach it and was so shy and so reluctant to intrude on their lives that she never made use of it. Instead she stayed in her room and lived on sliced white bread and the jars of Cheese Whiz – a thick, processed cheese spread – that her mother sent her. Thankfully Cheese Whiz did not make up her entire diet, and for her main meal she ate a hot, three-course lunch – soup, meat and two veg, and a steamed pudding – in the Dining Block at Rowntree's every day. The food had always been subsidized by the company and remained very good value at around half a crown (twelve and a half pence) a week – the same price that Maureen's school dinners had been.

At first, in the evenings, curled up in her room, she listened to pop music on Radio Luxembourg, continually adjusting the dial to try to get a stronger signal as it was often barely audible among the haze of static and competing foreign language stations. Her landlord had lent her the radio, and when it fell silent one night she assumed that she had broken it. She was too timid to tell him and from then on she sat in her room in silence. Only much later, after she had moved out of her digs, did she realize that it was actually a battery-operated radio and all that had happened was that the batteries had gone flat. That was how naive and innocent she was in those early days. Even after she had left home, her parents, and particularly her mother, continued to have a strong and occasionally overpowering influence on their daughter. However, like many other children of strict upbringing, when the parental controls were lifted, the first tastes of freedom could be dizzying and were sometimes embraced with a headlong, reckless enthusiasm, whatever the consequences. Maureen was now getting ready to make up for lost time.

She was still only fifteen when she started going out with her first boyfriend, Peter, who worked at the Co-op Dairy down the road from the factory. They met at a dance and their first date was at the Odeon cinema. She cannot remember what film was playing, but then, as she says with one of her trademark wicked grins, 'We were in the back row, so I didn't see much of the film!' He was three years older than her and a 'rocker', with blue jeans, black leather jacket and a BSA Gold Flash motorbike. Although crash helmets were available then, few self-respecting motorcyclists and certainly no rockers would have been seen wearing one, and Maureen used to ride pillion on Peter's motorbike with her long hair flying in the wind behind her. He drove a Co-op van during the working day and would sometimes pick Maureen up in it and take her for a spin at lunchtime, though she had to sit on the floor and keep her head down until they got out of York because he would have been sacked if he had been caught taking passengers in the van.

Peter was a huge rock 'n' roll fan and had seen Bill Haley during his 1957 tour of Britain, when Haley's brand of rock 'n' roll had fans jiving in the aisles and the self-appointed guardians of British morals frothing at the mouth. Maureen wasn't a Haley fan – she thought he looked less like a rock god and more like an overweight, kiss-curled salesman at a plumbing supplies convention – but like most girls of her age, she worshipped Elvis and she loved to go jiving. Most Saturday nights Peter would take Maureen to one of the local dances, and though they would sit out the waltzes and foxtrots, as soon as a rock 'n' roll song started, he would pull her to her feet and out onto the dance floor and they would jive, her skirt whirling out as he spun her around. However, she says, 'One of my most abiding memories of my relationship with Peter is the number of pairs of earrings I went through. I have pierced ears and every time I went out with him, I seemed to lose an earring because he always wore pullovers and my earrings would keep catching in them.'

After a few weeks in Smartie Packing, Maureen was beginning to match and even exceed the speed of the experienced workers and she found it a lovely department to work in. There was very little noise in the days before it was all mechanized. In other departments the girls could barely hear themselves think for the din of the machines, but in Smartie Packing, 'it was nice and quiet,' she says. 'You could have a conversation with your workmates without shouting your head off to make yourself heard. We did different jobs all the time as well, which made the work much less monotonous. As well as packing, we did wrapping, and all sorts of other jobs, and in spring and in early winter we would sometimes go upstairs and do Easter eggs or Christmas specialties as well. We did Smarties eggs, but there were also small chocolate ones that we packed in a kind of egg box, just as if they were fresh eggs.'

She ate lunch in the Dining Block with her friends every day, and after they had eaten they would go downstairs and watch a film or go dancing for twenty minutes before it was time to go back to work. They danced to rock 'n' roll music, wearing skirts they'd made themselves out of a yard of material, with layer upon layer of petticoats under their skirts that would spin out as they danced.

Despite the strict company rules and regulations, like fashion-conscious women in all industries, Rowntree's employees tended to push the boundaries of what was permissible, and Maureen was no exception. The main reason for the company rule requiring women to wear turbans was not so much the fear that stray hairs would get into the product, though that certainly was a concern, but that loose, unbound hair might become tangled in the machinery, with potentially fatal consequences. Women on the production lines were instructed to wear their turbans pulled right down so that no hair at all was showing, but if Maureen was planning to go out in the evening (and now she had made some friends and had a boyfriend she usually was), she went to work with curlers in her hair, covered by her turban, but always with a bit of her fringe showing; all the girls she worked with used to do the same thing. If they were not wearing curlers, they used to wear their turbans pushed right back on their heads, with even more of their hair showing. Later, invisible hairnets were introduced, and then the girls back-combed their fringes and wore their turbans so far back on their heads that they were almost invisible from the front.

On Saturday afternoons Maureen and the rest of the girls would go into town:

> *... with our gondola baskets and a plastic flower stuck on the side – we all did the same thing – and stilettos that usually needed heeling. We even wore stilettos to work, everybody did it. A lot of the girls had their hair back-combed as well, but I never could because my hair was too fine. Even one of the overlookers, I think her name was Gloria, used to have her hair back-combed once a week. Her hair was blonde and she had two kiss curls at the front and her hair piled up in a 'beehive', and it always looked immaculate. Mind you, she put so much lacquer on it that it would last a week like that before it had to be done again. She would take her turban off after a day's work and there was still not a hair out of place. I think she went to bed with a pair of knickers on her head to keep her hair right, but that was quite common then, I did it myself often enough. Lots of the girls had their hair in beehives, and some of them would lacquer it and keep it like that for weeks on end. There were always rumours going around that someone had seen beetles or cockroaches inside a*

girl's beehive, though I suspect that it was just a bit of an urban myth.

I really liked the fashions in those days and used to love getting dressed up. I was pretty good at dress-making and could make all my own clothes. We wore stockings and suspenders, stilettos, and we always wore gloves, usually white ones, and shoes and handbag to match. We all wore skirts under our overalls and hooped petticoats. My digs were just over the bridge from Rowntree's and the boys used to love watching me run down the bridge in the morning! I was never late for work, but I usually cut it pretty fine and often had to run the last couple of hundred yards. The hoops would ride up while I was running so there'd be a lot of wolf whistles from the boys and some of them would get a right eyeful.

When we were going out dancing at night we had the big full net petticoats, layers of them, which would flare out around you as you danced and looked fabulous. I loved those, worn under a skirt with a tiny nipped in waist and a big flared skirt. I was still living in digs when tights came in and we all thought what a great invention they were, though I don't think the boys were as keen on them as we were – stocking tops were a big deal for boys! Then it went to hot pants with a little dress over the top and big platform shoes, and miniskirts of course, which I loved as well.

When miniskirts came into fashion, the younger Rowntree's girls used to sew their skirts 'as tight and as short as we dared', as one recalls. 'We'd pluck our eyebrows down to almost nothing, because that was the fashion then, and dye our hair – I had mine two-tone for a while, blonde at the front and brown at the back – and then back-comb it right high.'

Surprisingly, given the strict rules and regulations covering most areas of their employees' working lives, Rowntree's did not seem to concern themselves too much about even the most extreme fashions. The girls could wear pretty much whatever they liked under their overalls, and were even allowed to totter round on stilettos or platform heels, which on a factory floor surrounded by fast-moving and highly dangerous machinery would give a modern safety officer heart failure. The only thing that Maureen remembers the overlookers being very quick to clamp down on was love bites. 'If anyone came in with a love bite showing – and it was something I never had – they had to wear a scarf or a polo neck, or they would be sent home, or sent to the Medical department to have a huge plaster put over it. Because we were making things that people were going to eat, they were very hot on skin complaints of any sort, but I think the fuss about love bites was really more of a moral thing than any concern about broken skin near the chocolates.'

In February 1961, Maureen's sister Shirley started work at Rowntree's as well and began sharing the room that Maureen rented. Although they were not making any greater use of the facilities, such as they were, the landlord promptly put up the rent by 50 per cent to fifteen shillings a week. Shirley was eighteen months younger than Maureen, and before leaving school she had been quite emphatic that, whatever else she did in life, she would not be going to work in a factory like her big sister, because she wanted 'a bit better than that' for herself. She had learned typing at school and could have tried for an office job but, realizing that the typing pool at an office or a small factory, or a job answering the phone and typing letters for a country solicitor, would not pay anywhere near as much as she could earn working on the production line at Rowntree's, she shelved her reservations, swallowed her pride and applied for a job at the factory.

Other girls, like one of Maureen's contemporaries, Sheila Hawksby, defied their parents' hopes that they would 'better themselves' when they opted for the higher wages at Rowntree's rather than higher status but lower paid work elsewhere. Some of Sheila's friends were already working at Rowntree's and she decided she wanted to work there too, even though it was not what her parents, and her mother in particular, had wanted for her after her expensive private education. When she told them, although her father reluctantly accepted her decision, her mother 'went berserk'. However, Sheila did not back down and now says, 'I'm only sorry that when I finished at Rowntree's forty-two and a half years later, they weren't still alive to see that it hadn't worked out too badly for me after all.'

Like Maureen before her, Shirley was desperately homesick and lonely at first. From being part of a large family in a small village to being virtually on her own in a huge factory in a strange town, and having to live in digs as well, was a real shock to her system. Even though she was sharing with her sister, Maureen was rarely there in the evenings and, without any friends of her own, Shirley spent night after night on her own. 'I remember the loneliness more than anything,' she says. 'My sister was living the life, out with her boyfriend every night until midnight, but I was very young and very shy, and my first few months at the factory were absolutely miserable.' With very little money, she could not go out much even if she had made friends to go with, so instead she just stayed in on her own every night, sitting up in bed, writing her diary, mostly written in pencil as pens were expensive in those days, and reading book after book.

She had no money to spare for buying books, but the works library proved a godsend for her. Set up by Joseph Rowntree in 1885 with some of his own money and a grant from the Pure Literature Society to purchase 'suitable' books, it was a typically philanthropic gesture by Joseph, albeit one that was slightly tarnished by his insistence on deducting a penny a week from the wages of every employee to help pay for the upkeep of the library.

However, like Maureen when she started working at Rowntree's, Shirley had every reason to be grateful for Joseph Rowntree's legacy, because almost every day she would go to the works library at lunchtime or after work and collect two new books from the well-stocked shelves. At the foot of the stairs in the library there was a large portrait of Joseph's son, Seebohm, with eyes that seemed to follow you as you passed it. Shirley found the portrait a little disconcerting, if not sinister, unlike one of the cleaners who used to strike up a conversation with the portrait as she swept the stairs every morning, telling Seebohm's image, 'You would turn in your grave if you could see the place now.'

Having selected her books, Shirley would take them back to her digs. After a frugal tea of bread spread with potted meat (she bought a loaf of bread and two ounces of potted beef every Monday for one shilling and fivepence halfpenny – about one pound ten today – that lasted her until she went home for the weekend on Friday night), she would tuck herself into bed with a hot-water bottle, read her books and 'cry for my family' until she fell asleep.

When Shirley had gone for her interview at Rowntree's, Maureen had told her, 'You'll be okay so long as you're not in Cream Packing,' so Shirley's heart sank when they told her that was where she would be working. Overlookers, charge-hands and teachers had always been promoted from the production line and, in most departments, relations with their workmates remained fairly friendly even after they had 'crossed the line' to join the bosses. Maureen had found all of the teachers and overlookers in the Smarties department to be quite amicable, but there was a very different atmosphere in the Cream Packing department.

She had warned Shirley about one notorious overlooker in particular, a woman called Noreen, who was 'an absolute dragon' and ruled the Cream Packing department with a rod of iron, although in her defence, with a roomful of teenage girls to control, her job cannot always have been easy. She was quite tall and, though she was not particularly powerfully built, she had a look about her that would have curdled milk. 'Everybody talked about Noreen,' Maureen says, 'and you'd be hard put to find anyone with a good word to say for her. She was a complete cow without any redeeming features at all, as far as we could tell. If you were nice to her she was suspicious, and if you didn't behave you got into trouble.'

As a result of Maureen's warning, Shirley was wary of Noreen when she started, but even so, she felt that Noreen was 'on her case' more than any of the other girls, though she admits that most of the other girls also felt singled out and victimized by Noreen, and sometimes Shirley didn't do herself any favours. One of the greatest crimes in the Rowntree's rule book was to be caught eating the chocolates, and when Shirley was working on Easter eggs, one of her workmates threw a piece of broken egg at her while they were having their tea break. Shirley broke off a piece and ate it before throwing the rest of it back. When she looked up, the dreaded overlooker, Noreen, was bearing down on her. 'Are you eating?' Noreen said. Shirley could feel her face going red. Her mother had always told her that the worst possible thing was to tell a lie, so she quickly swallowed the chocolate then opened her mouth wide and said, 'Pardon?' Noreen gave her a filthy look and stalked off towards the other end of the room.

Shirley and another young packer were also hauled up before Noreen when two of the Black Magic boxes they had been packing were found to be missing the makeweight chocolates that were supposed to be added when the boxes were light. For some reason, the Brazil nut centres always caused problems and the check-weigher who stood at the end of the conveyor belt and weighed their work to make sure that they had packed the right quantity of sweets or chocolates, and that each box had the necessary minimum weight printed on the outside of it, would be calling out 'lights' or 'heavies' as the boxes passed her. Whenever the call was 'lights', another packer had to add an extra chocolate as a makeweight.

On this occasion, Noreen accused Shirley and the other young packer of eating the makeweights and gave them a warning that any repetition would lead to a suspension, though that threat, whether or not it was subsequently carried out, was often used as much to send a warning to the others as to punish the wrongdoer herself. 'People were always being suspended or threatened with suspension,' Maureen said, 'and it was a big thing for them, because they'd lose a day's pay.' In Cream Packing you could even be suspended for singing. Working in the Smarties department, Maureen and the other girls used to sing all the time, and it was the same in most of the other departments – workers could sing all day long if they wanted to, because it was felt to be good for productivity and morale.

But in the Cream Packing department, Noreen would only let the girls sing for the three-quarters of an hour that *Music While You Work* was playing over the loudspeakers.

Although there was a programme of the same title on the BBC Light Programme (the forerunner of Radio 1 and Radio 2), Rowntree's *Music While You Work* was home-produced, from a room in the main corridor, where originally a woman employee, and later a man, played records that were relayed over the Tannoys to the various departments. Workers could leave requests, and if it was someone's birthday or anniversary the Rowntree's disc jockey would play them a record. Employees could also take in their own records and ask for them to be played, and there was huge excitement in 1962 when Sue Mizzi's husband, who was in the Army and stationed on a base with US soldiers, sent her a copy of the new Elvis record 'Return to Sender', which hadn't been released in Britain at the time. Sue took it into the factory and as soon as it was played, she was surrounded by girls asking her how she had got hold of it and whether she could get them a copy, too.

While other workers carried on singing even after *Music While You Work* had finished – one of them, Joyce Burnett, says she and her friends 'used to sing from going in first thing in the morning to coming out at night' – in Cream Packing, as soon as the programme had ended, Noreen banned the girls from singing and threatened them with suspension if they carried on. Some of the girls responded with a defiant little ditty of their own:

> Music While You Work *has ended,*
> *If you sing, you'll get suspended.*

There were worse punishments than suspension for those who fell foul of the overlookers. Girls were sometimes sacked for taking chocolates, though there was a suspicion that this was used as a means of getting rid of poor or troublesome workers as much as a reflection of the crime. While working on the Kit Kat line, one woman, Joan Drake, noticed a worker being frogmarched away by two burly men. She later found out that they were private detectives hired by Rowntree's, and the man was said to have had eighty bars of chocolate hidden inside his overalls. She never saw him at the factory again. On another famous occasion the police were summoned and a woman worker was actually arrested in front of her colleagues for taking chocolates, though in her case it was again not a matter of her pinching an occasional chocolate from the production line but of smuggling out large quantities and selling them. Once more, there was a suspicion that the arrest had been carried out in such a public way as a warning to the rest of the workforce.

Sometimes there were other things than Noreen's arbitrary rules, foul temper and threats of suspension for Shirley to worry about. She was working on the line one day with a stack of large wooden trays full of chocolates piled up alongside her work table. The girl across from her suddenly looked up and gave a scream. When Shirley followed her gaze, she saw that the chocolates that she was about to pack into the boxes seemed to be moving. When she took a closer look, she discovered that the tray was alive with brown beetles. They turned out to be flour beetles, which eat a wide range of foods, including chocolate. That batch of chocolates had to be destroyed, the production line halted and Shirley and the other girls transferred to other duties for the rest of the day, while the cleaning and maintenance staff cleaned everything until it shone and fumigated the storeroom where the beetles had been hatching.

Until they got used to the work, Shirley and the other new girls on the production line in Cream Packing used to end each day with an aching back from stooping over their table or conveyor belt for hours on end; Maureen still sees women today who have a permanent stoop from the years that they spent working on the line at Rowntree's. The work was hard and relentless with never a moment to relax, but Shirley tried to console herself with the thought that since she never had time to bite her nails any more, after years of ugly, badly bitten nails, hers were now growing nicely; she even bought some nail polish to celebrate.

Maureen was still often out with Peter in the evenings, but on other nights she and Shirley would go out together. The two sisters were very different, 'chalk and cheese', Maureen says, 'but with only eighteen months between us, we grew up close and we stayed very close, best friends as well as sisters'. They did not have a lot of money, but they used to find ways to go out nearly all the time, doing things that did not cost much, or were even free, like cake-decorating classes at Rowntree's and the dance classes that they went to five nights a week. They did not drink – their parents did not approve and they were too young anyway – so their only expense was an occasional glass of orange juice. There were many other ways of filling their off-duty hours without spending money. As an older employee, Dot Edwards recalls, 'Rowntree's laid on plenty of entertainment in your time, though not in theirs of course. There were all sorts: classes in just about everything you could think of, outings, films and plays, and sports and swimming galas.'

Maureen and Shirley also did classes during Day Continuation at Rowntree's, which now occupied one day a week for girls aged sixteen and under. First thing in the morning there was an assembly, and then a series of classes that might include PT, cookery, sewing, woodwork, singing, dancing, art, maths, biology or English. The classes were very popular with the girls, not only because they were a change from factory routine, but also because on Day Continuation they started the working day an hour or so later than usual and then went home at 4.20 p.m., an hour and ten minutes earlier than when they were working on the production line. 'We loved our day release classes,' Maureen says. 'We had the chance to wear something nice for a change because, as we weren't going on the production line, we didn't have to wear the usual overalls and turban. We got a bit of a lie in because we didn't start till half past eight or nine o'clock, we had a tea break in the afternoon as well as the morning, which we never got on our normal work days, and we finished early as well. They had a lovely gym there and we had a wonderful deep, hot bath at the end of PT.'

The baths, in a series of small bathrooms, were compulsory and had already been run for them when the girls returned to the changing rooms, and unlike some of their workmates at Rowntree's, they were not rushed in and out of the baths within two minutes, so they had plenty of time to enjoy the hot water. A bath was a rare treat for Maureen and Shirley, since unless they paid through the nose for it, there was no provision for them to have anything other than a cold-water wash at their digs. Other employees were also allowed to use the baths on payment of a modest fee, though fewer now needed to make use of that facility than in the pre-war and immediately post-war years when, with few houses having bathrooms and greedy boarding house keepers charging their lodgers as much as a shilling for a bath, Rowntree's workers could use the baths at work for just twopence, though they did have to provide their own soap and towel.

If Rowntree's attempts to give their young employees a continuing education were generally welcomed, the company's concern for their welfare could sometimes be over-intrusive. More than one young girl was reported to her parents by her overlookers for being spotted 'mixing with the wrong type of person', even if the sighting had occurred outside working hours in the girl's own free time. Maureen and Shirley escaped such unwelcome attention, and that was perhaps just as well, because in addition to going to the 'respectable' dances at the New Earswick Folk Hall, Maureen also once took Shirley to the De Grey Rooms, a place their mother had forbidden them to go because she had heard bad things about it and thought it was a den of iniquity. They went anyway, but took the precaution of telling their mother that they were going to a dance at the Folk Hall.

Maureen wore a brand-new yellow shift dress that had cost her nineteen shillings and elevenpence (about eighteen pounds today) and a new pair of shoes that were three pounds. Her mum always insisted that Maureen got her shoes from Saxones, which she felt was better quality than most of the other stores, but three pounds was more than Maureen's entire weekly wage, so she went in and chose a pair, put a deposit on them and then went back every week to pay off a bit more until she had cleared the cost and could take them home.

The De Grey Rooms were by then some way past their prime, with peeling wallpaper, damp stains on some of the walls and moth-eaten curtains at the windows, but with the lights turned low and a spotlight sparkling from the revolving glitter ball hanging from the ceiling, they had a certain tawdry glamour. Maureen and Shirley had a great time, dancing non-stop all evening, but it turned out that their mother might have been right, if not about the De Grey Rooms, then about the surrounding area, because her daughters were 'kerb-crawled' as they walked back through the darkened streets afterwards and were scared out of their wits, though in the end they got home safely. It was a long time before either of them could be persuaded to go back to the De Grey Rooms after that.

Maureen had three best friends: Rita, Helen and Maggie. Rita and Helen were country girls like Maureen; they used to like going to classes and were rather quiet and shy. Maggie was much more interested in a good night out. Maureen says:

> *She was totally different to me, but we got on like a house on fire. I have never smoked and I didn't touch alcohol until after I was married, whereas Maggie used to drink and smoke, had her hair dyed blonde, and did all the things that my mother used to hate. She went to dance classes with Shirley and me just once, because it wasn't her sort of thing at all, but we'd go to the Empire ballroom together, another place that my mother certainly did not approve of. Maggie was very slim and a tiny little thing, and a real magnet for boys. She had a baby outside marriage to a man who was a gorgeous-looking lad. He looked like a pop star and she was determined to have him, and by the time they eventually got married, she already had a daughter by him and was pregnant with another child, a son. However, they didn't stay married for long because her husband had a serious drink problem and eventually became one of York's*

'famous alcoholics'. I saw him not so long ago. He came up to me, breathing alcohol fumes all over me even though it was only half past nine in the morning, and said, 'Don't I know you?' So I said, 'I don't think so,' and just kept on walking.

14

Dorothy

In 1956, while she was working in Cream Packing, Dorothy met a good-looking, dark-haired young man called Rodney Pipes. He had been away doing his National Service for two years, but when he came out of the Army, he began working at Rowntree's and was assigned to the machines in Dorothy's department on shift work. He came from Crayke, near Easingwold, and he used to cycle into work every day, nearly thirty miles there and back. If one of the girls on the machines failed to turn up for work, one of the men would often be put on the conveyor to make up the numbers. It was the first time in Rowntree's history that men had ever been on the machines; it had always been women's work before then.

Dorothy found herself working next to Rodney one day. They chatted away and, she says:

Rod and I just seemed to click. From then on he was always following me about, wherever I'd go, he'd be there as well. I was already going out with a boy at the time, but I gave him up to go out with Rod. The other girls had seen us looking at each other, and put two and two together, so they'd try and fix it so that he had to come on the machine where I was – even the overlooker was in on it! After a while they took Rodney off

> *that job and he went on to taking the goods away from the end of the machines, but when* Music While You Work *was on – and us girls used to sing our heads off to it – if a soft song came on that both Rod and I liked, the girls would all say, 'He's here!' and I'd look up and he'd be stood at the end of the machine, waving to me.*

The Tannoy system was normally used only to play music, but Rowntree's made an exception in 1955 when the local football team, York City, which had spent most of its life in the basement divisions of the Football League, got to the semi-final of the FA Cup – it was the first time in its entire history that the club had done so. Rowntree's broadcast the semi-final match against mighty Newcastle United live over the Tannoys at the factory. 'Every single person in the factory was listening,' Dorothy says, 'even if, like me, they didn't really like football. It was a real novelty.' When York drew the first match, Rowntree's also broadcast the replay, but the fairytale ended there as Newcastle won two–nil.

Once a year in March, everyone who worked at Rowntree's was paid a bonus, a share of the profits the company had made that year, in proportion to their normal earnings. It was a very welcome lump sum, because few of Rowntree's employees were able to save much out of their modest weekly wages, and the bonus often enabled them to pay the deposit on a 'big ticket' item, like a holiday or a washing machine. 'I used to laugh at my grandmother at bonus time,' Dorothy says, smiling at the memory. 'My dad had still kept on living at my grandma's, and when it came to the time for the profit share, she always had her clean pinny on and there'd be something special for his dinner. But he always looked after her anyway, he really did.

He never remarried, and because she'd taken care of us while he was away in the Army, he made sure to look after her; I think he felt very beholden to her.' Thanks to the bit of extra made from the profit-share scheme, at Easter their dad always made sure that there was something extra for their grandmother, and a shiny new pair of shoes for the girls.

'That bonus was a nice, tidy sum of money,' Dorothy says, 'and at Easter 1957, Rod and I got engaged with our share. I was twenty-one on 4 July 1957 and Rod and I got married on the twenty-seventh, at Clifton Church.' In her flat near the city centre, among all the photographs of her children and grandchildren, Dorothy still has a lovely wedding photograph of her and Rod cutting the cake on their big day. They are both breaking into laughter and look as if they could not possibly be any happier. She did not have the luxury of buying a new wedding dress and instead obtained her dress from one of the girls at work, but you would not know that to look at it – it fits her as if it was made for her. She looks radiant in the white, high-necked gown with long sleeves and dozens of satin-covered buttons running up the front of the dress to a satin collar.

'It's funny,' she says, 'because the first time I ever saw that photograph of us cutting the cake was when it appeared in the local paper. Like Rod's family, the wedding photographer, Mr Caperly, also came from Crayke. He was very keen, in fact perhaps too keen, because he even followed us down to the station when we set off on honeymoon, and he was so pleased with that particular photograph that he put it in the window of his shop to advertise his services. He didn't even do us a copy of the print and I didn't get hold of it for years. When I finally did, it still had his advertising label stuck across the bottom of the picture.'

The reception was at a church hall in Water Lane, and because they did not have much money, all the food was home-made. Rod's mum and a lot of her friends and neighbours all got together and baked, and they arranged some transport and brought it all through to York from Crayke. 'They'd gone to a lot of trouble,' Dorothy says, 'with sandwiches and savouries, and they even brought little jellies with piped cream on top. They were set in little waxed paper bowls and somehow they all survived the journey in one piece. So that was our wedding.'

Dorothy and Rod went to Torquay for their honeymoon, and they had deliberately timed their wedding so that they could go on honeymoon during the Rowntree's holiday week, so they did not have to take any extra time off work. It was an attitude that would have delighted Joseph Rowntree, whose strong social conscience went hand in hand with a truly Victorian determination to extract, not just the last grain of cocoa from his raw material, but also the absolute maximum amount of work from those in his employ. One of his granddaughters used to delight in telling the tale of one of Joseph's employees who asked him for time off work because he was getting married the next morning. Joseph was said to have replied, 'Very well, and as it is such an important occasion, I won't expect you in until the afternoon.'

Dorothy and Rod may have had the holiday week for their honeymoon, but they set off with nothing at all in their pockets, Dorothy says, 'because we'd already spent almost all our wages and spare money on the wedding, the train tickets and the bed and breakfast for our honeymoon. I had kept a few shillings back for spending money, but just as I was leaving the house to go to the station, my grandmother asked me for the money for my keep. As I'd just got married, I thought she might have let me off it that week, but no, so that cleaned me out as well.'

When they got on the train to Torquay, there were three girls from the same department at Rowntree's as Dorothy, who had all had the same idea and got married on that same day. So they all finished up in the same carriage, on the same train together, going to Torquay for their honeymoons. The guard who came round to check their tickets got chatting to them and when he discovered that they worked at Rowntree's, he told them another tale about Joseph Rowntree. 'My dad knew him,' the guard said, 'and he said he was the most upright man he ever met. One of the other guards ushered Mr Rowntree into a first-class carriage of a crowded train one day. When he protested that he only had a third-class ticket, the guard said, "It's all right, Mr Rowntree, don't let that worry you, sir," and he slammed the door and waved the train off. You couldn't change carriages once the train was moving, so he just had to sit there, but do you know what?' He paused to make sure he had their attention. 'The next time Mr Rowntree caught the train, he bought a first-class ticket and then insisted on sitting in third class to make up for the other journey.'

'All right if we go first class to make up for that, then?' Rod said, but the guard just smiled and moved on.

When they got to Devon, Rod and Dorothy stayed at a bed and breakfast place just outside Babbacombe and, she says, 'It was lovely. It was really hot that week and it was just like being abroad. I came back ever so tanned, but Rodney was very fair-skinned and he came back still looking just like a pint of milk. We really enjoyed it and we always said we'd go back to Babbacombe one day, but sadly we never managed to.'

When they heard that Dorothy and Rod were getting married, her friends came from all over the factory to bring little presents for them. 'We'd just got our first little house,' Dorothy says, 'a two-up, two-down terraced house in Nunnery Lane, and they were coming up and saying, "Make use of this, we don't need it," and just bringing us all sorts of things. They set us up in our home really.' That house had cost them £500. They managed to save enough for the deposit and then paid the rest off at so much a week. There was no bathroom and an outside toilet in the yard, and no central heating of course, something only wealthy people could afford. There was just a coal fire in the kitchen, so in winter there was often ice on the inside of the windows as well as on the outside. They had a tin bath and, in later years, Dorothy used to put it outside in summer, like a paddling pool for the children to play in. There was a fire oven to cook with, and they had no labour-saving devices at all. The house was classified as slum housing and, says Dorothy, 'I suppose it was pretty primitive by modern standards, but we were as happy as Larry there. We had to move in the end though, because they were going to pull the houses down, but a friend from work who lived up at Muncaster heard of a house that was coming vacant up there, and she told me about it, so we got in quick, got the house and moved up there.'

Dorothy worked at Rowntree's for another year after they were married. She could only work part time, though, as the company rule preventing married women from working full time remained in force, and she left when she became pregnant with their first child, a boy they christened Gary. She says:

Before I left, the other girls were giving me clothes and all sorts of little things for the baby. That was what they were like, they were just really kind, generous people. I remember when Pauline Musgrave, who worked at Rowntree's and was a really good swimmer, was picked to go to the Helsinki Olympics in 1952, and we had a collection for her, to fund her so she could go, because she wouldn't have been able to afford it otherwise. We had very good healthcare at Rowntree's, everything was there for you and you really were looked after. When I was pregnant, I wasn't put on lifting or anything like that, I just did what I could manage to do, and they made sure I went for my medicals and things like that. Mind you, there was no swinging the lead. My dad had an accident at work and crushed his hand in the machine, so he was off work for a while on sick pay, but if you were off sick, you could only go out until a certain time of night. If you were seen out late at night when you were supposed to be off sick, they'd want to know why and they'd say, 'If you're well enough to go out, you're well enough to go to work,' and they would stop your sick pay.

Fortunately for her dad, his injuries were treated swiftly by one of Rowntree's team of nurses, who worked shifts so that there was always someone available if accidents happened during the evening or night shifts. He was then sent to the City General Hospital for further treatment, carried there in Rowntree's own ambulance. His injuries, though serious, were not permanent and he was back at work within a few weeks.

Gary was born in 1958 and a second boy, Graham, followed in 1961, but by then Dorothy's father had died. He had never remarried and had never had a home of his own, preferring to live with his mother until she died, after which he moved in with Dorothy's sister in Huntington Road. He was kind and loving to his daughters, but he was a reticent character who kept his thoughts and feelings very much to himself, and he took a lot of family secrets to the grave. Dorothy says:

> *He was a quiet man, very tall and quite well made. He was a gentle giant and a lovely dad, but he was quiet. He never used two words where one would do; my grandmother used to say, 'If words were coins, he'd not have spent his first pound yet.' He never, ever spoke about the war and what he'd done in it, and he never told me anything about my mum either. I still don't know the first thing about her. I was given a photograph not so long ago of my mother and my sister on the beach at Scarborough before I was born. Although my mum has her arms folded in front of her, so it's hard to be sure, I'd love to think she was pregnant with me when the picture was taken – my sister looks to be about five years old in the picture, and that's the age difference between us. It's one of the few photographs I have of my mum. Although my sister's much older than me, she was still only seven when my mum died and she doesn't really remember her either, so we know almost nothing about her. Maybe in later years my dad would have opened up more and told us things and we would have got to talk about her, but it wasn't to be. I was just six weeks off having my second boy when my dad had a heart attack and died. He was only fifty-one.*

Dorothy decided not to go back to work again until 1967, when Gary was nine and Graham seven, by which time she'd been away from the factory for almost ten years. She had made a conscious decision to be at home with her family and to make the most of the boys' early years. 'I'd had quite a break,' she says, 'but I went back to Rowntree's and after all that time there were still all the same women there, still doing the same jobs, so I was straight back into the swing of it. I began working in Enrobing, just doing afternoons, and I was paid one pound seventeen and six a week for fifteen hours, so it wasn't a great wage, but it was a little extra towards the family budget, and I was back at home by the time the boys came in from school.'

Dorothy was skilful and experienced enough to adapt to working on the enrober again without any problems, but it could be a daunting experience for some of the younger girls, largely because, as Sue Mizzi recalls, 'There were four right well-known women who worked there. Everyone was frightened of them, though no one knew why, or if they did, they weren't telling.' When Sue and her friend were sent to work there, no one, least of all the intimidating foursome, told them what they were supposed to be doing, so her friend just pointed towards them and said to Sue, 'Let's just copy them.' They did exactly that and, perhaps as a result, they got on like a house on fire with the fearsome foursome, though at the end of the shift they were still little wiser about what their job was supposed to be, nor whether they had been doing it right or wrong.

When Dorothy had been working in Enrobing for a while, she was transferred to packing After Eight mints. Rowntree's still did not have a machine that could feed the chocolates into the small brown envelopes, so all the packing was done by hand. The After Eights used to come down the conveyor and the packers had to pick the mints up, slip them into the envelopes and then put them into the cartons, exactly twenty-six in each one. 'It got a bit monotonous now and again,' Dorothy says, 'but you moved around the conveyor so you did different jobs on the machine, which made it a bit more interesting.'

However, Dorothy had not been working there long when she had to hand in her notice yet again after discovering to her considerable surprise that she was once more pregnant, with her third boy, Julian. 'When I left,' she says, 'they were all teasing me and saying, "Don't worry, come straight back and bring him in with you, we can wash all his nappies in the big sink in the corner there!" where we used to clean the pans that had chocolate in them.' Not long after the birth she did go back again, though not with Julian in tow. She worked in Enrobing again at first, and then went into the Smarties department, and, she says, 'It was an education, the way they were made.' Tubes of Smarties had previously been filled by hand, work which was so repetitive and mechanical that even the most conscientious worker was sometimes tempted to improvise a little just to alleviate the boredom. Sarah James, whose mother worked in the Gum department on the Smarties production line, was 'amazed to hear my mother talking of deliberately putting all the same coloured Smarties together in one tube rather than mixing them all up. My mum! Hardly a rebel!'

Now the company was mechanizing the process and bringing in new machines to produce giant-sized tubes of Smarties as well as the standard tubes, and a whole new team of women was brought together to work on the product. None of them had ever done any of the work before. 'These tubes came through on the conveyor belt,' Dorothy recalls, 'and you had to take them off three at a time, put them in a rack and pass them to the next person to Sellotape the end of the tube and then pass them on again to the packers. Well, I'm not kidding you, you only needed the Sellotape to go a bit wrong and you would start falling behind, but the tubes were still coming down the belt and they started to pile up. We'd be covered in bits of Sellotape with tubes still coming down the belt and falling off onto the floor. We didn't know what to do and we couldn't stop laughing about it, so the overlooker really got cross with us. Eventually we did get the hang of it, but while we were learning it was hilarious.'

Another girl sent to work in Packing and Despatch found Sellotape to be just as much of a health hazard there. She was armed with a Sellotape 'gun' and told that her job was to seal boxes ready for despatch. Unfortunately she had never seen a Sellotape gun before and didn't know how to work it. When the first box came down the line she started the tape all right and stuck one end of it to the box, but she didn't know how to stop it and the tape 'just kept going on and on and on. Before long it was not only stuck to the box, it was also stuck to me, and in fact it was stuck to just about everything else as well.' By now she was blushing crimson and every eye in the room was on her. Finally one of the other women came down and said, 'Don't you know what to do?' She shook her head, saying, 'Nobody showed me.' The woman showed her how to do it in two seconds flat, and having disentangled herself from the Sellotape, she managed to do the rest of her boxes without further mishap.

It was a measure of the contentment that Dorothy had found in her family life with Rod that she could take in her stride things that would have had her in tears when she was younger. She loved her work and the company of the women she worked alongside, but the best moments of the day were always those that she spent in the company of her family.

Dorothy continued working at Rowntree's until 1976, when she was forty, and she then left the company for the last time. 'I had to finish then,' she says, 'because my youngest, Julian, had started going to school and I wanted to be there to see him off to school in the morning and be there again when he finished in the afternoon – you couldn't afford to pay people to look after your children then, and there were no family members to do it for me, like my grandmother had done for my father – so I needed to work hours that fitted in with that. There were no shifts like that at Rowntree's so I left the factory for the last time and found other work.'

The 'Swinging Sixties' were long over and in their off-duty hours, in place of miniskirts and bouffant, heavily lacquered beehive hairstyles, the younger Rowntree's girls were now beginning to appear for work in punk-style clothing and with spiky, heavily gelled and highly coloured hairstyles. One girl in the department did not want to waste her money on hair colouring, and so bleached the ends of her hair blonde by dipping it into a bucket of Domestos.

Alongside the superficial changes, Dorothy had also noticed a difference in the atmosphere inside the factory. Although there was far less tension between management and unions at Rowntree's than in many other British industries, the factory was not immune to the disputes and industrial strife that was scarring the 1970s, and the sense of being part of a community of workers that had always marked out Rowntree's in the past was now fast fading.

'It was a shame that I had to leave in one way,' Dorothy says, 'because I was never happier than I was at Rowntree's, and it had been such a lovely atmosphere, but that did change a lot after Mackintosh came in.' In 1969, Rowntree's merged with the Halifax toffee maker Mackintosh. Coachloads of Rowntree's employees went to the House of Commons to petition against the merger, and they arrived back in York really late at night, but still had to go into work as usual early the next morning. As soon as they got there, they were greeted by workmates saying, 'You did a lot of good, didn't you?' It turned out that the merger had gone through the previous evening, while they were still on their way back from London. One woman spoke for many when she lamented the change, remembering how at one time, 'I couldn't get to work quick enough to get to chat with my friends and enjoy all the jokes. It changed after the Rowntree-Mackintosh merger, though. It wasn't the friendly, family firm it was before.'

Dorothy agrees:

There just didn't seem to be the same friendliness after that. It wasn't just that the Rowntree's company was beginning to change by then, because some of the people who worked there were also very different from the ones I'd worked with when I was young. I was working on Smarties by then and some of the women on the machines were lunatics. It was all piecework and they wanted to earn the money, so if they got someone who was a bit slow with them, they used to play hell. That's what finished me in the end, because they got greedy. For the sake of two or three pence, these girls were getting nasty with someone who was doing their best but was still learning, and they'd be saying, 'Oh, don't have her on here, we don't want her.'

I feel sorry for eighteen-year-olds now though, because things are much worse now; there just aren't the jobs any more. When I was young we could just walk out of school and go straight into a job. There were three confectionery companies in York: Rowntree's, Terry's and Craven's; there were the railways, the carriage works, the glass works, the button factory, Armstrong's and a lot of other smaller factories you could work in, but now, even with a good education, what is there at the end of it? It's soul-destroying to see it – what have we done to the place?

15

Maureen

A few months after Shirley had joined her in York, when Maureen was still seventeen, their mum and dad borrowed £100 as a deposit on a Victorian house on East Parade in the Heworth district of the city, and moved there with the girls' brothers and youngest sister. The family was then reunited, with Maureen and Shirley able to move out of their digs and live with their parents again. On the day they moved, 15 April 1961, they were full of excited chatter and laughter as they packed their suitcases, but no matter how carefully they folded them, they now had far more clothes than they could squeeze into their cases. 'We'll have to make two trips,' Maureen said, but now that they were on the brink of leaving their hated digs, neither of them could bear the thought of having to return once more. Instead, in fits of laughter, they began dressing themselves in layer after layer of their most bulky clothing.

With a final look around the room, they stumbled down the stairs, bumping their bulging suitcases from step to step, then dropped the key on the hall table and slammed the door behind them for the last time. Their elation soon began to fade. They could not afford to take a taxi and now faced a two-mile walk from their digs to the house at Heworth wearing several layers of clothes and carrying their leaden suitcases. Even worse, it was unusually hot for so early in the year, with the sun burning down out of a cloudless sky. They plodded slowly up the road, pausing frequently to rest their aching arms and wipe the sweat from their brows. Every time they heard a vehicle approaching, they gazed behind them, desperately hoping that some knight in shining armour, though more likely in a Ford Popular, would take pity on them and give them a lift, but each time the car swept past and disappeared into the distance in a cloud of dust and exhaust fumes. The girls trudged onwards, their footsteps slowing with almost every yard and the rest breaks becoming more and more frequent, and longer and longer. It took them two hours to cover the two miles, and by the time they got to the new house, both of them were drenched in sweat and almost collapsing from exhaustion.

Having moved back in with their parents, they paid their mum one pound a week for their board and lodging. Most of the girls who worked at Rowntree's had to pay a lot more than that to their mothers, but Maureen and Shirley's mum refused to take any more from them, leaving them with what seemed to them then to be a lot of spending money. Until he moved to York, their dad had been working at Northern Dairies at Holme on Spalding Moor, and he used to cycle all the way there from Hayton, nearly ten miles away, in all weathers. Life became a lot easier for him after they moved into the city, because he took a job at Rowntree's as well, working in the Smarties department like his eldest daughter, so she would often see him during the day. It was a relief to both girls to be back home with their parents, not least because there was now something a lot more substantial than Cheese Whiz or potted meat on the table for their tea every night.

It was a nice area and a lovely house, though even in the early 1960s it was still by no means unusual to find houses with only the most minimal facilities. The house in East Parade had a bathroom with a bath in it, but there was no hot water supply other than a back boiler on the kitchen fire, so if there was no fire lit, the only way to get water for a bath was to heat it in saucepans on the stove or in the washing machine and then carry it up to the bathroom one pan at a time. 'I was usually the one who had to do it,' Maureen remembers, 'because, though she probably wouldn't admit it, Shirley was a bit lazy and it was hard work carrying all that water upstairs. So almost every time, she was happy to share my bathwater. I'd go first, which was only fair having done all the work, but then she'd say, "Oh, leave the water in," and no matter how dirty it was, she would be straight in after me.' They used to use the washing machine when they were washing their hair as well, bending over the sink and rinsing their hair with water from the outlet pipe of the washer.

There was an outside toilet in the yard, but almost invariably the light was not working because every time a light bulb went anywhere in the house, someone would pinch the bulb from the toilet to replace it. The girls hated going to the outside loo, especially after dark, but Shirley hated it the most because she was frightened of spiders and the loo was full of them. There was rarely any proper loo paper, and Maureen or one of the other children would have the job of tearing up squares of newspaper and spiking them on a nail sticking out of the back of the toilet door. Even when there was the luxury of a toilet roll, it was always an Izal one, with hard, shiny paper that was, if anything, even less pleasant to use than old newspaper.

Maureen and Peter had been going out together for over two years and had even got engaged, but they eventually split up, mainly because someone else had caught Maureen's eye. She told Peter she was finishing with him and started going out with a boy who had a scooter instead of a motorbike. 'So I went from a rocker to a mod,' she says now with a laugh. Even though mods looked smarter, tending to wear sharp suits rather than the leather jackets and jeans that bikers wore, it's doubtful whether Maureen's parents would have been much more approving of their daughter's choice of a mod boyfriend than they were of a rocker. A series of bank holiday riots at seaside resorts in the early 1960s, with running battles between groups of mods and rockers, and the resulting lurid media coverage, had led to calls from MPs and police for tougher penalties on hooliganism, and much soul-searching about the decline of the 'moral fibre of the nation'. In that feverish climate, the mere sight of a group of rockers on their bikes or mods on their scooters was enough to provoke something approaching horror in the hearts of the older generation. Maureen's church-going, strongly moral and conservative parents certainly fitted that description, but in the event she managed to persuade them that her new boyfriend was a steady, respectable lad, and not some feral hooligan.

In addition to changing boyfriends, Maureen was also ready for a change in her working life and she left Rowntree's before she was eighteen years old. 'Silly girl,' she says now, shaking her head at the memory. Had she stayed there until her eighteenth birthday, she would have been on the full adult rate of pay, much more than she could earn anywhere else in York. She was a fast worker and a real hard grafter and Rowntree's were so eager to keep her that they offered her the chance to work anywhere she wanted in the factory, from the production line to the offices, but 'nearly eighteen, nearly ready to go onto the big money, I was stupid and I turned them down', she says.

Maureen was bored with the work she was doing at Rowntree's and had made up her mind that it was time for a change, so she left the factory to go and work as a waitress at Shepherds Café in The Shambles in the centre of York. It was one of the most atmospheric streets in Britain, where each storey of the medieval buildings jutted out beyond the one below so far that they cast the pavements into shadow, and it was said that you could reach out of the window on one side and shake hands with your neighbour across the street. Such sights, as well as the glories of the Minster, were beginning to draw tourists to the city, and the number of cafés and restaurants to serve them was growing, but wages in catering were very low and Britons had not really embraced the concept of tipping at the time – some still haven't! – so Maureen's earnings were a lot lower than they would have been had she stayed at Rowntree's.

After Maureen left, Shirley didn't stay at the factory very long either, going off to work at Terry's instead. Although Rowntree's and Terry's were direct competitors, the companies' rivalry never really involved their employees. 'There wasn't really any rivalry,' Maureen says, 'because you could get a job anywhere in those days. You could walk out of one job and into another one the next day, so no one really thought about rivalry or anything. We'd meet women from Terry's when we were out and they were friendly enough. You just worked where the money was best or where it suited you best.' However, Shirley did not stay very long at Terry's either, and walked out on them after a dispute with an overlooker. 'She's a bit fiery, is Shirley,' Maureen says. 'She's not so bad now, but she used to be really fiery; I think it's the red hair that does it.'

Soon after starting work at the café, Maureen parted company with her mod boyfriend and, through an introduction from one of the other waitresses, she then met and began going out with a boy called Brian, who was serving in the Air Force and based near York at Church Fenton. They had a whirlwind romance and were married when she was eighteen, by which time she was already carrying her first child, a son they named Brian after his father. They split up just two years later when she was twenty, even though there was a second son, Peter, on the way by then – 'life in the fast lane', she says now with a wry smile. Her husband had been given a short-term posting to Huntingdon and Maureen's mum persuaded – in fact ordered – her not to go with him, insisting that with one baby and another on the way, she needed to be at home so her mother could help to look after them. Maureen's husband was probably already having an affair while he was in Huntingdon because, as she says, 'He always used to buy me presents when he was doing something naughty, and every other day he used to send me a couple of little bottles of Tia Maria through the post that he must have bought in the NAAFI at his base, so I was already thinking that something was up.'

He left the Air Force soon afterwards and returned to York where he started working as a bus driver, but it didn't stop him from 'playing away', and when Maureen discovered that he was having an affair with a bus conductress, she threw him out and started divorce proceedings. What made it even worse in Maureen's eyes was that the bus conductress was 'an old woman, or that's how it seemed to me at the time, because I was only twenty and she was thirty-two, so she seemed old to me, and yet there was my husband having an affair with her.'

Attitudes were fast changing but, like with illegitimacy, there were still traces of the old stigma attached to divorce in those days, and it was not a pleasant experience for her. 'It wasn't good, that's for sure,' she says, suppressing a shudder even now at the memory of the acrimonious divorce, and the financial hardship and social problems it caused her. Divorced women in those days were often regarded with suspicion, if not outright hostility, by other women. There was a crude stereotype of divorcees as 'fast' and predatory towards married men, and now that Maureen was separated from her husband, the reaction of some women she'd thought of as friends was hurtful. However, others rallied round and supported her through those difficult times as she went through with the divorce, got herself a council flat and moved there with her two sons.

Despite the continuing problems in other areas of women's lives, that in itself was an indication of how far women had progressed. There is a gap between all generations, but arguably there has never been such a gulf as that which separated the pre- and post-war generations. Only twenty years separated Madge and Florence from Maureen, but it might as well have been a century, given how much the lives of women had been transformed in that time.

There was still a long way to go, but access to reliable contraception meant that, though it had not vanished entirely, for the first time the fear of unwanted pregnancy had been greatly diminished. When single, Maureen had been free to have a number of boyfriends without being labelled as 'easy'. When her marriage did not prove successful, divorce was no longer seen as a personal disgrace, and nor was Maureen as utterly financially dependent on her husband as Madge had been on hers. The rights of married women to have their own money and their own bank accounts, to work full time and pursue long-term careers if they wished, and to receive maintenance for their children from their former husbands and support from the state if it was needed, were no longer in doubt.

Despite these changes in society's attitudes, in practice life as a single parent on a low income was never less than a struggle for Maureen, but she coped, and within two years she was married again, though this time, she says, the decision to get married owed more to a lobbying campaign by her mother and grandmother than to her being head over heels in love. By now her brothers and sisters were old enough to babysit for her, but her parents, determined that she should have no opportunities to bring further unhappiness on herself nor 'shame' on her family through extra-marital affairs, continued to play a powerful role in her life and would only allow her brothers and sisters to babysit for her on nights when she was being chaperoned by her parents. 'I was only allowed to go out if I went with them,' she says. 'I could go to the working men's club with them at the weekend, but I had to stay at their house on those nights to rule out any chance of a bit of "hanky panky" with anyone I might have met while I was out, not that there was much chance of that when I was only out at a working men's club and under the constant, watchful gaze of my parents.'

However, she did meet her second husband, Michael, at the club. He was out for the evening with his brother and sister-in-law and they all got talking together. Maureen's parents approved of him and his relationship with Maureen developed from there. She went out with him a few times, but things might not have gone any further than that, had it not been for 'a bit of pushing' from her mother and grandmother. Maureen got on well enough with Michael and he was a pleasant, kind man, though undemonstrative and perhaps even a little dull; there was certainly no fire burning in Maureen's heart, just the words of her mother and grandmother echoing in her ears: 'Those boys need a father. When you've got two kids, you can't afford to be too fussy. He's a nice man and he's got a nice car, so what are you waiting for?' In the end she bowed to the pressure, convinced herself that they must be right, and married him.

They had two children together – a boy, Glen, and a girl they named Beverley – a brother and sister for her two sons from her first marriage. Maureen had gone back to work in 1974 when Beverley was two, mainly because she wanted, but could not afford, an automatic washing machine. She had a twin tub, but washing for four children, including nappies for the youngest, was hard work, so she thought, 'Right, if I want an automatic, I've got to work for it,' and she went back to Rowntree's twelve years after she had walked out. They were pleased to see her; there were still overlookers there who remembered her as an excellent worker, and in any case, although the dark clouds of world recession were looming, the last echoes of the boom years of the 1960s and early 1970s meant that Rowntree's were still hiring almost anyone who came through the door at the time.

Increasing affluence, falling prices and much greater availability of consumer goods and labour-saving devices were changing women's daily lives in ways that would have been barely credible to their parents' generation. Central heating was no longer found only in the houses of the well off, almost every home contained a television, even if many were still the old black-and-white sets rather than the newer, more expensive colour televisions and air travel and holidays abroad were no longer the exclusive preserve of the rich. Fridges and freezers had replaced meat-safes and larders; boilers, washboards, possers and all the other paraphernalia of hand-washing had given way first to twin tubs and then automatic washing machines; hand-operated carpet sweepers had been replaced by electric vacuum cleaners; and convenience foods, disposable nappies and a host of other things were making the tasks of keeping a house and raising children far less all-consuming and exhausting than had been the case in the pre-war years.

Although a married woman with children, Maureen was also now able to work full time if she chose. Rowntree's policy of only employing single women for full-time work had been creaking from the 1950s onwards. In the immediate post-war period, with the country almost bankrupt and crippled with stupendous debts, the domestic economy had stagnated for a while, but there had been such a desperate need for hard currency that there was a frantic export drive from all branches of British industry, including Rowntree's. Rationing continued for several years after the war, but Rowntree's avoided some of the problems caused by sugar shortages by helping to develop a new artificial sweetener, and as soon as restrictions began to be lifted, demand for confectionery soared as people flocked to indulge themselves in the little luxuries that had so long been denied to them.

The runaway demand at home and abroad – production almost doubled between 1950 and 1960 – left Rowntree's struggling to keep pace. With the rest of the British economy booming as well and jobs around every corner, it had become increasingly difficult to hire enough workers and the company experienced such a shortage of labour that it began actively recruiting workers from other districts, and even from overseas. The company was also willing to vary its normal working hours to accommodate the women who formed an ever-growing proportion of the workforce, and the evening 'twilight shift' from 6 p.m. to 9.30 p.m. was introduced, specifically to cater for married women with young children. 'They were that desperate for staff,' one of them recalls, 'that you could practically choose your own hours.'

In 1964, Miss Vale of the Rowntree's Employment department had even gone all the way to Malta to recruit girls to come and work at Rowntree's, because there were just not enough girls in Britain willing to work at the factory. She returned with a contingent of Maltese girls, some of whom worked for a year or two but then went back, while others made York their permanent home. Miss Vale was the head of the Women's Employment department but, like her predecessor, Miss Sherlock, she had been able to rise to those heady heights within the company only because she had chosen to remain single. Had she married, her career at Rowntree's would have peaked at a much lower level. However, the pressure to find more workers at last led to the policy of barring married women from full-time employment being ended in 1966. The Miss Vales and Miss Sherlocks of the future would now be able to combine marriage with a career.

Miss Sherlock was a legendary character and, as well as being head of the Women's Employment department, she also organized everything from the rents for the Rowntree's allotments to the company holidays. Workers would sign up for a holiday in Belgium, France, Switzerland or wherever that year's destination was to be, and would then contribute a weekly amount to the holiday fund to pay for it. Rowntree's also ran trains to Scarborough once a year for the annual works outing, with several trains needed to carry the numbers of employees who took part. Individual groups of workers would also organize trips on their own behalf, independent of anything Miss Sherlock and Rowntree's might be planning. The foilers (the women who wrapped the Kit Kat bars in aluminium foil) organized a trip to Blackpool one year that was known as 'The Foilers' Follies'. They arrived back at four o'clock in the morning, half asleep and already hungover, but still clutching their sticks of souvenir Blackpool rock.

Maureen went back to work on the Smarties production line in 1974, but she found that times had changed and it was no longer the same quiet workplace she had been used to. When she had first started at Rowntree's, it had all been hand-work, but by the time she went back for her second spell, the work had become heavily mechanized, and the noise of the machines meant she had to shout to talk to her neighbours on the line. However, unlike many married women, who tended to struggle when they returned to the factory after a long absence, she had no trouble getting back up to speed and seemed to pick it up straight away. Her job was often to stand in what was called 'the hole', topping up tubes of Smarties that the machines had not filled correctly. There was also a section on the floor above, used to pack the giant-sized Smarties tubes, where the work involved filling and weighing the large tubes and capping and Sellotaping the tops to seal them. The women moved around, swapping roles to alleviate the boredom of the work, and one of Maureen's preferred jobs was doing 'bitumen wrapping' – wrapping the outers in waterproof tar paper to protect them from damp while in storage or transit – which still involved some elements of skill and variety that had been almost entirely eliminated from other stages of the production process.

Every now and again there would be a new product, and workers from different departments would be transferred to the new line ready for the launch, sometimes in an air of secrecy that MI5 would have struggled to match. Some did not take off and were discontinued, but others, including the Yorkie bar, launched in 1976, were huge successes. Aimed at men, it was marketed as a chunkier, more 'butch' alternative to Cadbury's Dairy Milk, with television advertisements showing lorry drivers biting into Yorkie bars as if they were Desperate Dan eating a steel girder or a cow pie. A huge billboard was also erected at York railway station, greeting arriving passengers with the slogan: 'Welcome to York, where the men are hunky and the chocolate's chunky'. The word 'York' was formed from a three-dimensional image of a Yorkie bar, with the '–ie' part missing, as if bitten off by a giant.

Maureen worked at Rowntree's for another five years, until she left again in 1979. 'I worked evenings from 6 p.m. to 9.30 p.m.,' she says, 'and I found it a bit of a struggle getting the tea over with and the kids settled, and then setting off to work, and when a job came up at a York hospital, working during the day, in school hours, I took it.' In retrospect, it was probably not the best time to join the public sector, because the effects of the 'Winter of Discontent' were still being felt, including strikes by train drivers, refuse collectors, gravediggers, ambulance drivers and NHS ancillary workers, who blockaded hospital entrances in pursuit of their pay claim and forced many hospitals only to admit emergency cases. Margaret Thatcher's election victory that year heralded a relentless round of cuts to public expenditure, and though Maureen spent ten years as a hospital worker, the health authority, struggling to balance its budget as the squeeze on public sector spending tightened, was laying off an ever increasing number of workers. The consequence for those who remained in employment was that more and more work was piled onto them and, in the end, in 1989, Maureen said, '"I'm not having this," and I gave a month's notice.'

She was already working in a pub in the evenings to earn a little extra money, but she was beginning to feel she had been hasty in quitting her main job without another one to go to, when a friend told her that Rowntree's were taking on temporary workers for the Christmas rush. So she went back to the factory once more, although this time she worked in the Cream Packing department. The notorious overlooker, Noreen, was still in charge, but 'She was okay with me,' Maureen says, 'mainly because I think she'd grown old and mellowed quite a lot by the time I was in Cream Packing, so I didn't really see the worst of her. I knew her by reputation though, and Shirley had worked under her for a while when she really was the dreaded Noreen.'

Rowntree's had been taken over the previous year. After the Swiss-German confectioner Jacob Suchard had carried out a 'dawn raid' on Rowntree's shares in 1988, Suchard's Swiss rivals Nestlé, the world's largest food producer, launched a rival bid. There was vociferous opposition from the Rowntree's board of directors, the workforce, the people of York, the City Council, Labour and Conservative MPs and the trustees of several of the Rowntree's charities, but despite pressure from many of his own backbenchers, Lord Young, then the Secretary for Trade and Industry, refused to refer the bid to the Monopolies Commission and the takeover duly went ahead. By the time Maureen returned to the factory the following year, she could detect a marked difference in the working atmosphere.

Shirley had also gone back to Rowntree's with Maureen and they worked together on the conveyor belt. Once more they had no trouble in picking up the pace of production line work, but Rowntree's blanket recruitment of workers to cope with the seasonal demand for chocolates meant that, either through a lack of skill or simple laziness, a lot of the other new recruits were not up to the job. Maureen says:

Without bragging, we were two of the hardest working people there. There were a few older women there who were top dogs and didn't normally like working with temps, but they didn't mind us because we were grafters. We could keep pace with them and we never took time off, so they'd even ask for Shirley and me to go on the machines with them, but they didn't like most of the temps, and with good reason, because a lot of them were bone idle. We'd been brought up to be hard-working and to take pride in what we did, but most of the temps were just there for the money and would do as little as they could get away with. You could be off sick for two days on full pay without having to produce a doctor's note, and some of them were taking days off almost every week, whereas in all the time we worked there, Shirley never took a day off at all and the only day off I ever took was my very last day before I finished, when I had a really stinking cold. Yet we weren't treated any better for working hard than some of the temps who were skiving and taking days off all the time. Nonetheless, the money we were earning was amazing and we would have stayed as long as they wanted us, but unfortunately we were only temps and as soon as the Christmas rush was over, we were laid off.

Sadly, by then Maureen's second marriage was heading for divorce. She was now in her late forties and she and Michael had been married for twenty-five years, but although they had been happy enough in the early stages of their marriage, it was never a Burton and Taylor romance, and as the years went by they found that they had less and less in common, and spent less and less time in each other's company. 'By the time we'd been together a few years, there was more life in a tramp's vest than there was in our bed at night,' Maureen says with a mischievous grin. 'We'd had separate bedrooms for a few years and when it got to our silver wedding, he said to me, "What do you want to do?" I didn't have to think about that for long, and I just said, "I want to get a divorce. We owe it to each other."'

They had an amicable divorce and soon afterwards Michael met somebody else, got engaged and then remarried. 'I wasn't bothered about any of that,' Maureen says, 'but Michael just didn't bother about any of the kids after the divorce; they never saw him at all. Beverley has a little girl, Millie, of her own now, who's going on for four years old and he's never even seen her, but he's the one who's missing out, because she's gorgeous.'

To make ends meet, Maureen had found a steady job in a cake shop, albeit at a lot less money than she had been earning at Rowntree's, but when they contacted her to ask her to come back again as a temp for the Easter rush, she turned them down at first, feeling it would be foolish to give up a full-time job for the precarious prospect of temporary work at Rowntree's, no matter how well paid it might be. However, in the end she decided to risk it and went back to the company for a fourth time. This time she was working in the Melangeur department, where the chocolate was made, but she found the work monotonous in the extreme, and there was even less of the camaraderie with the other women that she had so enjoyed when she had first worked there thirty years before, and in the end she left the factory for the final time in 1995, and spent the last ten years of her working life on the checkout at a Sainsbury's supermarket, before retiring in 2005.

Epilogue

Many of the women workers at Rowntree's believed that the sense of being part of a family business and a caring community of workers and managers was lost when the Rowntree family's close personal connection with the company ended; as one of their women employees said, 'It was never the same place after that.' Fears for the future were heightened when Rowntree-Mackintosh was the subject of a hostile takeover. Suchard made the first bid, but Nestlé then stepped in as 'white knights' and bought the company on much more favourable terms for Rowntree's shareholders and employees. Although many in York opposed any takeover at all, it is undeniable that the Nestlé bid was the more palatable option. (When Suchard, as part of Kraft, took over the other York chocolate factory, Terry's, they closed it down altogether.) The company was known as Nestlé-Rowntree for a number of years, but the Rowntree branding was eventually dropped.

Some of the people in York who had opposed the takeover reacted as if it were almost a bereavement, the loss forever of a vital part of their city and their lives. There were even fears that the factory would be closed and production transferred to Nestlé plants overseas. Pessimists approaching the site today might at first feel that their gloomy predictions have been vindicated, for parts of the complex of great red-brick buildings constructed on Joseph Rowntree's orders in the 1890s, and extended over the following half-century, have already been demolished and the remainder are now deserted, boarded up and fenced off, with 'For Sale' boards around them. 'When I die I'm going to haunt the Rowntree's factory,' says one long-term former employee, 'but there's not much left for me to haunt now. They've pulled down most of the old buildings where I worked. I can't understand why they did it, because they were beautiful buildings and if they wanted flats to sell, those buildings would have been perfect for that.'

Other parts of Rowntree's have also gone, like Dunollie, the Cocoa Works Rest Home in Scarborough, while the closure of the girls' Day Continuation School in 1970 seemed to many employees to symbolize the last rites for the old Rowntree's way of doing things, though, since the school-leaving age had been raised and the company no longer employed fourteen-year-olds, it was arguable that Day Continuation classes were no longer of use anyway. Nonetheless, that feeling was accentuated when the entire Guides department was closed down, and after ninety years of feeding the hungry workers, the Dining Block served its last meal in 2002 and is now part of the Nuffield Hospital. Even more recently, in 2012 the Rowntree's playing fields to the north of the factory were sold to York St John University.

However, the story is not all doom and gloom. Although production of some brands has indeed been moved elsewhere – Black Magic, Dairy Box and Smarties are no longer produced in York – Nestlé has invested approximately £200 million in new buildings and equipment in the city, and production now takes place in far more modern and energy-efficient surroundings than the cavernous rooms and draughty corridors of the old factory. It is one of the largest confectionery factories in the world, and as well as Aero, POLO mints, Milkybar and Yorkie bars, the factory produces one billion Kit Kats a year, making it one of the world's most popular confectionery brands. Even now the workforce still numbers close to 2,000, and the factory remains today, as it was 100 years ago, York's largest private employer.

Part of Joseph Rowntree's legacy also remains. The charitable trusts that bear his name continue his efforts to alleviate poverty, improve social housing and promote international peace, social justice and democratic reform. New Earswick is still there too, and continues to be a lovely place to live, a thriving village with its shops, post office and Folk Hall still intact, though in a sign of the times that would no doubt have had Joseph spinning in his grave, the sale of alcohol, banned under the covenant establishing the villages, was overturned in 1978 when 87 per cent of the villagers voted for its repeal, so that alcoholic drinks could be sold at dances and at other events in the Folk Hall.

The shop in York where the Rowntree's story began is still standing, though in another indicator of changing times, it now houses not a cocoa and chocolate emporium but a branch of Pizza Hut. Chocolate is still part of the fabric of the city, however, and visitor attractions, such as York's Chocolate Story, the York Cocoa House and the Rowntree's display at the York Castle Museum, testify to its enduring importance. To the shame of the city, however, nowhere in York is there a blue plaque to testify to the historic importance of the shop at 28 Pavement, Tanners Moat by the riverside, the Haxby Road factory, the New Earswick Folk Hall, or any of the multitude of other York buildings that played a part in the story of Rowntree's and the city it has dominated – and nurtured – for well over a century.

Although the company is now known as Nestlé, the citizens of York continue to refer to the factory as 'Rowntree's', even though it is now a quarter of a century since the takeover, and there is still immense local pride in the contribution to the city made by successive generations of the Rowntree family, their company and their charitable foundations.

The Rowntree's legacy perhaps lives on most strongly through the memories of those who worked there. Like Madge, Florence, Eileen, Dorothy and Maureen, the vast majority of former employees still feel great affection for the place where they spent their working lives. 'Working at Rowntree's was the happiest time of my life,' says Kath. 'We used to laugh and joke till tears rolled down our faces. It was more than just a job, it was a way of life, and our fellow workers were like family to us.' Another of her generation, Dot, adds, 'It was lovely working at Rowntree's. Some people used to play stink about it, but I never did. I don't care what anybody says, the management at Rowntree's were very, very good to the staff. We used to have our fall-outs sometimes and I'd mutter to myself, "I hate this so and so place," but I'd always be there the next morning and always looking forward to the day. I never regret a single day I spent at Rowntree's – never.'

For some of the younger employees, working at the factory may be 'just a job', but some of the women there still share the affection for the place that the earlier generations felt. 'When you think about it,' Sue Mizzi says, 'for a lot of people in York, this was their life … and it's been my life as well.' Aged sixty-nine, but still working as a cleaner at the factory, she is hoping they won't ever make her retire. 'The Queen's still working,' she says, 'and she's eighty-six, and if they can't make her finish work, they can't make me finish either.' Another employee from the company's Golden Age, Margaret, says, 'Rowntree's played a huge part in my life, from the beginning of my life, throughout my working life, and almost to the end of my life. Rowntree's is York; or at least, it was York.'

* * *

Although Michael remarried, Maureen remained on her own for a while and found that 'I quite liked it, to be honest. It was nice really, just looking after myself for the first time in many years, and pleasing myself – I could clean up and know it would stay that way – so I don't quite know how I got myself back into the position of being in a relationship again, but somehow it happened!' This time, twice burned, Maureen was in no hurry to get married to her new partner, Bob, but despite or perhaps because of that, the relationship has endured and they are still together now. She has been retired for seven years, but even now, aged sixty-seven, she has not given up work entirely, and does a few hours' private cleaning a week just to top up her pension. She still likes to go dancing as well when she gets the chance, though since her partner doesn't dance, she doesn't get many opportunities these days.

Looking back over her life, she says:

I've got loads of regrets in one way: I shouldn't have left Rowntree's; I shouldn't have got married at eighteen, though I suppose I must have had my reasons at the time; I should have got a bigger pension [part-time women workers couldn't join the Rowntree's pension plan and Maureen did not begin paying into a pension until she was working at Sainsbury's at the very end of her working career]. That part of my life is past now, but it's been a good life and an interesting one … sometimes too interesting! And whatever regrets I might have, they are nothing compared to the happiness I've had from my life. I couldn't be happier with my children and grandchildren, so I suppose I can't regret any of the steps that got me here, even the ones that really were mistakes. I've never been to a Rowntree's reunion, which I suppose is a shame in some ways, but I still bump into people I knew from there regularly around York, and it's always great to see them and have a chat about old times and a few laughs as well.

* * *

Rod left Rowntree's before Dorothy retired, and went to work for the council until he had to retire through ill health. They had been married for thirty-eight years when he died in 1995, aged sixty-two. The year after Rod's death, Dorothy's youngest son and his wife took her to Spain for a break, and organized and paid for everything. 'I'd never been abroad,' Dorothy says. 'In fact I'd never even been in an aircraft before, and I was a bit frightened when we took off but once we were up above the clouds, I relaxed and started to enjoy it, so much so that I said to my son, "If we get any higher, we'll be in heaven. I hope to God your dad doesn't come knocking on the plane window!"'

Dorothy's family remain very close and tight-knit. 'We were all brought up', she says, 'that if one member of the family was in trouble, everyone would rally round and help out, and that's what it's like to this day; I just like to have my family around me.' She regularly looks after her grandchildren and great-grandchildren and, she says, 'Although at times you think, "Oh God, I need five minutes here," I really like my family close by. I always try and see the good side of people as well. Some of my family tell me that I'm too trusting, but I can't change that and nor do I want to; the way I was brought up is the way I am. I know that things aren't like that any more, but I grew up in a different era, when you could go out or pop to the shops, leave your front door wide open and know that nothing would be touched.'

After she finished at Rowntree's, Dorothy worked as a home help until she retired, but she says:

I was quite sad about it really. As a home help I was just going round on my own all the time and I missed the atmosphere and the laughs of working with a lot of people. So although in one way I was glad to leave Rowntree's when I did, because it was no longer the place I remembered from when I was young, it was bittersweet as well because I'd had some very happy times there and I'd made some friends for life. Even the overlookers, once you got used to them, they were friends to you, though mind you, friends or not, you still had to abide by the rules. I worked with a lot of nice women there, and I'm still friends with many of them now, including two or three of them who were there almost from when I first started, back in 1950 when I was just a girl of fourteen. There were four of us who always seemed to be working together on the Smarties machines and we still all meet up and go out for lunch together. They were very happy times at Rowntree's and I've never regretted working there for a single moment.

* * *

Eileen retired in 1980 and, like many of her friends and workmates, it was a bittersweet moment when the time came to go. Eileen had also noticed a change in the atmosphere of Rowntree's once the family were no longer directly involved in running the business:

When I worked in the offices in the 1950s, a lot of the Rowntree family were still working there – Philip, Peter and Christopher Rowntree all worked there when I was there, and it was a very happy place when the family were in charge, but I think it changed after the merger with Mackintosh [in 1969]. The old Rowntree family cared about their workers, they really cared about their people, and I think that was lost when it ceased to be a family business and became just a business.

Relations were brilliant in the factory in my day. You had the odd spark, that was natural – I mean, there were 13,000 people working there at one time – but generally it was a good place to work. Supervisors, overlookers and charge-hands came from among the people working on the line – from there you applied to become a charge-hand – and for the most part they were fine. There was only one charge-hand I remember, who used to march up and down the conveyor and she really was like a 'death guard', everyone was a bit frightened of her. I had a bit of a go with her one day and she didn't like you to stand up to her – so she definitely didn't like me – and she could be nasty at times, but she was the only one, the others were all fine. It was a happy factory, not a miserable one; you didn't dread going to work, you looked forward to it.

I still see people in town that I knew at Rowntree's, though I can't remember half of them to be honest, but they say,

'Hello Eileen,' and I say 'Hello' back and then try and remember who they are. I went on a Rowntree's pensioners' trip about three years ago and a lady came up to me and said, 'Eileen Morgan!' I looked at her but I couldn't recognize her so I said, 'I'm sorry, I don't know who you are.' She said, 'Tang Hall Junior School.' I said, 'I left there when I was eleven, sixty-five years ago, how on earth did you recognize me?' And she said, 'Well, your hair's white now of course, but otherwise you haven't changed a bit.'

I made friends at Rowntree's who I'm still friends with now, and I do remember them! I have two really good friends who I met when I was on the cleaning staff in 1980 and they still come to see us. And one of them comes every week and takes me shopping, because we haven't got a car. One of the first people I met when I went back in 1961 was a girl I'd known as a child, but only to say 'Hello' to. We made friends and I'm still friends with her now. She comes to see me every few weeks and we have a real get-together for three or four hours and it's lovely. And when I hear music now, it often reminds me of different people I used to work with, who all had their favourite songs when we had the music playing and we all used to sing as we worked.

* * *

Florence retired from Rowntree's in 1983 when she was sixty – there was no choice about it, all their employees had to retire at that age. Then, at sixty-one and a half, chafing at the inactivity and in need of some extra money to make ends meet, she applied for a job as a cleaner at the University of York. When she went for the interview, the manager said to her, 'Will you tell me why you want to come and work here?'

'Yes, because I need the money,' Florence said.

'Fair enough,' he said and hired her on the spot. It was hard physical work, but she kept on doing it, riding her bike there and back as well, until 1993, when she turned seventy and retired for the last time. Her husband, Arthur, had already stopped work well before then and was not in the best of health by the time Florence retired. He had undergone two major heart operations, including one in which they'd fitted a metal valve to regulate his heartbeat. 'When he first had it fitted,' Florence recalls with a laugh, 'we were lying in bed that night and it was making so much noise that it was just like listening to someone playing table tennis. But it settled down after a day or so and after that you could barely hear it at all.' Arthur had always been a dapper dresser and a handsome man with perfect teeth, but after his two heart operations he was on Warfarin for years to thin his blood and in the end, she says, it rotted his teeth. By the time his heart finally gave out in 2005, they had enjoyed fifty-eight very happy years together.

Florence has no regrets at all about her life with Arthur, and very few about her working life at Rowntree's. 'I'd have liked to have had the chance to go to Dunollie some time – the Rowntree's rest home in Scarborough,' she says, 'but I was never poorly, so I never got the chance to do that. I did go to a reception in Harrogate when I'd done my twenty-five years working for Rowntree's. They gave me an inscribed gold watch to commemorate it. I still wear it and it still keeps good time.'

Rowntree's also paid for Florence to go to the Crown Hotel in Scarborough for a weekend on her retirement from the firm in 1983 – they did the same for everyone who had reached retirement age, though few of them could have matched Florence's forty-six-year span of service with the firm. On retirement, as the *Cocoa Works Magazine* faithfully reported, in addition to any presentations from the company, men were usually given 'a gift of banknotes collected in the department' by their workmates, but women were more likely to receive a gift of china or glassware than hard cash.

Women receiving a company pension automatically became members of the Rowntree's Pensioners Club, which helped them to keep in touch with former workmates and offered them the chance to take part in classes ranging from ballroom dancing to cake decorating. The club also organized a number of day trips and longer outings. However, the tea sets and the weekends away for retirees did not continue long beyond Florence's own retirement, and the practice of sending former workers a Christmas card and a ten-pound voucher, allowing them to use a 'waste card' to purchase cheap misshapes, was also discontinued as, one by one, the things that exemplified Rowntree's traditional care for their employees were discontinued as cost-saving measures. Thatcherism and the 'Big Bang' in the City of London were now in full swing, heralding a more money-driven, selfish era, and Rowntree's brand of liberalism and paternalism seemed old-fashioned and even archaic to the hard-nosed global businessmen of the coming age.

Increased mechanization was also making the work that women carried out at the factory ever more repetitive and monotonous. When Madge and Florence began working at Rowntree's before the war, virtually everything – piping, marking, packing, labelling – was done by hand, and jobs like box-making and hand-packing were highly skilled. Some of it, like lifting up the outers and stacking them, was heavy work, too. Until the 1950s, women might well have packed a complete box of chocolates by themselves, 'cupping' them by putting them into the frilled paper cups and then packing the box in a strict pattern. They took a real pride in their work and the skills that they had mastered.

However, the company gradually introduced machine-packing instead, and in the 1950s the individual paper cups were replaced by VFP (Vacuum Formed Plastic) packing, and from then on women would just place one or two chocolates in the plastic trays as they went past on the conveyor belt. 'You just sat there and did the same thing over and over again, all day long,' Dot Edwards says. 'One American visitor told me he thought the girls doing the packing were all robots. They'd put you on a chair and say, "Put that caramel in that mould," and you'd do that all day, unless you swapped jobs with a friend. Mind you, no one minded who you swapped with as long as the box was correct when it got to the end of the line. As they brought in more machines, they also gradually closed the floors of the Cream Block. When I started there were still four floors working, but by the time I left there was just the ground floor.'

The de-skilling of women's work, the redundancies and the progressive loss of the 'family feeling' that had once so distinguished Rowntree's from other factories, inevitably brought in their wake a much faster staff turnover. It had ceased to be a family business for the Rowntrees long ago, and was now no longer the family business of any members of Florence's family either. Only one of her three children, Malcolm, worked at the factory; he spent twenty-five years there, before taking redundancy and starting a minibus company. Her eldest daughter, Carol, now retired herself, was a teacher; her younger daughter is a teaching assistant and Florence herself is perfectly content that her own time at Rowntree's is in the past. 'I don't know that I'd like to go back there now,' she says. 'I think we definitely had the best days of Rowntree's, but they were happy times and I've great memories of it. The friends I had at work I'm still friends with now, or those that are left anyway. I go to keep-fit with them at the bowls club at New Earswick on Tuesday mornings – I can't do it all now, but I do what I can – and I go to Movement to Music on Thursday afternoons. It's nothing serious, just a bit of fun, but then like we say, "We don't come for gold medals, we just come for fun."' They even did a performance in their leotards on the Rose Lawn in front of the Rowntree's factory once, bringing back memories of those long-ago days, when in her green tabard and navy-blue knickers, and her face burning from embarrassment, Florence and her young workmates had done their Greek dancing class while derogatory comments from all the male Rowntree's workers within range echoed in her ears. When Florence's Movement to Music class of retirees performed there, it was such a burning hot day that they had medical staff standing by in case any of the women collapsed from the heat! 'We were doing it to a record on a record player,' Florence says, 'and it was so hot that the record warped in the heat and the music was speeding up and slowing down so badly that we had to stop, though by then we were laughing so much we couldn't do it anyway.'

Florence is eighty-nine now, and was still riding her push-bike when she was eighty-two, but her children eventually persuaded her to stop because there was too much heavy traffic on the roads and she had had one too many near misses with lorries thundering past. 'I used to go to line dancing, too, until I was eighty-eight,' she says, 'but I've given that up as well now, though I hope I live a little bit longer. Arthur used to tell me I'd live to a hundred and I used to say, "No, you'll outlive me, but I'll tell you what, if you go before me, I'll be a merry widow!'"

* * *

Madge finished her long career at Rowntree's working as an examiner, checking the quality of the work as it was coming off the end of the production line, and she kept doing it until 1978, when she had to retire because she had reached the compulsory retirement age of sixty. Even with seven years' absence from the factory while her three daughters were babies, she had still worked at Rowntree's for a total of thirty-nine years and was not ready to go at all, but that company rule was unbreakable. Many of her generation were just as upset to be retiring. 'I didn't want to leave at all,' Dot Edwards says, 'a lot of us didn't, but you had no choice, you had to retire when you got to sixty. I was really upset to go and I really missed the atmosphere and the friendliness and everything. There was a bit of bitchiness, like you always find in a crowd of women, but not a lot. It was a real family place; all the families used to work there.' Of Madge's three daughters, Fay only worked at Rowntree's as a holiday job, but the youngest, Lynne, worked there and met her future husband at the factory. Her other daughter, Hazel, opted not to go to Rowntree's and instead began her working life at York's other chocolate company, Terry's.

By the time Madge retired, Bill's health had not been good for a few years – he smoked and drank heavily, which cannot have helped – and finally, after he had gone into Killingbeck Hospital for an operation, the surgeon took Madge to one side and said to her, 'I'm afraid there's nothing more we can do for him.' When Madge told Bill that, he said, 'Well, I might as well be at home then,' and discharged himself from hospital. So Madge took him home and looked after him until he died. She was no longer young herself and it was hard physical work caring for him – 'I used to lift him out of bed onto the commode,' she says, 'and then lift him back in again, and do everything for him' – but somehow she coped. Although the doctors had said that Bill had only months to live, in fact he lasted for over two years after that, before eventually dying at the age of sixty-five. Madge says:

> *I'm not religious or anything. I don't believe in God, but I do think that there's something there, and I do believe in fate. Everything's planned out for you somehow. As my husband was dying, I could hear him muttering, 'Let me in. Let me in. I ain't a Roman Catholic, I'm Church of England.' So he was having trouble getting through those gates. Anyway, eventually they must have let him through. It was real windy outside, it was rattling the windows and whistling round the chimney, and my husband was making this awful noise with his breathing, so I went into the other bedroom, just to get a bit of rest. When I woke up, the wind had dropped and, as I lay there, everything was so quiet that I knew he must have gone. I went and had a look at him and then I went into Lynne, who was staying with me at the time. I woke her up and told her, 'Your dad's gone.'*

In the stillness of the night, the two women went downstairs and sat together at the kitchen table, talking quietly. They had a glass of sherry to steady their nerves, and during those peaceful moments they shared many memories, some good and some not so good. After perhaps half an hour, Madge drained the last of her sherry and then she went back upstairs and laid out his body herself, the last task she would ever have to perform for him. She washed and shaved him and combed his hair, then dressed him in his best suit, shirt and tie, and polished his shoes and put them on his feet. By that time dawn was breaking and she sent Lynne to telephone the doctor and the undertaker. There were few mourners at the funeral other than Madge and her daughters.

It had been anything but an easy life for Madge with Bill, but she made up her mind to make up for it as much as she could in the years she had left, and in her words, 'I've had a life since he's been gone and I've had a real good time.' She went to Spain for a holiday and liked it so much that she went back again and again, and in the end she decided to live there permanently. At first she just tested the waters by renting a caravan for a month, on a site between Alicante and Benidorm with about fifty people already living there. They were all British and she found them such a good group of people and enjoyed the lifestyle so much that she bought a mobile home of her own and began living there all the year round.

She was already eighty years old when she bought the mobile home, but she remained in Spain for another eight years and loved every minute of it. It is testament to her strength of character – not to mention her physical fitness and strength – that she embraced such an adventure at that late stage in her life. There was a social club nearby where she would go dancing and join in the karaoke sessions and, she says, 'I used to like getting dressed up and acting daft.' After all the years of hard work, at home and at Rowntree's, those years in Spain were truly happy and carefree for Madge. She made many good friends and at one time she even thought that true love had come knocking at her door, when she began seeing a man who was British but had been living in Spain since his previous relationship had ended acrimoniously.

Madge was very happy with him, so much so that she thought she would be spending the rest of her days with him, but that came to a sudden end when they returned to England together on a visit. Madge went to see her daughters in York, while he went to his home town, ostensibly to see his sons. On the day they were due to fly back to Spain together, her daughter Hazel received a note from the man – he did not even have the guts to tell Madge himself, or to write to her direct – saying that he would not be going back to Spain with her as he had moved in again with his previous partner. Madge's tone as she tells the story today reflects the bafflement she felt then and still feels now.

Despite that blow, she was still loving her life in Spain, but then, aged eighty-eight, she suffered a bout of food poisoning. She got up in the middle of the night and went to the bathroom, but after washing her hands, as she turned to reach for the towel, she fainted and fell back, cracking her head against the edge of the washbasin. The next thing she knew she was lying on the floor. She managed to get back into bed, but when she woke in the morning she found the pillow was saturated with blood from where she had split her scalp open. A friend took her to the doctor to get the wound stitched, but the incident made her realize how vulnerable she would be if she had another accident or her health started to fail. After thinking hard about it, she decided that the time had come for her to go home and, not without some sadness, for her years in Spain had been some of the happiest of her long life, she sold her mobile home and moved back to York.

Madge now lives in sheltered housing on the outskirts of the city in a flat bought for her by her three daughters, who all live nearby. Among her possessions is the carriage clock she won in the schools baking competition eighty years ago. It is still keeping perfect time, although it no longer has pride of place on the mantelpiece in her pristine flat, and has been relegated to a table beside an armchair.

Even in her nineties, Madge remains fiercely independent, full of energy, humour and a zest for life. She has always had perfect eyesight and never had to wear glasses, and although she is now facing an operation for cataracts, she's coping with that with her customary jaunty optimism. Apart from her twice-weekly keep-fit sessions in the communal area, she busies herself walking to the local shops, and even sometimes picks up items for less active neighbours who are ten and twenty years her junior.

She has lived two full lives, one before and another after her husband's death, and has managed to pack enough experiences into the second one to fill another three or four lifetimes on top; she is an inspiration to everyone she meets. She loved every minute of her long career at Rowntree's, and the friends she made there, even though with each passing year, fewer and fewer are left. Even now, aged ninety-four, she is still insisting, 'I enjoyed every hour of my time at Rowntree's and I'd go back there today, if only they'd have me!'

Rowntree's Timeline

1725 Mary Tuke opens a grocer's shop in Walmgate, York.
1822 Joseph Rowntree Senior opens a grocer's shop at 28 Pavement, York.
1862 Henry Rowntree buys the Tukes' cocoa business.
1864 Henry Rowntree opens a factory at Tanners Moat.
1869 Joseph Rowntree Junior joins the business to save it from bankruptcy.
1881 Rowntree's Fruit Pastilles are launched.
1893 Rowntree's Fruit Gums are launched.
1887 Elect Cocoa is launched.
1889 Joseph Rowntree Junior's son Seebohm joins the business.
1890 Construction work begins on the Haxby Road factory.
1901 Seebohm Rowntree publishes a study of poverty in York. Joseph Rowntree buys a 150-acre estate as the site for a model village, New Earswick.
1909 Yearsley swimming pool is completed and presented by Rowntree's to the City of York.
1923 Joseph Rowntree steps down as chairman and is succeeded by Seebohm.
1925 Joseph Rowntree dies.

1933 Black Magic chocolates are launched.
1935 Chocolate Crisp is launched. Joseph Rowntree Theatre opens.
1936 Dairy Box is launched.
1937 Chocolate Beans are renamed Smarties and relaunched. Chocolate Crisp is renamed Kit Kat.
1941 George Harris becomes the first non-Rowntree family member to be chairman.
1942 The old Tanners Moat factory is destroyed in the great German air raid on York.
1948 POLO mints are launched.
1952 George Harris is forced to step down as chairman.
1954 Seebohm Rowntree dies.
1962 After Eight mints are launched.
1969 Rowntree's merges with Mackintosh to form Rowntree-Mackintosh.
1976 Yorkie bar is launched.
1988 Nestlé launches a successful takeover bid for Rowntree-Mackintosh. The company is renamed Nestlé-Rowntree.
2006 Nestlé-Rowntree announces the loss of 645 jobs as production of Smarties and Black Magic is moved abroad. Kit Kat and POLO mints continue to be produced in York.
2008 Rowntree name is dropped and the company is renamed Nestlé Confectionery (UK).
2012 150th anniversary celebrations of the founding of Rowntree's.

Acknowledgements

Our greatest and most heartfelt thanks go to the remarkable and inspiring women who shared their stories with us in the course of researching this book. Our thanks not only to the five 'principal characters' – Madge Burrow, Florence Davies, Eileen Kelly, Dorothy Pipes and Maureen Hayfield – but to the many other women who worked at Rowntree's, and to their sons, daughters, nephews, nieces and friends who made contact with us on their behalf. Our sincere thanks to Caroline and Alistair Appleby, Joan and Phil Barnes, Gwen Barrass, Mick Beard, Maureen Blashill, Joyce Burnett, Carol Mackenzie, Marjorie Chapman, Sharon Cowell, Dorothy Edwards, Cherrill Frensham, Shirley Goodyear, Brenda Gray, Marjorie Harrison, Ann Hartley, Sheila Hawksby, Mr Horwell, Sarah James, Lisa Kennedy, Joan Martin, Sue Mizzi, Chris Moorey, Marjorie Parsons, Audrey Peace, Elsie Lilian Scaife, Dorothy Stokes, Mrs Storrs, Madge and Liz Tillett, Hazel Tooth, Muriel Warwick, Kath Webster, Beryl and Denis Woodcock, and to those who preferred to remain anonymous, with our sincere apologies to anyone we may have inadvertently missed.

We are also indebted to the following for their help and advice: Emma Robertson, author of *The Romance of the Cocoa Bean* and founder of the website www.cocoareworks.co.uk;

Beckie Senior, Sam Spencer, Helen Askham and the staff of York's Chocolate Story; Sophie Jewett of the York Cocoa House; David Brooks of the Dean Court Hotel in York; Professor Gweno Williams of York St John University; Graham Relton of the Yorkshire Film Archive; Bridget Morris of The Rowntree Society; the staff of the New Earswick Folk Hall; Bernard Drury of the Nestlé Rowntree Bowling Club; Mike Race of the York Oral History Society; the staff of the Fountains Learning Centre, York St John University; York Central Library; the York Castle Museum and the Library and the Borthwick Institute at the University of York; The Press, York; BBC Radio York; Steve Cook and David Swinburne of the Royal Literary Fund; and above all to Alex Hutchinson, Heritage Assistant at Nestlé's York factory, whose knowledge of the old Rowntree's factory, its personalities and production methods was invaluable, and to her colleagues James Maxton, Corporate Communications Manager, and Sally Pain, Head of Corporate Communications.

Our thanks also to Mark Lucas and Alice Saunders at Lucas Alexander Whitley, and at HarperCollins, our gratitude to Iain MacGregor, Jamie Joseph and Holly Kyte in the Collins editorial team, Sarah Patel in publicity, and all those in production and design who worked on the book.